GOODSON MUMBA

Professional Property Management

Achieving Excellence in Real Estate

Copyright © 2024 by Goodson Mumba

All rights reserved. No part of this publication may be reproduced, stored or transmitted in any form or by any means, electronic, mechanical, photocopying, recording, scanning, or otherwise without written permission from the publisher. It is illegal to copy this book, post it to a website, or distribute it by any other means without permission.

First edition

ISBN: 9798335228930

This book was professionally typeset on Reedsy. Find out more at reedsy.com

Contents

Preface iv
Acknowledgement vii
Dedication viii
Disclaimer ix
1 Chapter 1: Introduction to Property Management 1
2 Chapter 2: Building a Strong Foundation 18
3 Chapter 3: Acquiring Properties 37
4 Chapter 4: Onboarding New Properties 54
5 Chapter 5: Marketing and Leasing 76
6 Chapter 6: Tenant Relations 100
7 Chapter 7: Financial Management 126
8 Chapter 8: Maintenance and Repairs 151
9 Chapter 9: Legal Aspects of Property Management 176
10 Chapter 10: Technology in Property Management 202
11 Chapter 11: Managing Commercial Properties 229
12 Chapter 12: Sustainable Property Management 256
13 Chapter 13: Handling Difficult Situations 282
14 Chapter 14: Scaling Your Property Management Business 306
15 Chapter 15: Achieving Excellence in Property Management 329
About the Author 354

Preface

The real estate industry is a cornerstone of our economy, and at its heart lies the pivotal role of property management. Property managers are the unsung heroes who balance the needs of property owners with those of tenants, ensuring properties are well-maintained and profitable. It is a role that demands a diverse skill set, unyielding dedication, and a passion for excellence. This book, "Professional Property Management: Achieving Excellence in Real Estate," is crafted to be your definitive guide in mastering this multifaceted profession.

My journey in property management began years ago, navigating the complexities of tenant relations, maintenance issues, and financial management. Over time, I learned that excellence in this field is not merely about managing properties efficiently; it's about creating thriving communities, fostering strong tenant relationships, and staying ahead of industry trends. This book distills those lessons, providing a roadmap for both new and seasoned property managers who aspire to reach the pinnacle of their profession.

"Professional Property Management: Achieving Excellence in Real Estate" is organized to cover every aspect of property management comprehensively. We start by laying a strong foundation, introducing the core principles and historical context that have shaped modern property management. From there, we explore essential topics such as legal frameworks, financial management, tenant relations, and marketing strategies. Each chapter is designed to build your knowledge progressively, equipping you with the tools you need to excel.

A recurring theme throughout this book is the pursuit of excellence. Excellence is not a static goal but a continuous journey of improvement. It requires setting high standards, embracing best practices, and constantly seeking innovation. To illustrate these points, the book includes real-world case studies of property managers who have achieved remarkable success. These examples serve not only to educate but also to inspire you to implement strategies that drive outstanding results.

We are at the dawn of a new era in property management, characterized by rapid technological advancements and a growing emphasis on sustainability. This book addresses these future trends, exploring how property managers can leverage technology and implement sustainable practices to stay competitive. From Proptech innovations to green building initiatives, we delve into the future of property management and how you can lead in this evolving landscape.

I owe a debt of gratitude to the mentors, colleagues, and clients who have shared their insights and experiences with me. Their contributions have enriched this book and helped shape its content. I also extend my thanks to the dedicated professionals who reviewed early drafts and provided invaluable feedback.

It is my hope that this book serves as a beacon for your professional journey. Whether you are embarking on a new career in property management or seeking to refine your existing skills, "Professional Property Management: Achieving Excellence in Real Estate" is here to guide you. Let this book be your companion as you strive to achieve excellence and make a meaningful impact in the world of real estate.

To the pursuit of excellence,

Goodson Mumba

Acknowledgement

I would like to eternally and gratefully acknowledge the Almighty God for the infinite intelligence from His universal mind where we draw from all that we come to know and are yet to know. May I also acknowledge and thank everyone that has played a part in my journey of life in terms of spiritual, moral, emotional and material support.

Dedication

I extend my sincerest gratitude to my beloved wife, Edith Mumba, and our children, Angelina, Lubuto, Letticia, Lulumbi, and Butusho, for their unwavering support and understanding throughout the conception, writing, and eventual publication of this book, despite the sacrifices and challenges they endured.

Disclaimer

This book is a work of fiction. Names, characters, businesses, places, events, and incidents are either the products of the author's imagination or used in a fictitious manner. Any resemblance to actual persons, living or dead, or actual events is purely coincidental.

1

Chapter 1: Introduction to Property Management

Defining Property Management

Jack Miller stood at the edge of a high-rise balcony, the city sprawled out beneath him like a glittering tapestry. The view was breathtaking, but Jack's mind was focused on the task at hand. He had just accepted the position as the lead property manager for Blackwood Real Estate, a portfolio of properties as diverse as the city itself.

As he turned to face the assembled team of eager assistants and seasoned professionals, he knew this first meeting was crucial. They needed to understand what property management truly entailed.

"Good morning, everyone," Jack began, his voice carrying a blend of authority and enthusiasm. "Before we dive into the specifics of our projects, let's take a step back and define what property management is."

The room quieted, all eyes on Jack. He walked to a

whiteboard and wrote the words "Property Management" in bold letters.

"Property management," he said, underlining the words, "is the administration, operation, and oversight of real estate properties on behalf of an owner. It involves handling the day-to-day responsibilities to ensure the properties are well-maintained, profitable, and compliant with laws."

He paused, scanning the room to make sure everyone was following. "But it's more than just a job. It's about creating value. For the property owners, for the tenants, and for the community."

Jack moved to the next point, writing it on the board. "At its core, property management encompasses four key areas: Administration, Finance, Tenant Relations, and Maintenance. Let's break these down."

"First, Administration," Jack continued. "This includes all the paperwork, the leases, the compliance with laws, and the overall organization of property operations. Without proper administration, chaos would ensue."

He could see nods of understanding and a few scribbled notes. "Second, Finance. Managing the financial aspect means ensuring rent is collected, bills are paid, and the property remains profitable. It's the backbone of any successful property management strategy."

"Third, Tenant Relations. This is where our people skills come into play. We need to understand our tenants' needs, resolve conflicts, and maintain high occupancy rates through excellent customer service."

"Finally, Maintenance. Ensuring that properties are safe, functional, and appealing is critical. This involves everything from routine inspections to emergency repairs."

Jack took a deep breath, feeling the weight of the responsibility but also the excitement of the journey ahead. "Property management is not just about managing buildings; it's about managing relationships and resources. It's about taking a holistic view to maximize the value and appeal of properties while ensuring a positive experience for tenants."

He could see the recognition in their faces, the realization of the complexity and the importance of their roles. "If we can excel in these areas, we won't just be property managers; we'll be stewards of our clients' investments and champions of our tenants' living and working environments."

The room erupted into discussions and questions, the team already brainstorming ideas and strategies. Jack smiled, knowing they were off to a promising start.

In this moment, the foundation was laid—not just for managing properties, but for achieving excellence in every aspect of their work.

Historical Overview of Property Management

As the room buzzed with the energy of Jack's initial presentation, he knew it was time to provide some context, a backdrop to their mission. He wanted his team to appreciate the roots of their profession and understand how far it had come.

Jack raised his hand slightly, and the room fell silent again. "Before we move forward, let's take a step back in time. To understand where we're going, it's crucial to know where we've been. Let's delve into the history of property management."

He clicked a remote, and the screen behind him lit up with an image of an ancient Roman villa. "Property management is not a modern invention. It dates back to ancient civilizations. In Rome, large estates called 'latifundia' were managed by overseers known as 'vilicus.' These managers were responsible for the estate's agricultural production and maintenance, much like today's property managers."

The screen transitioned to a medieval castle. "In the Middle Ages, estates and manors required similar oversight. Landlords would employ stewards to manage their properties, collect rents, and ensure the land was productive. These stewards were precursors to modern property managers, handling both the financial and operational aspects of large estates."

He noticed a few nodding heads, and a glimmer of curiosity sparked in others. "Fast forward to the Industrial Revolution," Jack continued, as the screen showed crowded cityscapes and early apartment buildings. "Urbanization led to a boom in rental properties. As cities grew, so did the need for organized management of these buildings. The role of the property manager became more formalized, with responsibilities expanding to include tenant relations, rent collection, and maintenance."

Jack moved to the next slide, showing a bustling city street from the 1950s. "Post-World War II, property management evolved significantly. The rise of suburban developments and commercial properties created new challenges and opportunities. Property managers were now crucial in maintaining the quality and value of properties amidst rapid growth and changing demographics."

He paused, letting the weight of this historical journey sink in. "And here we are today," he said, as the screen displayed a modern skyline. "In the 21st century, property management has become a sophisticated profession. We deal with advanced technology, complex regulations, and diverse tenant needs. But at its heart, our work still revolves around the same principles that guided ancient and medieval managers: maintaining value, ensuring productivity, and fostering good relationships."

Jack stepped away from the screen, looking directly at his team. "Understanding this history gives us a sense of purpose and continuity. We're part of a long tradition of individuals dedicated to preserving and enhancing the places where people live and work. As we move forward, let's honor that legacy by striving for excellence in everything we do."

The room was silent, but Jack could see the impact of his words in their expressions. They were no longer just employees at the start of another job; they were part of a historical continuum, entrusted with a vital role in society.

Jack smiled, feeling the connection between the past and the present. "Let's carry this knowledge with us as we tackle the challenges ahead. Remember, we stand on the shoulders of those who came before us. Let's make them proud."

The atmosphere in the room shifted, a renewed sense of purpose taking hold. Jack had not only defined what property management was but had also woven their roles into the rich tapestry of history, inspiring his team to achieve greatness in their shared journey.

Types of Properties Managed

Jack Miller felt the momentum building in the room. He had laid the foundation by defining property management and exploring its history. Now, it was time to delve into the diverse types of properties they would be managing, each with its own unique challenges and rewards.

He clicked the remote, and the screen displayed a collage of different buildings and properties. "As property managers, our expertise spans a wide array of property types. Let's explore these in detail."

The first image zoomed in on a sleek, modern apartment building. "Residential properties," Jack began. "These include single-family homes, multi-family units, and high-rise apartment buildings. Our goal here is to ensure a safe, comfortable living environment for tenants. This involves everything from handling maintenance requests to organizing community events."

Jack could see a few team members nodding, some with experience in residential management. He clicked to the next image, showcasing a bustling office building. "Commercial properties. These include office buildings, retail spaces, and mixed-use developments. Managing these properties requires a keen understanding of business needs, lease negotiations, and maintaining spaces that enhance productivity and customer appeal."

The room buzzed with interest as Jack moved to the next slide, which displayed an industrial park. "Industrial properties," he continued. "Think warehouses, manufacturing facilities, and distribution centers. These properties have specific requirements, such as ensuring compliance with safety regulations and managing large-scale maintenance operations. The logistics can be complex, but the rewards are significant."

The screen transitioned to a picture of a luxurious resort. "Hospitality properties," Jack said, his tone warm. "Hotels, resorts, and vacation rentals. Here, customer service is paramount. We need to provide exceptional experiences for guests, which means maintaining high standards of cleanliness, comfort, and amenities."

Jack noticed a spark of excitement in one of the new hires, likely someone with a background in the hospitality industry. He clicked to the next image, a serene senior living community. "Specialty properties," he explained. "This category includes senior living facilities, student housing, and affordable housing projects. Managing these properties often involves additional layers of care and consideration, from health and safety protocols to community-building activities."

He paused to let this variety sink in, the screen now showing a diverse cityscape with all these property types interwoven. "Each type of property we manage has its own set of challenges and opportunities. Whether we're ensuring the smooth operation of an office building or creating a welcoming home for families, our role remains vital."

Jack stepped away from the screen and faced his team. "Understanding these different property types allows us to tailor our approach. It helps us anticipate issues and create solutions that fit each unique context. The better we understand the properties we manage, the better we can serve our tenants and clients."

He could see the gears turning in their minds, the realization of the complexity and diversity of their work taking hold. Jack knew this understanding would be crucial as they moved forward.

"Our strength lies in our versatility and our ability to adapt," Jack concluded. "As we continue to explore the nuances of each property type, remember that every challenge we face is an opportunity to excel and make a difference."

The room filled with a renewed sense of purpose and excitement. They were ready to embrace the diverse world of property management, equipped with knowledge and a shared commitment to excellence.

Jack felt a deep sense of satisfaction. The journey was just beginning, but he could already see the potential in his team. Together, they would navigate the complexities of various properties, striving for excellence at every turn.

Roles and Responsibilities of a Property Manager

Jack Miller watched the excitement grow in the room. His team was starting to grasp the vast landscape of property management, from its definition and history to the diverse types of properties they would handle. Now, it was time to drill down into what they, as property managers, were expected to do every day.

"Alright," Jack said, pulling the team's attention back to the front of the room. "We've talked about what property management is and the types of properties we manage. Now, let's dive into the heart of our work: the roles and responsibilities of a property manager."

He clicked the remote, and the screen displayed a pie chart divided into several sections. "Property management is a multifaceted role. Let's break it down."

The first section of the chart highlighted. "1. Financial Management," Jack began. "This is the backbone of our responsibilities. It includes budgeting, setting rental rates, and ensuring rent is collected on time. We also handle accounts payable, monitor financial performance, and provide regular financial reports to property owners."

He saw a few team members nodding, particularly those with accounting backgrounds. "Accurate financial management keeps properties profitable and ensures funds are available for maintenance and improvements."

The next section highlighted. "2. Tenant Relations," Jack continued. "This is all about maintaining positive relationships with our tenants. It involves screening prospective tenants, managing lease agreements, handling tenant complaints, and resolving conflicts. Good tenant relations can significantly reduce turnover rates and improve tenant satisfaction."

A murmur of agreement swept through the room. Jack knew many had experienced the challenges of tenant relations firsthand.

The third section lit up. "3. Maintenance and Repairs. This is crucial for maintaining property value and ensuring tenant safety and satisfaction. We schedule regular inspections, coordinate repairs, and handle emergencies. This includes everything from fixing a leaky faucet to overseeing major renovations."

He clicked to the next section. "4. Legal Compliance. Property managers must stay abreast of local, state, and federal laws governing property management and landlord-tenant relationships. This includes understanding fair housing laws, safety regulations, and lease enforcement. Non-compliance can lead to costly legal issues."

The team members leaned in, recognizing the importance of staying informed and compliant.

The fifth section highlighted. "5. Marketing and Leasing. To keep properties occupied, we need effective marketing strategies. This includes creating compelling listings, using various advertising channels, and showing properties to potential tenants. Once we attract interest, we manage the leasing process from start to finish."

Jack noticed a few smiles—marketing and leasing were often seen as the more dynamic aspects of property management.

The final section lit up. "6. Risk Management. This involves identifying potential risks, such as safety hazards or financial vulnerabilities, and implementing strategies to mitigate them. This also includes having appropriate insurance coverage and developing emergency preparedness plans."

He turned off the projector and faced the team. "These are the core responsibilities of a property manager, but our role often requires us to wear many hats. We might be financial analysts, mediators, marketers, and maintenance supervisors all in one day."

Jack walked closer to his team, ensuring his words resonated. "Our job is demanding, but it's also incredibly rewarding. We have the power to make a significant impact on the lives of our tenants and the success of our property owners. Every decision we make, every problem we solve, contributes to the overall value and functionality of the properties we manage."

He paused, letting the weight of these responsibilities settle in. "Remember, excellence in property management comes from understanding and mastering these roles. Each task, no matter how small, plays a part in our overall success."

The room was silent, each team member processing the depth of their responsibilities. Jack could see determination in their eyes—an acknowledgment of the challenges ahead and a readiness to tackle them.

Jack smiled, feeling the collective commitment. "Let's embrace these roles with professionalism and dedication. Together, we will achieve excellence in property management."

The atmosphere was charged with purpose. Jack knew his team was ready to take on their roles, armed with the knowledge and a clear understanding of their responsibilities. The foundation was set, and the journey toward excellence had begun.

Skills Required for Effective Management

Jack Miller took a moment to observe his team. He could see their commitment and readiness to embrace their roles and responsibilities. Now, it was time to equip them with the skills necessary to excel.

"Alright, team," Jack said, his voice filled with enthusiasm. "We've discussed what property management entails, its history, the types of properties, and our responsibilities. Now, let's talk about the skills required to manage effectively."

He clicked the remote, and the screen displayed a list of skills. "Effective property management requires a unique blend of skills. Let's break these down."

The first skill highlighted. "1. **Communication.** Clear and effective communication is crucial. Whether we're negotiating lease terms, resolving tenant complaints, or coordinating with contractors, how we communicate can make or break a situation. Always aim for clarity, professionalism, and empathy."

Jack noticed Sarah, his assistant, nodding. She had always

been a strong communicator, adept at de-escalating tense situations with tenants.

The next skill illuminated. "2. **Organization.** Property management involves juggling many tasks simultaneously. From keeping track of maintenance schedules to ensuring timely rent collection, strong organizational skills are essential. Use tools and systems to stay on top of everything."

He saw David, the new hire with a background in logistics, scribbling notes furiously. Organization was his forte, and Jack was eager to see him apply those skills here.

The third skill lit up. "3. **Problem-Solving.** Unexpected issues will arise, whether it's a burst pipe at 2 AM or a tenant dispute. Effective problem-solving means thinking quickly, staying calm under pressure, and finding practical solutions that work for everyone involved."

Jack remembered a night when he had to deal with a flooded basement. His quick thinking had saved the property from severe damage and impressed the tenants with his swift action.

The fourth skill highlighted. "4. **Financial Acumen.** Understanding budgets, financial reports, and market trends is vital. We need to make informed decisions that impact the property's profitability and ensure financial stability for our clients."

Lisa, the team's financial whiz, smiled. She had a knack for making sense of complex financial data and translating it into actionable strategies.

The fifth skill lit up. "5. **Attention to Detail.** Small details can have significant impacts. Whether reviewing lease agreements, conducting property inspections, or managing maintenance schedules, attention to detail ensures nothing slips through the cracks."

Jack thought of the time he had caught a small clause in a lease that could have cost the company thousands. His meticulous nature had paid off, and it was a trait he encouraged in his team.

The final skill illuminated. "6. **Adaptability.** The property management landscape is ever-changing, from new regulations to market shifts. Being adaptable means staying informed, learning continuously, and being ready to pivot strategies when necessary."

He could see the recognition in their faces, understanding that adaptability was key to staying ahead in their field.

Jack turned off the projector and faced his team, the atmosphere charged with readiness and determination. "These skills are our tools. Mastering them will not only help us manage properties effectively but also differentiate us as top-tier professionals in the industry."

He stepped closer, making sure his words resonated. "Communication, organization, problem-solving, financial acumen, attention to detail, and adaptability. Focus on developing these skills, and you'll not only meet the demands of our job but exceed expectations."

Jack paused, letting the importance of these skills sink in. "Remember, each skill complements the others. Together, they form the foundation of effective property management. Let's commit to honing these skills and supporting each other in our continuous improvement."

The room was filled with a collective sense of purpose. Jack knew his team was not only ready but eager to develop the skills necessary for excellence. They were equipped with the knowledge and understanding needed to tackle any challenge.

Jack smiled, feeling the anticipation in the room. "Let's get to work. Excellence is not a destination but a continuous journey, and we're on this path together."

With that, the team was energized, ready to embrace their roles with the skills that would ensure their success. The journey towards effective management had truly begun, guided by a clear vision and a shared commitment to excellence.

The Future of Property Management

Jack Miller felt the energy in the room reach its peak. His team had absorbed the foundational elements of property management, the historical context, and the essential skills needed to excel. Now, it was time to look forward and explore the future of their profession.

"Alright, team," Jack began, capturing their attention once more. "We've covered a lot of ground today. But as we master the present, we must also anticipate and prepare for the future. Let's talk about where property management is headed."

He clicked the remote, and the screen displayed an image of a futuristic city skyline, blending technology with sleek, sustainable buildings. "The future of property management is shaped by emerging trends and innovations. Understanding these will help us stay ahead of the curve."

The first trend highlighted on the screen. "1. **Technology Integration.** From smart home devices to property management software, technology is revolutionizing our industry. Automation tools can streamline rent collection, maintenance requests, and even tenant screening. Embracing these technologies will make us more efficient and responsive."

Jack noticed his team leaning in, intrigued by the possibilities. Sarah, always tech-savvy, had been advocating for new software solutions, and Jack was eager to see her ideas implemented.

The next trend illuminated. "2. **Sustainability.** Green building practices and sustainable management are not just trends but necessities. Energy-efficient appliances, renewable energy sources, and eco-friendly materials are becoming standard. Tenants and property owners alike are demanding environmentally responsible practices."

He saw Lisa nodding; her passion for sustainability had already led to successful green initiatives in their properties. Jack was proud of how these efforts had enhanced both property value and tenant satisfaction.

The third trend lit up. "3. **Flexible Workspaces.** The rise of remote work has transformed commercial real estate. Flexible office spaces, co-working environments, and adaptable layouts are the future. We need to cater to businesses that require dynamic and scalable office solutions."

David, with his background in logistics and adaptive planning, seemed particularly excited about this. Jack knew his skills would be invaluable as they navigated these changes.

The fourth trend highlighted. "4. **Data-Driven Decision Making.** Utilizing data analytics can provide insights into market trends, tenant preferences, and operational efficiency. By leveraging big data, we can make informed decisions that optimize property performance and tenant satisfaction."

Jack recalled a recent project where data analysis had helped them adjust rental rates competitively while maintaining high occupancy. The impact had been immediate and positive.

The fifth trend illuminated. "5. **Enhanced Tenant Experiences.** The tenant experience is becoming central to property management. From personalized services to community-building activities, creating a positive living and working environment is crucial. Happy tenants stay longer and contribute to a property's reputation."

He noticed smiles around the room. They all remembered the holiday event that had brought tenants together, fostering a sense of community and increasing overall satisfaction.

The final trend lit up. "6. **Regulatory Changes.** Laws and regulations are constantly evolving. Staying ahead of these changes is vital to ensure compliance and avoid legal pitfalls. We must be proactive in understanding new legislation and adapting our practices accordingly."

Jack turned off the projector and faced his team, the anticipation of the future palpable. "The landscape of property management is changing rapidly. By embracing these trends, we position ourselves as leaders in the field. Our ability to adapt, innovate, and stay informed will define our success."

He stepped closer, making eye contact with each team member. "The future is not something to fear but to welcome. It's an opportunity to grow, improve, and lead the industry. Let's commit to continuous learning and innovation. Let's be the ones who shape the future of property management."

The room was silent, each person reflecting on the journey ahead. Jack could see the determination in their eyes—a readiness to embrace change and drive progress.

"Remember," Jack concluded, "excellence is a journey, and the path forward is filled with opportunities. Let's seize them together, with confidence and vision. The future of property management starts now, with us."

The atmosphere was electric, charged with purpose and anticipation. Jack knew his team was ready to step into the future, equipped with knowledge, skills, and a shared commitment to excellence. Together, they would navigate the evolving landscape and lead the way forward.

The chapter ended with a sense of unity and optimism, setting the stage for a promising journey into the future of property management.

Chapter 2: Building a Strong Foundation

Legal and Regulatory Framework

Jack Miller stood at the head of the conference table, ready to address his team once more. Today's session was crucial—understanding the legal and regulatory framework that underpins property management. He knew this foundation was essential for their success.

"Good morning, team," Jack began, as the last few murmurs of conversation died down. "Today, we're going to discuss one of the most critical aspects of property management: the legal and regulatory framework. This is the bedrock upon which everything else is built."

He clicked the remote, and the screen behind him displayed a dense network of legal documents and regulations. "The laws governing property management are complex and varied. They protect the rights of property owners, tenants, and the broader community. Let's break it down."

CHAPTER 2: BUILDING A STRONG FOUNDATION

The first slide highlighted a federal courthouse. "1. **Federal Laws.** These include the Fair Housing Act, which prohibits discrimination based on race, color, national origin, religion, sex, familial status, or disability. Understanding and adhering to these laws is non-negotiable. Violations can lead to severe penalties."

Jack looked around the room, ensuring his team grasped the gravity of compliance. He remembered a colleague at another firm who faced a lawsuit due to a Fair Housing Act violation—a mistake that could have been avoided with proper knowledge and vigilance.

The next slide showed a state capitol building. "2. **State Laws.** Each state has its own set of regulations regarding security deposits, rent control, and tenant rights. For instance, California has strict rent control laws, while Texas has more landlord-friendly regulations. Knowing the state-specific laws where our properties are located is crucial."

He noticed David taking meticulous notes. Jack had always admired David's attention to detail, especially when navigating the intricacies of different state laws.

The third slide depicted a city hall. "3. **Local Ordinances.** Municipalities often have additional regulations, such as building codes, zoning laws, and noise ordinances. These can vary significantly from one city to another. Staying informed about local regulations ensures that our properties remain compliant and avoids costly fines or legal issues."

Jack recalled an incident in which a property he managed nearly faced shutdown due to a misunderstanding of local fire safety codes. It had been a wake-up call about the importance of local compliance.

The next image showed a balance scale. "4. **Lease Agree-**

ments. These legally binding contracts outline the terms and conditions of the tenancy. A well-drafted lease agreement protects both the landlord and the tenant. It should clearly state the rental terms, responsibilities for maintenance, and procedures for resolving disputes."

Jack glanced at Sarah, who had a knack for drafting clear, comprehensive lease agreements. Her expertise had saved them from potential disputes more than once.

The fifth slide highlighted an eviction notice. "5. **Eviction Processes.** Understanding the legal process for eviction is essential. Evictions must be handled according to the law, with proper notice and due process. Mishandling an eviction can lead to legal repercussions and damage our reputation."

He saw a few concerned looks and knew this was a delicate subject. Evictions were never easy, but understanding the legal framework ensured they were handled fairly and legally.

The final slide showed a handshake. "6. **Legal Counsel.** Sometimes, despite our best efforts, legal issues arise. Having a trusted legal advisor or attorney who specializes in property law is invaluable. They can provide guidance, represent us in disputes, and ensure our practices remain compliant with the ever-evolving legal landscape."

Jack turned off the projector and faced his team. "Understanding and adhering to these legal and regulatory frameworks is not just about avoiding fines or lawsuits. It's about building trust with our tenants and property owners, and operating with integrity."

He stepped closer, the importance of his words reflected in his tone. "A strong legal foundation ensures we can manage our properties effectively, ethically, and responsibly. It gives us the confidence to handle any challenges that come our way."

Jack could see the determination in their faces—a readiness to embrace the complexities of the legal landscape. "Let's commit to continuous learning and vigilance in this area. By staying informed and compliant, we protect our properties, our clients, and our reputation."

The room was silent, each team member processing the critical information. Jack knew they were ready to tackle the legal intricacies of property management with diligence and integrity.

"Remember," Jack concluded, "building a strong foundation starts with understanding the laws that govern our work. Let's ensure we uphold these standards in everything we do."

The session ended with a renewed sense of purpose. The team was equipped with the knowledge and commitment needed to navigate the legal framework, laying the groundwork for their journey toward excellence in property management.

Licensing and Certifications

The room was still humming with the weighty discussions of legal frameworks as Jack Miller prepared to move on to the next crucial topic. He could sense the team's focus sharpening, their minds keen to absorb more. Jack knew that a solid grasp of licensing and certifications would further cement their foundation in property management.

"Alright, team," Jack began, ensuring everyone was back in their seats and attentive. "We've tackled the legal and regulatory framework, but there's another vital component to building our foundation: licensing and certifications."

He clicked the remote, and the screen displayed an image of a professional certificate with a golden seal. "Licensing and certifications aren't just bureaucratic hurdles—they're critical to our credibility and professionalism. Let's explore why they matter and what we need."

The first slide highlighted. "1. **State Licensing Requirements.** Many states require property managers to hold a real estate broker's license or a property management license. This varies by state, so it's essential to understand the specific requirements where we operate. These licenses ensure we meet certain standards of knowledge and ethics."

Jack remembered the rigorous process he went through to obtain his own license. The education and exams had been challenging, but they ensured he was well-prepared for the complexities of the job.

The next slide displayed a classroom setting. "2. **Educational Programs.** To obtain and maintain our licenses, we often need to complete specific educational courses. These can cover a range of topics, from real estate law to property maintenance and tenant relations. Continuous education keeps us up-to-date with industry changes and best practices."

He saw Sarah nodding—she had just completed a course on sustainable property management and had shared valuable insights with the team. Jack knew that ongoing education was key to staying ahead in the industry.

The third slide depicted a professional conference. "3. **Certifications from Professional Organizations.** Certifications like the Certified Property Manager (CPM) from the Institute of Real Estate Management (IREM) or the Residential Management Professional (RMP) from the National Association of Residential Property Managers (NARPM) enhance our skills and credibility. They show our commitment to excellence and professional development."

Jack recalled the pride he felt when he earned his CPM designation. It had opened doors to new opportunities and provided a network of professionals he could rely on for advice and support.

The next image showed a renewal reminder on a calendar. "4. **License Renewal and Continuing Education.** Licenses and certifications need to be renewed periodically, often requiring continuing education credits. Staying on top of renewal deadlines and completing the necessary coursework ensures we remain in good standing and continue to grow professionally."

David, the meticulous planner, was already jotting down notes about upcoming renewal dates. Jack appreciated his proactive approach to ensuring compliance.

The fifth slide highlighted a mentor and mentee. "5. **Mentorship and Networking.** Engaging with mentors and industry peers through professional organizations provides valuable insights and support. Networking at industry events and participating in local chapters of property management associations can help us stay informed and connected."

Jack thought of his mentor, whose guidance had been instrumental in his early career. He encouraged his team to seek out mentors and build strong professional networks.

The final slide displayed a seal of approval. "6. **Ethical Standards and Accountability.** Many licensing bodies and professional organizations enforce a code of ethics. Adhering to these standards not only ensures legal compliance but also fosters trust with clients and tenants. Upholding ethical practices is paramount to our success and reputation."

Jack turned off the projector and faced his team, the importance of his words clear in his expression. "Licensing and certifications are more than just formalities. They are a testament to our dedication, professionalism, and commitment to continuous improvement."

He stepped closer, his voice filled with conviction. "By pursuing these credentials, we enhance our knowledge, build our credibility, and position ourselves as leaders in the field. Let's commit to staying informed, educated, and ethically grounded in all our endeavors."

The room was silent, the weight of the message sinking in. Jack could see the determination in their eyes—a collective readiness to invest in their professional growth and uphold the highest standards.

"Remember," Jack concluded, "building a strong foundation requires more than just knowledge and compliance. It requires a commitment to continuous learning and ethical excellence. Let's strive to achieve and maintain the credentials that set us apart as true professionals."

The session ended with a sense of purpose and direction. The team was equipped with the understanding and motivation needed to pursue the necessary licenses and certifications, laying the groundwork for their journey toward excellence in property management.

Establishing Business Goals and Objectives

Jack Miller could feel the team's energy as they delved deeper into building a robust foundation for their property management practice. Having covered legal frameworks and the importance of licensing and certifications, it was now time to align their efforts with clear, strategic goals and objectives.

"Okay, team," Jack said, bringing everyone's attention back to the front. "We've discussed the legalities and the need for credentials. Now, let's talk about something equally important: establishing our business goals and objectives."

He clicked the remote, and the screen displayed a mountain peak, symbolizing the pinnacle of success. "Setting clear goals and objectives gives us direction and purpose. It helps us measure our progress and stay focused on what matters most. Let's break this down."

The first slide highlighted a vision statement. "1. **Defining Our Vision and Mission.** Our vision is where we want to be in the future. It should inspire and motivate us. Our mission, on the other hand, defines our purpose and what we do every day to achieve that vision. Together, they provide a roadmap for our journey."

Jack glanced around the room, seeing nods of understanding. He remembered the day he and his founding partners crafted their vision and mission statements. It had been a pivotal moment, giving their business a clear sense of purpose.

The next slide showed a SMART goals chart. "2. **Setting SMART Goals.** Our goals need to be Specific, Measurable, Achievable, Relevant, and Time-bound. For instance, increasing our property portfolio by 15% within the next year is a SMART goal. It gives us a clear target and a timeframe."

Sarah, ever the planner, was already jotting down ideas. Jack knew she would be instrumental in turning their aspirations into actionable goals.

The third slide depicted a balance scale. "3. **Balancing**

Short-Term and Long-Term Goals. While it's important to have long-term ambitions, we must also focus on short-term objectives that keep us moving forward. This balance ensures we're making progress while keeping sight of our ultimate vision."

David, with his logistics background, understood the importance of balancing immediate tasks with future planning. Jack could see him mentally mapping out their goals.

The next image showed a diverse team in a brainstorming session. "4. **Involving the Team in Goal Setting.** Our goals should not be set in isolation. Involving the team in the process ensures buy-in and leverages diverse perspectives. It fosters a sense of ownership and accountability."

Jack remembered a brainstorming session where a junior team member's idea had led to a significant improvement in tenant satisfaction. Everyone's input was valuable.

The fifth slide highlighted a progress tracking board. "5. **Tracking Progress and Adjusting Goals.** Regularly monitoring our progress helps us stay on track and make necessary adjustments. Tools like performance dashboards and regular review meetings ensure we're aligned with our objectives."

Lisa, their financial whiz, smiled. She had recently introduced a new dashboard that had already proven invaluable in tracking their financial goals.

The final slide showed a trophy. "6. **Celebrating Achievements.** Recognizing and celebrating our achievements, both big and small, keeps morale high and motivates the team. Celebrations remind us of our progress and reinforce the behaviors that lead to success."

Jack turned off the projector and faced his team, the excitement in his voice clear. "Setting and achieving goals is not just about business success. It's about growing together as a team, staying motivated, and continuously improving."

He stepped closer, ensuring his words resonated. "Our vision and mission give us direction, but our goals and objectives drive our daily actions. Let's commit to setting meaningful goals and working tirelessly to achieve them."

The room was filled with a renewed sense of purpose. Jack could see the determination and excitement in their faces—a collective readiness to set ambitious goals and pursue them with vigor.

"Remember," Jack concluded, "establishing business goals and objectives is a dynamic process. It requires us to be strategic, collaborative, and persistent. Let's define our path and walk it together, step by step, toward excellence."

The session ended with an air of optimism and unity. The team was equipped with the knowledge and motivation needed to set clear, achievable goals, laying the groundwork for their journey toward excellence in property management.

Developing a Business Plan

Jack Miller felt a growing sense of accomplishment among his team as they absorbed the crucial lessons of building a solid foundation in property management. After establishing their business goals and objectives, it was time to discuss how to bring those goals to life through a well-crafted business plan.

"Alright, team," Jack began, his voice steady and confident. "We've identified our goals and objectives. Now, it's time to develop a business plan that will guide us in achieving them. This plan is our blueprint for success."

He clicked the remote, and the screen displayed a detailed blueprint of a skyscraper. "A business plan outlines our strategies, resources, and the steps we need to take to reach our goals. Let's break down the essential components."

The first slide highlighted a cover page with the title "Executive Summary." "1. **Executive Summary.** This is the most critical part of our business plan. It provides a snapshot of our business, including our mission, vision, key objectives, and strategies. Think of it as our business at a glance."

Jack remembered the countless hours spent perfecting their executive summary. It was the first impression for potential investors and partners, and it needed to be compelling.

The next slide displayed a chart showing market research data. "2. **Market Analysis.** Understanding the market is crucial. This section should include an analysis of the current market conditions, our target demographics, and competitive landscape. It helps us identify opportunities and threats."

Sarah, always analytical, was already thinking of ways to gather more comprehensive market data. Jack knew her insights would be invaluable.

The third slide depicted a detailed strategic plan. "3. **Marketing and Sales Strategy.** How do we plan to attract and retain clients? This section outlines our marketing campaigns, sales tactics, and branding efforts. It's about making sure we're visible and attractive to our target market."

Jack saw David nodding, his mind likely buzzing with innovative marketing ideas. David's creativity in past projects had already set them apart in the competitive landscape.

The next image showed an organizational chart. "4. **Organizational Structure.** This part defines our company's structure, detailing roles, responsibilities, and the chain of command. Clear structure ensures everyone knows their role and how they contribute to our goals."

Jack glanced at Lisa, who had been instrumental in refining their organizational structure. Her knack for clarity and efficiency had streamlined many of their operations.

The fifth slide highlighted financial projections. "5. **Financial Plan.** This section includes detailed financial projections, budgets, and funding requirements. It outlines how we plan to achieve financial sustainability and profitability. Investors and stakeholders will scrutinize this closely."

Lisa smiled, knowing her expertise in financial planning was about to be put to good use. Her accurate projections had kept them on track in challenging times.

The final slide showed a calendar with key milestones. "6. **Implementation Timeline.** A business plan needs a timeline for implementation. This section breaks down our goals into actionable steps with deadlines. It keeps us accountable and ensures we're making progress."

Jack turned off the projector and faced his team, his expression serious but optimistic. "A business plan is not just a document we file away. It's a living guide that directs our efforts and keeps us focused on our path to success."

He stepped closer, his voice filled with determination. "By developing a comprehensive business plan, we're not only setting our intentions but also preparing for the challenges ahead. It's about being proactive and strategic in everything we do."

The room was silent, each team member reflecting on the importance of a solid business plan. Jack could see the determination in their eyes—a readiness to map out their journey with precision and foresight.

"Remember," Jack concluded, "developing a business plan is a collaborative effort. It requires input from everyone and a commitment to our shared vision. Let's craft a plan that not only meets our current needs but also paves the way for future growth."

The session ended with a renewed sense of focus and purpose. The team was equipped with the understanding and motivation needed to develop a robust business plan, laying the groundwork for their journey toward excellence in property management.

Setting Up Efficient Office Systems

Jack Miller observed the eager faces around the conference table. The team had discussed the critical elements of legal frameworks, licensing, business goals, and crafting a solid business plan. Now, it was time to address the practical side of making their plans work: setting up efficient office systems.

"Team," Jack began, projecting a slide of a well-organized office. "We've laid out our goals and developed a business plan. The next step is to ensure our daily operations run smoothly. Efficient office systems are essential for productivity and success."

The first slide highlighted a desk with an array of labeled folders. "1. **Document Management System.** Managing documents effectively is crucial. A reliable document management system helps us store, organize, and retrieve documents quickly. It reduces clutter and ensures important files are easily accessible."

Jack remembered the chaos before implementing their current system. Papers would pile up, and finding critical documents was a time-consuming nightmare. Now, their digital document management system had streamlined everything, making retrieval quick and easy.

The next slide displayed a calendar and scheduling software. "2. **Scheduling and Task Management Tools.** To keep everyone on track, we need tools that help us schedule meetings, set deadlines, and manage tasks. Tools like Asana, Trello, or even a well-maintained shared calendar ensure we stay organized and meet our deadlines."

David, who thrived on organization, perked up. He had a knack for optimizing schedules and was already thinking of ways to enhance their current system.

The third slide depicted a telephone and an email inbox. "3. **Communication Systems.** Clear communication is key to efficient operations. Whether it's internal communication among staff or external communication with clients and vendors, we need reliable systems. Email, phone systems, and messaging apps like Slack help us stay connected and responsive."

Jack recalled times when communication breakdowns had led to missed opportunities and misunderstandings. Their new communication protocols had significantly improved team coordination and client satisfaction.

The next image showed a computer with various software applications open. "4. **Property Management Software.** Using specialized property management software can automate many tasks, such as rent collection, maintenance requests, and tenant screening. This not only saves time but also reduces errors and ensures consistency in our operations."

Sarah, their tech enthusiast, was already familiar with

several property management platforms. Jack knew she would lead the charge in selecting and implementing the best software for their needs.

The fifth slide featured a secure lock symbol. "5. **Data Security Systems.** Protecting our data is paramount. We handle sensitive information about properties, tenants, and finances. Robust data security measures, such as encryption, secure passwords, and regular backups, are essential to protect against breaches and data loss."

Lisa, who had a background in IT security, nodded in agreement. She had been advocating for stronger security protocols, and Jack was glad to see her expertise being recognized.

The final slide displayed an ergonomic office setup. "6. **Ergonomic and Efficient Workspaces.** A comfortable and efficient workspace boosts productivity and employee well-being. Investing in ergonomic furniture, good lighting, and a clean, organized environment can make a significant difference in how we work."

Jack looked around, seeing everyone envisioning improvements to their workspaces. A productive office wasn't just about tools and systems but also about creating an environment where the team could thrive.

He turned off the projector and faced his team, the importance of his message clear. "Efficient office systems are the backbone of our operations. They enable us to work smarter, not harder, and to deliver exceptional service to our clients."

Jack stepped closer, his voice steady and inspiring. "By setting up these systems, we're not just improving our workflow—we're building a foundation that supports our growth and excellence. Let's ensure our office systems are as strong and efficient as our vision and plans."

The room was silent, each team member considering the practical steps needed to enhance their office systems. Jack could see the determination in their eyes—a readiness to implement changes that would streamline their operations and boost their efficiency.

"Remember," Jack concluded, "setting up efficient office systems is a continuous process. It requires us to be proactive, adaptable, and committed to improvement. Let's create an office environment that supports our goals and enables us to achieve excellence."

The session ended with a renewed sense of focus on practical implementation. The team was equipped with the understanding and motivation needed to set up efficient office systems, laying the groundwork for their journey toward excellence in property management.

Networking and Industry Associations

Jack Miller could feel the energy and readiness of his team as they tackled each crucial component of building a strong foundation for their property management business. After discussing efficient office systems, it was now time to emphasize the importance of networking and industry associations.

"Team," Jack began, clicking the remote to display a vibrant networking event. "We've discussed how to streamline our internal processes. Now, let's talk about the value of networking and industry associations. Connecting with other professionals and staying active in the industry can open doors and provide invaluable insights."

The first slide highlighted a bustling conference hall. "1.

Industry Conferences and Trade Shows. Attending these events allows us to meet other professionals, learn about the latest trends, and discover new technologies. These gatherings are goldmines for networking and gaining fresh perspectives."

Jack remembered his first industry conference, where he had met a mentor who greatly influenced his career. Those connections had been instrumental in his growth and success.

The next slide displayed a group of professionals in a lively discussion. "2. **Professional Associations.** Joining associations like the National Association of Residential Property Managers (NARPM) or the Institute of Real Estate Management (IREM) provides access to resources, educational programs, and a network of peers. These organizations also offer certifications that enhance our credibility."

David, always eager to learn, was already considering which associations would provide the most value. Jack knew his enthusiasm would be infectious.

The third slide depicted a local meetup group. "3. **Local Networking Events.** Engaging in local events, such as chamber of commerce meetings or real estate investment clubs, helps us build relationships within our community. These connections can lead to new business opportunities and partnerships."

Sarah, who had a knack for community engagement, was already thinking about the next local event she could attend to represent their company.

The next image showed a mentor and mentee deep in conversation. "4. **Mentorship Programs.** Both finding a mentor and being a mentor can be incredibly beneficial. Mentors provide guidance and wisdom, while mentoring others helps us develop leadership skills and gives back to the community."

Jack smiled, thinking of his own mentors who had guided him through challenging times. He encouraged his team to both seek mentors and offer their own experiences to newcomers in the industry.

The fifth slide highlighted a webinar. "5. **Online Communities and Webinars.** Participating in online forums, webinars, and social media groups can expand our reach and keep us informed about industry trends and best practices. These platforms offer flexibility and a wealth of information."

Lisa, who was tech-savvy, saw the potential in leveraging online platforms to stay connected and informed. Jack appreciated her ability to integrate digital tools into their networking strategy.

The final slide showed an award ceremony. "6. **Awards and Recognition Programs.** Applying for industry awards not only motivates us to strive for excellence but also enhances our reputation. Recognition from reputable organizations can significantly boost our credibility and attract new clients."

Jack turned off the projector and faced his team, the importance of his message clear. "Networking and industry associations are more than just social activities. They are strategic moves that position us as leaders and innovators in property management."

He stepped closer, his voice filled with passion. "By actively participating in these networks, we gain knowledge, build relationships, and create opportunities for growth. Let's commit to engaging with our industry and community to drive our business forward."

The room was silent, each team member reflecting on the

importance of building strong professional networks. Jack could see the determination in their eyes—a readiness to connect, learn, and grow through active participation in their industry.

"Remember," Jack concluded, "networking and involvement in industry associations are continuous efforts. They require us to be proactive, open-minded, and engaged. Let's build a network that supports our goals and propels us toward excellence."

The session ended with a renewed sense of purpose and a plan to actively engage in their industry. The team was equipped with the understanding and motivation needed to build valuable networks and participate in industry associations, laying the groundwork for their journey toward excellence in property management.

3

Chapter 3: Acquiring Properties

Market Research and Analysis

Jack Miller stood at the front of the room, his gaze sweeping over the eager faces of his team. They had moved beyond laying the foundation and were now ready to explore the exciting realm of acquiring properties. But before diving in, they needed to understand the importance of market research and analysis.

"Team," Jack began, his voice filled with enthusiasm. "Today, we embark on the journey of acquiring properties—a pivotal step in our growth. But to do this successfully, we must first delve into the intricacies of market research and analysis."

He clicked the remote, and the screen illuminated with a map of their target market. "Market research is the compass that guides our decisions. It helps us understand the current landscape, identify opportunities, and mitigate risks. Let's break it down."

The first slide highlighted a graph showing market trends.

"1. **Understanding Market Trends.** We need to stay abreast of market trends such as rental rates, vacancy rates, and property values. Analyzing historical data and projections allows us to anticipate market fluctuations and make informed decisions."

Jack remembered a time when they had overlooked a downward trend in rental rates, resulting in a property acquisition that underperformed. Market research would ensure they avoided such pitfalls in the future.

The next slide displayed a chart of demographic data. "2. **Demographic Analysis.** Understanding the demographics of our target market—such as age, income levels, and household size—helps us tailor our property offerings to meet the needs of potential tenants. It ensures our properties remain attractive and in demand."

Sarah, with her keen eye for detail, was already jotting down notes on demographic trends. Her insights would be crucial in identifying lucrative opportunities within specific demographic segments.

The third slide depicted a competitive analysis table. "3. **Competitive Analysis.** We need to know our competition inside and out. Analyzing competing properties—such as their amenities, rental rates, and occupancy rates—helps us position our properties strategically and differentiate ourselves in the market."

David, always strategic in his approach, was already brainstorming ways to gain a competitive edge. Jack knew his analytical mind would be invaluable in dissecting their competitors' strengths and weaknesses.

The next image showed a risk assessment matrix. "4. **Risk Assessment.** Every property acquisition comes with risks, from economic downturns to unforeseen maintenance issues. Conducting a thorough risk assessment allows us to identify potential threats and develop strategies to mitigate them. It ensures we proceed with caution and foresight."

Lisa, their financial guru, nodded in agreement. She had a knack for evaluating risk factors and devising contingency plans, ensuring their investments were as secure as possible.

The fifth slide highlighted a SWOT analysis diagram. "5. **SWOT Analysis.** By analyzing our strengths, weaknesses, opportunities, and threats, we gain a comprehensive understanding of our position in the market. This helps us capitalize on our strengths, address our weaknesses, seize opportunities, and prepare for potential challenges."

Jack saw nods of understanding around the room. Their SWOT analysis sessions had led to valuable insights and strategic decisions in the past.

The final slide displayed a checklist titled "Key Considerations." "6. **Key Considerations.** Finally, we must consider various factors such as location, property condition, financing options, and regulatory requirements. Each property acquisition is unique, and thorough consideration of these factors ensures we make sound investment decisions."

Jack turned off the projector and faced his team, the importance of his message resonating in the air. "Market research and analysis are the foundation of successful property acquisitions. They provide us with the knowledge and insights needed to make informed decisions and navigate the complexities of the real estate market."

He stepped closer, his voice filled with conviction. "By conducting thorough research and analysis, we minimize risks and maximize opportunities. Let's commit to approaching each property acquisition with diligence, foresight, and strategic thinking."

The room was silent, each team member absorbing the gravity of their task. Jack could see the determination in their eyes—a readiness to embark on this journey armed with knowledge and insight.

"Remember," Jack concluded, "market research and analysis are ongoing processes. They require us to be proactive, adaptable, and informed. Let's dive into our market research with enthusiasm and dedication, laying the groundwork for successful property acquisitions."

The session ended with a renewed sense of purpose and a plan to delve into market research with vigor. The team was equipped with the understanding and motivation needed to analyze their target market thoroughly, laying the groundwork for their journey toward excellence in property acquisition.

Property Acquisition Strategies

Jack Miller stood before his team, the excitement palpable in the air as they delved deeper into the intricacies of acquiring properties. Having discussed the importance of market research and analysis, it was now time to explore the various strategies they could employ to acquire properties successfully.

"Team," Jack began, his voice infused with anticipation. "Now that we understand our market and have identified opportunities, let's explore the strategies we can use to acquire properties strategically. Each strategy has its own benefits and considerations, so let's dive in."

CHAPTER 3: ACQUIRING PROPERTIES

He clicked the remote, and the screen displayed a list of property acquisition strategies. "Property acquisition strategies are the blueprints for achieving our investment goals. Let's examine some of the most common ones."

The first slide highlighted "Direct Purchase." "1. **Direct Purchase.** This involves buying properties directly from sellers, whether they are individual homeowners, real estate agents, or other investors. Direct purchase gives us full control over the transaction process and allows for negotiation to secure favorable terms."

Jack recalled the thrill of negotiating their first direct purchase. It had been a steep learning curve, but the satisfaction of sealing the deal had made it worthwhile.

The next slide displayed "Off-Market Deals." "2. **Off-Market Deals.** Off-market properties are not listed publicly and may require more effort to find. However, they often present unique opportunities and less competition. Building relationships with property owners, networking within the industry, and leveraging off-market databases can uncover hidden gems."

Sarah, with her knack for networking, saw the potential in exploring off-market deals. She made a mental note to expand their network and uncover lucrative opportunities.

The third slide depicted "Distressed Properties." "3. **Distressed Properties.** These properties are typically under financial distress or in poor condition. Acquiring distressed properties can be an opportunity to add value through renovations or repositioning. However, it requires careful due diligence and a solid renovation plan."

David, always drawn to strategic challenges, saw the potential in acquiring distressed properties. He began brainstorming ways to turn them into profitable investments.

The next image showed "Partnerships and Joint Ventures." "4. **Partnerships and Joint Ventures.** Collaborating with other investors or real estate firms allows us to pool resources, share risks, and access expertise. Partnerships can provide access to larger deals and diversify our investment portfolio."

Lisa, with her financial expertise, recognized the benefits of partnerships in accessing larger investments. She began considering potential partners who could complement their strengths and goals.

The fifth slide highlighted "Real Estate Investment Trusts (REITs)." "5. **Real Estate Investment Trusts (REITs).** Investing in REITs provides exposure to a diversified portfolio of properties without the need for direct ownership. REITs offer liquidity, passive income, and professional management, making them an attractive option for investors seeking diversification."

Jack emphasized the importance of considering REITs as part of their investment strategy. While they offered benefits, he reminded the team to conduct thorough research before investing.

The final slide displayed "Auction Properties." "6. **Auction Properties.** Properties sold at auctions can offer opportunities for acquisition at below-market prices. However, the auction process can be competitive and require quick decision-making. Proper research and preparation are essential for success in this strategy."

Jack turned off the projector and faced his team, the excitement evident in their expressions. "Each property acquisition strategy offers unique advantages and challenges. By understanding our options and aligning them with our investment goals, we can make informed decisions that propel us toward success."

He stepped closer, his voice filled with confidence. "Let's explore these strategies with enthusiasm and discernment, leveraging our market knowledge and strategic thinking to acquire properties that align with our vision and objectives."

The room was buzzing with anticipation as each team member considered the strategies presented. Jack could see the determination in their eyes—a readiness to explore new avenues and seize opportunities in the real estate market.

"Remember," Jack concluded, "property acquisition is a dynamic process that requires flexibility and adaptability. Let's embrace these strategies as tools to achieve our investment goals and build a strong portfolio."

The session ended with a renewed sense of purpose and a plan to explore various property acquisition strategies. The team was equipped with the understanding and motivation needed to pursue opportunities and expand their presence in the real estate market.

Due Diligence Processes

Jack Miller stood before his team, their attention focused as they continued their exploration of property acquisition strategies. Having discussed the importance of market research and analysis, and strategies for acquiring properties, it was now time to delve into the crucial aspect of due diligence processes.

"Team," Jack began, his tone serious yet determined. "As we navigate the path of property acquisition, one of the most critical steps we must take is conducting thorough due diligence. This process ensures we make informed decisions and mitigate risks. Let's explore the key elements of due diligence."

He clicked the remote, and the screen displayed a checklist titled "Due Diligence Processes." "Due diligence is the backbone of our decision-making process. It involves investigating every aspect of a property to ensure its suitability and viability as an investment."

The first slide highlighted "Financial Due Diligence." "1. **Financial Due Diligence.** This involves analyzing the financial records of the property, including income, expenses, taxes, and cash flow projections. We must verify the accuracy of financial statements and assess the property's financial performance to determine its potential return on investment."

Jack emphasized the importance of financial due diligence in assessing the profitability of a property. He recalled a time when meticulous financial analysis had revealed hidden expenses that could have derailed their investment.

The next slide displayed "Physical Inspection." "2. **Physical Inspection.** Conducting a thorough inspection of the property is essential to identify any structural issues, maintenance needs, or code violations. Hiring qualified inspectors to assess the property's condition ensures we uncover any hidden defects that could affect its value or safety."

Sarah, who valued attention to detail, nodded in agreement. She understood the importance of a comprehensive physical inspection in uncovering potential risks and liabilities.

The third slide depicted "Legal and Title Due Diligence." "3. **Legal and Title Due Diligence.** We must review the property's legal documents, including deeds, titles, surveys, and zoning regulations. This ensures the property has clear title ownership and is free from legal encumbrances or disputes that could jeopardize the transaction."

David, always meticulous in his approach, recognized the significance of legal due diligence in protecting their interests. He made a mental note to engage legal experts to scrutinize the property's legal documents thoroughly.

The next image showed "Environmental Assessment." "4. **Environmental Assessment.** Assessing environmental risks such as contamination, hazardous materials, or regulatory compliance issues is crucial, especially for properties with industrial or commercial use. Conducting environmental assessments helps us identify potential liabilities and comply with environmental regulations."

Lisa, their financial expert, saw the potential financial implications of environmental liabilities. She knew the importance of conducting thorough environmental assessments to avoid costly surprises down the line.

The fifth slide highlighted "Market and Comparable Analysis." "5. **Market and Comparable Analysis.** Analyzing market trends and comparing the property to similar properties in the area helps us determine its market value and potential appreciation. This ensures we make informed decisions regarding pricing and negotiation."

Jack stressed the importance of understanding the property's market context to assess its investment potential accurately. He encouraged the team to conduct in-depth market analysis to validate their investment assumptions.

The final slide displayed "Tenant and Lease Audits." "6. **Tenant and Lease Audits.** Reviewing existing lease agreements, tenant profiles, and rental histories provides insights into the property's income stability and tenant satisfaction.

Identifying potential lease risks or opportunities allows us to proactively address them during the acquisition process."

Jack turned off the projector and faced his team, the gravity of the due diligence process evident in his expression. "Due diligence is our safeguard against costly mistakes and unforeseen risks. By conducting thorough investigations in these key areas, we protect our investments and set ourselves up for success."

He stepped closer, his voice resonating with conviction. "Let's approach due diligence with diligence, attention to detail, and a commitment to excellence. By leaving no stone unturned, we ensure our property acquisitions are founded on solid ground."

The room was silent, each team member absorbing the importance of due diligence in their acquisition process. Jack could see the determination in their eyes—a readiness to approach their due diligence processes with rigor and thoroughness.

"Remember," Jack concluded, "due diligence is not just a checklist—it's a mindset. Let's embrace this mindset as we conduct our due diligence processes, ensuring each property acquisition is backed by thorough research and analysis."

The session ended with a renewed sense of purpose and a plan to embark on their due diligence processes with diligence and dedication. The team was equipped with the understanding and motivation needed to conduct comprehensive due diligence, laying the groundwork for successful property acquisitions.

CHAPTER 3: ACQUIRING PROPERTIES

Negotiation Techniques

Jack Miller stood at the front of the room, his team's attention fixed on him as they continued their journey through the complexities of property acquisition. Having covered the crucial aspects of due diligence processes, it was now time to equip them with the essential skill of negotiation.

"Team," Jack began, his voice projecting confidence and authority. "Negotiation is an art form—a skill that can make or break a property acquisition deal. It's the bridge between our research and analysis and the realization of our investment goals. Let's explore the key negotiation techniques that will empower us to secure favorable deals."

He clicked the remote, and the screen displayed a list of negotiation techniques. "Negotiation is the cornerstone of successful property acquisitions. Mastering these techniques allows us to navigate the complexities of the negotiation process with finesse and confidence."

The first slide highlighted "Preparation and Information Gathering." "1. **Preparation and Information Gathering.** Before entering into negotiations, we must thoroughly prepare by gathering information about the property, the seller, and the market. Knowledge is power in negotiation, and being well-prepared gives us a strategic advantage."

Jack emphasized the importance of preparation in negotiation. He recalled a deal where their meticulous research had uncovered a seller's urgent need to close quickly, giving them leverage in negotiations.

The next slide displayed "Setting Clear Objectives and Priorities." "2. **Setting Clear Objectives and Priorities.** It's essential to define our objectives and priorities before entering into negotiations. What are our must-haves, nice-to-haves, and deal-breakers? Setting clear parameters helps us stay focused and assertive during negotiations."

Sarah, who valued clarity and focus, nodded in agreement. She understood the importance of setting clear objectives to guide their negotiation strategy effectively.

The third slide depicted "Active Listening and Empathy." "3. **Active Listening and Empathy.** Effective negotiation is not just about making demands—it's also about understanding the other party's perspective. Active listening and empathy allow us to build rapport, identify common ground, and find mutually beneficial solutions."

David, with his knack for building relationships, recognized the power of empathy in negotiation. He made a mental note to listen actively and seek understanding during their negotiations.

The next image showed "Creative Problem-Solving." "4. **Creative Problem-Solving.** Sometimes, negotiations reach an impasse. In such situations, we must employ creative problem-solving techniques to explore alternative solutions and find win-win outcomes. Thinking outside the box can break deadlocks and unlock hidden value."

Lisa, their problem-solving expert, saw the potential in approaching negotiations with creativity and flexibility. She began brainstorming innovative solutions to potential negotiation challenges.

The fifth slide highlighted "Assertiveness and Confidence." "5. **Assertiveness and Confidence.** Confidence is key in negotiation. We must assertively advocate for our interests while remaining respectful and professional. Confidence breeds credibility and can sway negotiations in our favor."

Jack stressed the importance of projecting confidence in negotiation. He encouraged the team to exude assertiveness while maintaining a collaborative demeanor.

The final slide displayed "Effective Communication and Body Language." "6. **Effective Communication and Body Language.** Communication is not just about what we say—it's also about how we say it. Clear and concise communication, coupled with positive body language, builds trust and fosters productive negotiations."

Jack turned off the projector and faced his team, the gravity of their task evident in his expression. "Negotiation is a delicate dance—a balance between assertiveness and empathy, strategy and flexibility. By mastering these techniques, we can navigate negotiations with finesse and achieve our desired outcomes."

He stepped closer, his voice resonating with determination. "Let's approach our negotiations with confidence, preparation, and a commitment to win-win outcomes. By honing our negotiation skills, we position ourselves for success in the competitive real estate market."

The room was silent, each team member absorbing the importance of negotiation techniques in their acquisition process. Jack could see the determination in their eyes—a readiness to apply these techniques with skill and finesse.

"Remember," Jack concluded, "negotiation is an ongoing process—it's not just about closing deals, but also about building relationships and fostering trust. Let's embrace these techniques as tools to achieve our investment goals and forge successful partnerships."

The session ended with a renewed sense of purpose and a plan to apply negotiation techniques effectively in their property acquisitions. The team was equipped with the understanding and motivation needed to navigate negotiations with confidence and skill, laying the groundwork for successful acquisitions in the dynamic real estate market.

Closing the Deal

Jack Miller stood before his team, their anticipation palpable as they neared the culmination of their journey through the complexities of property acquisition. Having covered negotiation techniques and financing options, it was now time to focus on the pivotal moment of closing the deal.

"Team," Jack began, his voice steady and resolute. "Closing the deal is the culmination of our efforts—a moment where preparation meets opportunity. It's the final step in our journey towards acquiring properties, and it requires careful attention to detail and effective execution. Let's explore the key aspects of closing the deal."

He clicked the remote, and the screen displayed a checklist titled "Closing the Deal." "Closing the deal is the ultimate goal of our acquisition process. It involves finalizing the transaction, transferring ownership, and ensuring all legal and financial requirements are met."

The first slide highlighted "Documentation and Paperwork." "1. **Documentation and Paperwork.** Closing a real estate deal involves a significant amount of paperwork, including purchase agreements, deeds, mortgage documents, and title insurance. Ensuring all documentation is accurate and complete is essential for a smooth closing process."

Jack emphasized the importance of meticulous attention to detail in preparing and reviewing the necessary documents.

He recalled a time when a minor oversight in paperwork had delayed their closing process, highlighting the importance of thoroughness.

The next slide displayed "Funding and Financing." "2. **Funding and Financing.** Securing funding for the property purchase is crucial. Whether through cash reserves, bank loans, or alternative financing options, having the necessary funds in place ensures we can proceed with the transaction smoothly. Coordinating with lenders and financial institutions is key to securing favorable financing terms."

Sarah, their finance expert, nodded in agreement. She understood the importance of having financing arrangements in place well in advance to avoid any last-minute complications.

The third slide depicted "Title and Property Transfer." "3. **Title and Property Transfer.** Transferring ownership of the property requires a clear title and legal documentation. Conducting a title search and obtaining title insurance protects against any claims or encumbrances on the property. Working with a qualified title company ensures a seamless transfer of ownership."

David, with his legal expertise, recognized the significance of ensuring a clear title and smooth property transfer. He made a mental note to engage reputable title services to handle the transfer process.

The next image showed "Escrow and Closing Agents." "4. **Escrow and Closing Agents.** Utilizing escrow services and working with experienced closing agents facilitates the closing process. Escrow agents act as neutral third parties, holding funds and documents until all conditions of the transaction are met. Closing agents oversee the signing of documents and ensure compliance with legal requirements."

Lisa, their detail-oriented team member, saw the value in entrusting the closing process to experienced professionals. She began researching reputable escrow and closing agents to handle their transactions.

The fifth slide highlighted "Final Walkthrough and Inspections." "5. **Final Walkthrough and Inspections.** Conducting a final walkthrough of the property ensures it meets the agreed-upon condition and specifications. Any discrepancies or issues discovered during the walkthrough can be addressed before closing. Inspections, such as termite inspections or structural assessments, provide additional assurance of the property's condition."

Jack stressed the importance of conducting thorough final inspections to ensure the property meets their expectations. He reminded the team to schedule inspections well in advance to allow time for any necessary repairs or negotiations.

The final slide displayed "Closing Costs and Fees." "6. **Closing Costs and Fees.** Closing a real estate deal incurs various costs and fees, including legal fees, title insurance, appraisal fees, and property taxes. Understanding and budgeting for these costs ensures we are financially prepared for closing day. Negotiating with service providers for competitive rates can help minimize closing expenses."

Jack turned off the projector and faced his team, the gravity of their impending transactions evident in his expression. "Closing the deal is the final hurdle in our property acquisition process. It requires precision, diligence, and effective coordination to ensure a successful outcome."

He stepped closer, his voice filled with determination. "Let's approach the closing process with confidence and attention to detail, ensuring all aspects of the transaction are handled with care. By executing each step meticulously, we finalize our acquisitions and move one step closer to achieving our investment goals."

The room was silent, each team member absorbing the importance of closing the deal with precision and efficiency. Jack could see the determination in their eyes—a readiness to navigate the final stages of their acquisitions with determination and focus.

"Remember," Jack concluded, "closing the deal is not just a formality—it's the culmination of our hard work and dedication. Let's embrace the closing process with enthusiasm and professionalism, ensuring each transaction is completed with integrity and excellence."

The session ended with a renewed sense of purpose and a plan to approach their closing processes with diligence and attention to detail. The team was equipped with the understanding and

4

Chapter 4: Onboarding New Properties

Initial Property Inspections

Jack Miller gathered his team in the conference room, excitement buzzing in the air as they embarked on the next phase of their property management journey. Having successfully closed deals and acquired new properties, it was time to focus on the crucial process of onboarding. And it all began with the initial property inspections.

"Team," Jack began, his voice filled with anticipation. "Onboarding new properties is the gateway to our success as property managers. It's where we lay the groundwork for exceptional management and tenant satisfaction. Let's delve into the first step: initial property inspections."

He clicked the remote, and the screen illuminated with a checklist titled "Initial Property Inspections." "Initial property inspections are our opportunity to assess the condition of the property, identify any maintenance needs, and lay the

CHAPTER 4: ONBOARDING NEW PROPERTIES

foundation for effective management."

The first slide highlighted "Exterior Inspection." "1. **Exterior Inspection.** We begin by examining the exterior of the property, assessing its curb appeal, landscaping, and structural integrity. This allows us to identify any visible maintenance issues, such as peeling paint, damaged siding, or overgrown vegetation."

Jack emphasized the importance of making a strong first impression with the property's exterior. He recalled a time when a well-maintained exterior had attracted high-quality tenants and boosted property value.

The next slide displayed "Interior Walkthrough." "2. **Interior Walkthrough.** We then conduct a thorough walkthrough of the interior spaces, inspecting each room for signs of wear and tear, water damage, or safety hazards. This includes checking the condition of flooring, walls, ceilings, fixtures, and appliances."

Sarah, with her keen eye for detail, nodded in agreement. She understood the importance of identifying any interior issues that could impact tenant satisfaction and retention.

The third slide depicted "Mechanical Systems Inspection." "3. **Mechanical Systems Inspection.** Assessing the functionality of mechanical systems, such as HVAC, plumbing, electrical, and security systems, is crucial. Any signs of malfunction or deterioration should be addressed promptly to ensure tenant comfort and safety."

David, always analytical in his approach, recognized the significance of maintaining reliable mechanical systems to minimize disruptions and costly repairs.

The next image showed "Safety and Compliance Checks." "4. **Safety and Compliance Checks.** Ensuring the property meets all safety and compliance standards is non-negotiable. This includes checking smoke detectors, carbon monoxide detectors, fire extinguishers, and ensuring compliance with local building codes and regulations."

Lisa, their compliance expert, nodded in agreement. She understood the importance of prioritizing safety and compliance to mitigate risks and liabilities.

The fifth slide highlighted "Documentation and Reporting."
"5. **Documentation and Reporting.** Documenting our findings through detailed inspection reports is essential. These reports serve as a baseline for property maintenance and provide documentation of the property's condition at the time of onboarding. Clear and concise reporting ensures transparency and accountability."

Jack stressed the importance of thorough documentation to track maintenance needs and monitor property condition over time. He reminded the team to maintain detailed records to facilitate effective property management.

The final slide displayed "Action Plan and Prioritization."
"6. **Action Plan and Prioritization.** Based on our inspection findings, we develop an action plan to address maintenance needs and prioritize repairs. This ensures that critical issues are addressed promptly, while less urgent tasks are scheduled for future maintenance cycles."

Jack turned off the projector and faced his team, the gravity of their responsibility evident in his expression. "Initial property inspections set the tone for our management approach. By conducting thorough assessments and developing actionable plans, we demonstrate our commitment to proactive maintenance and tenant satisfaction."

He stepped closer, his voice filled with conviction. "Let's

approach our initial property inspections with diligence and attention to detail, ensuring each property is primed for success from day one. By laying a strong foundation, we set ourselves up for excellence in property management."

The room was silent, each team member absorbing the importance of their role in onboarding new properties effectively. Jack could see the determination in their eyes—a readiness to tackle the challenges and opportunities that lay ahead.

"Remember," Jack concluded, "initial property inspections are just the beginning of our journey with each property. Let's approach them with enthusiasm and professionalism, knowing that our efforts will pave the way for long-term success."

The session ended with a renewed sense of purpose and a plan to conduct initial property inspections with diligence and care. The team was equipped with the understanding and motivation needed to set their properties on the path to excellence in management and tenant satisfaction.

Creating a Management Plan

Jack Miller gathered his team once again in the conference room, the energy buzzing as they delved further into the onboarding process of their newly acquired properties. Having completed the initial property inspections, it was time to craft a comprehensive management plan to ensure the smooth operation and optimization of each property.

"Team," Jack began, his voice filled with purpose. "Creating a management plan is the cornerstone of our approach to property management. It's where we outline our strategies, goals, and processes to maximize the value and performance of each property. Let's dive into the second step: creating a management plan."

He clicked the remote, and the screen illuminated with a checklist titled "Creating a Management Plan." "A management plan serves as our roadmap for success, guiding our actions and decisions throughout the lifecycle of each property."

The first slide highlighted "Tenant Experience and Satisfaction." "1. **Tenant Experience and Satisfaction.** At the heart of our management plan is a focus on tenant experience and satisfaction. We aim to create a positive living environment for our tenants, fostering a sense of community and addressing their needs promptly and effectively."

Jack emphasized the importance of prioritizing tenant satisfaction to enhance retention rates and attract high-quality tenants. He recalled a time when exceptional tenant service had led to glowing reviews and increased referrals.

The next slide displayed "Maintenance and Repairs Protocol." "2. **Maintenance and Repairs Protocol.** Establishing a proactive maintenance and repairs protocol is essential for preserving property value and minimizing disruptions. This includes scheduling regular maintenance checks, promptly addressing repair requests, and maintaining clear communication with tenants."

Sarah, with her organizational skills, nodded in agreement. She understood the importance of implementing a structured maintenance plan to ensure properties remained in top condition.

The third slide depicted "Financial Management and Budgeting." "3. **Financial Management and Budgeting.** Sound financial management is crucial for the success of each property. This includes budgeting for expenses, tracking income and expenses, and optimizing revenue streams. We aim to maximize profitability while ensuring financial stability and transparency."

David, always attentive to financial matters, recognized the significance of effective budgeting and financial oversight. He made a mental note to implement rigorous financial controls to optimize property performance.

The next image showed "Leasing and Marketing Strategy."
"4. **Leasing and Marketing Strategy.** Developing a targeted leasing and marketing strategy helps us attract and retain quality tenants. This includes identifying target demographics, utilizing digital marketing channels, and implementing effective leasing processes to minimize vacancies and maximize rental income."

Lisa, their marketing expert, saw the potential in leveraging digital marketing tools and data-driven strategies to attract prospective tenants. She began brainstorming innovative approaches to enhance property visibility and leasing success.

The fifth slide highlighted "Compliance and Regulatory Compliance." "5. **Compliance and Regulatory Compliance.** Ensuring compliance with local laws, regulations, and housing standards is non-negotiable. This includes staying up-to-date with changing regulations, obtaining necessary permits and licenses, and maintaining accurate records to demonstrate compliance."

Jack stressed the importance of prioritizing compliance to mitigate legal risks and liabilities. He reminded the team to stay vigilant and proactive in adhering to regulatory requirements.

The final slide displayed "Emergency Response and Crisis Management." "6. **Emergency Response and Crisis Management.** Preparedness is key in managing emergencies and crises effectively. This includes developing emergency response plans, conducting regular drills, and maintaining communication channels with tenants and emergency services."

Jack turned off the projector and faced his team, the gravity of their responsibility evident in his expression. "A management plan is more than just a document—it's our commitment to excellence in property management. By outlining clear strategies and processes, we ensure each property operates smoothly and efficiently."

He stepped closer, his voice filled with determination. "Let's approach the creation of our management plans with diligence and foresight, knowing that our efforts will lay the foundation for long-term success."

The room was silent, each team member absorbing the importance of their role in crafting effective management plans. Jack could see the determination in their eyes—a readiness to tackle the challenges and opportunities that lay ahead.

"Remember," Jack concluded, "our management plans are living documents that evolve with each property. Let's approach them with enthusiasm and dedication, knowing that they are key to our success as property managers."

The session ended with a renewed sense of purpose and a plan to craft comprehensive management plans for each property. The team was equipped with the understanding and motivation needed to optimize property performance and tenant satisfaction through effective management planning.

Transitioning Tenants

Jack Miller reconvened his team in the conference room, their focus shifting to the critical task of transitioning tenants into their newly acquired properties. Having crafted comprehensive management plans, it was now time to ensure a seamless and positive experience for both existing and new tenants during the transition process.

"Team," Jack began, his tone determined. "Transitioning tenants is a pivotal step in our property management journey. It's where we bridge the gap between the old and the new, fostering continuity and trust while implementing our management strategies. Let's explore the third step: transitioning tenants."

He clicked the remote, and the screen illuminated with a checklist titled "Transitioning Tenants." "Transitioning tenants is about more than just changing keys—it's about ensuring a smooth and positive experience for everyone involved."

The first slide highlighted "Communication and Transparency." "1. **Communication and Transparency.** Clear and transparent communication is essential during the tenant transition process. We must keep tenants informed about upcoming changes, address any concerns promptly, and provide reassurance about the continuity of their living experience."

Jack emphasized the importance of maintaining open lines of communication to build trust and mitigate concerns among existing tenants. He recalled a time when proactive communication had eased tenants' apprehensions during a property transition.

The next slide displayed "Lease Renewals and New Agreements." "2. **Lease Renewals and New Agreements.** For existing tenants, we aim to facilitate smooth lease renewals or transitions to new lease agreements as needed. This includes reviewing lease terms, discussing any changes, and ensuring all parties are in agreement before finalizing arrangements."

Sarah, with her knack for detail, nodded in agreement. She understood the importance of ensuring lease agreements aligned with the management plan while respecting tenants' rights and preferences.

The third slide depicted "Welcome Packages and Orientation." "3. **Welcome Packages and Orientation.** Providing welcome packages and orientation sessions for new tenants helps them acclimate to their new living environment. This includes providing essential information about property amenities, community rules, and contact information for property management."

David, always focused on efficiency, recognized the value of welcoming new tenants and helping them feel at home from day one. He made a mental note to streamline the orientation process to ensure a seamless experience.

The next image showed "Tenant Feedback and Support." "4. **Tenant Feedback and Support.** Encouraging tenant feedback and providing ongoing support is crucial for fostering tenant satisfaction and retention. We must be responsive to tenant concerns, address issues promptly, and solicit feedback to continuously improve our services."

Lisa, their customer service expert, saw the potential in leveraging tenant feedback to enhance the tenant experience and strengthen community engagement. She began brainstorming ways to facilitate open communication and feedback channels.

The fifth slide highlighted "Community Building and Engagement." "5. **Community Building and Engagement.** Fostering a sense of community among tenants contributes to a positive living environment and enhances tenant satisfaction. This includes organizing community events, facilitating resident interactions, and creating opportunities for tenant collaboration and participation."

Jack stressed the importance of building a vibrant and supportive community within their properties. He encouraged the team to explore creative ways to engage tenants and foster a sense of belonging.

The final slide displayed "Follow-Up and Continuous Improvement." "6. **Follow-Up and Continuous Improvement.** After the transition process, we continue to follow up with tenants to ensure their needs are met and address any outstanding issues. Additionally, we use feedback and insights gathered during the transition to refine our processes and improve the tenant experience."

Jack turned off the projector and faced his team, the gravity of their responsibility evident in his expression. "Transitioning tenants is a pivotal moment in our management journey. By prioritizing communication, support, and community building, we ensure a positive experience for both existing and new tenants."

He stepped closer, his voice filled with determination. "Let's approach the tenant transition process with empathy, professionalism, and a commitment to excellence. By fostering a smooth and welcoming transition, we set the stage for long-term tenant satisfaction and retention."

The room was silent, each team member absorbing the

importance of their role in facilitating a seamless transition for tenants. Jack could see the determination in their eyes—a readiness to apply their expertise and compassion to ensure a positive tenant experience.

"Remember," Jack concluded, "our success as property managers hinges on the satisfaction and well-being of our tenants. Let's approach the tenant transition process with enthusiasm and dedication, knowing that each positive interaction contributes to our overall success."

The session ended with a renewed sense of purpose and a plan to execute the tenant transition process with care and professionalism. The team was equipped with the understanding and motivation needed to foster positive tenant experiences and build thriving communities within their properties.

Setting Up Maintenance Schedules

Jack Miller convened his team once more in the conference room, their attention now turning to the crucial task of setting up maintenance schedules for their newly acquired properties. Having addressed tenant transitions, it was time to ensure the properties remained in optimal condition through proactive maintenance planning.

"Team," Jack began, his voice resolute. "Setting up maintenance schedules is the backbone of our property management strategy. It's where we prioritize preventative care and proactive upkeep to preserve property value and tenant satisfaction. Let's explore the fourth step: setting up maintenance schedules."

He clicked the remote, and the screen illuminated with a

checklist titled "Setting Up Maintenance Schedules." "Maintenance schedules are our roadmap for preserving property condition and ensuring operational efficiency."

The first slide highlighted "Routine Maintenance Tasks." "1. **Routine Maintenance Tasks.** We begin by identifying routine maintenance tasks that are essential for property upkeep, such as HVAC system inspections, landscaping, gutter cleaning, and pest control. These tasks should be scheduled at regular intervals to prevent issues and prolong the lifespan of property components."

Jack emphasized the importance of proactive maintenance in preventing costly repairs and minimizing tenant disruptions. He recalled a time when routine inspections had identified a minor issue before it escalated into a major repair.

The next slide displayed "Seasonal Maintenance Considerations." "2. **Seasonal Maintenance Considerations.** Different seasons bring unique maintenance challenges. We must anticipate seasonal maintenance needs, such as snow removal in winter, gutter cleaning in fall, and irrigation system maintenance in spring and summer. By planning ahead, we ensure properties are prepared for seasonal changes."

Sarah, with her attention to detail, nodded in agreement. She understood the importance of adapting maintenance schedules to seasonal variations to mitigate weather-related risks and preserve property aesthetics.

The third slide depicted "Priority-Based Maintenance Planning." "3. **Priority-Based Maintenance Planning.** Not all maintenance tasks are created equal. We must prioritize tasks based on urgency, impact on tenant comfort and safety, and potential cost implications. This ensures we allocate resources effectively and address critical issues promptly."

David, always analytical in his approach, recognized the significance of prioritizing maintenance tasks to maximize operational efficiency and minimize risks. He made a mental note to develop a systematic approach to prioritize maintenance needs across their properties.

The next image showed "Vendor Management and Service Agreements." "4. **Vendor Management and Service Agreements.** Establishing relationships with reliable vendors and service providers is essential for executing maintenance tasks effectively. We must negotiate service agreements, coordinate scheduling, and maintain open communication to ensure timely and quality service delivery."

Lisa, their vendor management expert, saw the potential in leveraging strategic partnerships to streamline maintenance processes and minimize downtime. She began strategizing ways to optimize vendor relationships and negotiate favorable service agreements.

The fifth slide highlighted "Technology Integration for Maintenance Tracking." "5. **Technology Integration for Maintenance Tracking.** Leveraging technology solutions, such as property management software or maintenance management platforms, streamlines maintenance tracking and reporting. This allows us to schedule tasks, track work orders, and monitor property condition in real-time."

Jack stressed the importance of embracing technology to enhance maintenance efficiency and transparency. He encouraged the team to explore software solutions that could streamline their maintenance workflows and improve communication with tenants and vendors.

The final slide displayed "Continuous Evaluation and Optimization." "6. **Continuous Evaluation and Optimization.**

Maintenance schedules are not set in stone—they require continuous evaluation and optimization. We must regularly review performance metrics, solicit feedback from tenants and vendors, and adjust schedules as needed to ensure ongoing effectiveness and efficiency."

Jack turned off the projector and faced his team, the gravity of their responsibility evident in his expression. "Maintenance schedules are our commitment to proactive property care. By setting up comprehensive schedules and embracing technology solutions, we ensure our properties remain in optimal condition year-round."

He stepped closer, his voice filled with determination. "Let's approach maintenance scheduling with diligence and foresight, knowing that our efforts will preserve property value and enhance tenant satisfaction in the long run."

The room was silent, each team member absorbing the importance of their role in maintaining property integrity through proactive maintenance planning. Jack could see the determination in their eyes—a readiness to apply their expertise and innovation to ensure property longevity and tenant comfort.

"Remember," Jack concluded, "maintenance schedules are our proactive approach to property management. Let's embrace this responsibility with enthusiasm and dedication, knowing that each maintenance task contributes to our overall success."

The session ended with a renewed sense of purpose and a plan to implement comprehensive maintenance schedules for each property. The team was equipped with the understanding and motivation needed to prioritize preventative care and preserve property value through proactive maintenance planning.

Establishing Communication Protocols

Jack Miller reconvened his team once more in the conference room, their focus shifting to the crucial task of establishing communication protocols for their newly acquired properties. Having addressed maintenance schedules, it was now essential to ensure effective communication channels were in place to facilitate tenant interaction, resolve issues promptly, and maintain transparency.

"Team," Jack began, his voice filled with determination. "Effective communication is the cornerstone of successful property management. It's where we build trust, foster collaboration, and ensure tenant satisfaction. Let's explore the fifth step: establishing communication protocols."

He clicked the remote, and the screen illuminated with a checklist titled "Establishing Communication Protocols." "Communication protocols are our framework for maintaining open and transparent communication channels with tenants, vendors, and internal team members."

The first slide highlighted "Tenant Communication Channels." "1. **Tenant Communication Channels.** We begin by establishing clear channels for tenant communication, such as phone, email, and an online tenant portal. These channels should be easily accessible and well-publicized to ensure tenants can reach us with inquiries, requests, or feedback."

Jack emphasized the importance of accessibility and responsiveness in tenant communication. He recalled a time when timely communication had diffused a potential conflict and strengthened tenant trust.

The next slide displayed "Response Time Expectations." "2. **Response Time Expectations.** Setting clear expectations for response times is essential for managing tenant inquiries and requests effectively. We must establish guidelines for acknowledging and addressing tenant communications within a reasonable timeframe to demonstrate our commitment to tenant satisfaction."

Sarah, with her attention to detail, nodded in agreement. She understood the importance of managing tenant expectations and ensuring timely responses to maintain tenant trust and satisfaction.

The third slide depicted "Issue Resolution Protocols." "3. **Issue Resolution Protocols.** Establishing protocols for issue resolution ensures that tenant concerns are addressed promptly and efficiently. This includes triaging issues based on urgency, assigning responsibility for resolution, and communicating updates to tenants throughout the process."

David, always systematic in his approach, recognized the significance of implementing structured protocols to streamline issue resolution and minimize tenant disruptions. He made a mental note to develop a standardized workflow for handling tenant inquiries and requests.

The next image showed "Vendor and Contractor Communication." "4. **Vendor and Contractor Communication.** Maintaining open communication channels with vendors and contractors is essential for coordinating maintenance tasks and service delivery. We must establish clear lines of communication, provide detailed instructions, and follow up to ensure tasks are completed satisfactorily and on time."

Lisa, their vendor management expert, saw the potential in optimizing communication with vendors to enhance service quality and minimize downtime. She began strategizing ways to improve communication protocols and streamline collaboration with external partners.

The fifth slide highlighted "Internal Team Communication." "5. **Internal Team Communication.** Effective internal communication is vital for coordinating tasks, sharing information, and resolving issues efficiently. We must establish regular team meetings, utilize collaboration tools, and maintain open lines of communication to ensure alignment and synergy among team members."

Jack stressed the importance of fostering a culture of communication and collaboration within their team. He encouraged the team to prioritize transparency and information sharing to enhance operational efficiency and teamwork.

The final slide displayed "Feedback and Continuous Improvement." "6. **Feedback and Continuous Improvement.** Soliciting feedback from tenants, vendors, and team members is essential for identifying areas of improvement and refining communication protocols. We must regularly evaluate our communication practices, gather insights, and make adjustments to enhance effectiveness and satisfaction."

Jack turned off the projector and faced his team, the gravity of their responsibility evident in his expression. "Communication protocols are our commitment to transparency, responsiveness, and collaboration. By establishing clear channels and expectations, we ensure effective communication at every level of our property management process."

He stepped closer, his voice filled with determination. "Let's approach communication protocols with diligence and empathy, knowing that our efforts will foster trust, streamline operations, and enhance tenant satisfaction."

The room was silent, each team member absorbing the importance of their role in establishing effective communication protocols. Jack could see the determination in their eyes—a readiness to apply their expertise and communication skills to ensure property management success.

"Remember," Jack concluded, "communication is the key to our success as property managers. Let's embrace our role as effective communicators, knowing that each interaction contributes to tenant satisfaction and operational excellence."

The session ended with a renewed sense of purpose and a plan to implement comprehensive communication protocols for each property. The team was equipped with the understanding and motivation needed to prioritize transparency, responsiveness, and collaboration in their property management approach.

Documenting Property Information

Jack Miller gathered his team once again in the conference room, their attention now focused on the crucial task of documenting property information for their newly acquired properties. Having established communication protocols, it was imperative to centralize and organize essential property details to streamline operations and ensure compliance.

"Team," Jack began, his voice filled with purpose. "Documenting property information is the foundation of efficient property management. It's where we consolidate vital details, streamline processes, and maintain compliance. Let's explore the sixth step: documenting property information."

He clicked the remote, and the screen illuminated with a checklist titled "Documenting Property Information." "Documenting property information ensures that we have a comprehensive record of property details, maintenance history, and legal documentation."

The first slide highlighted "Property Details and Specifications." "1. **Property Details and Specifications.** We begin by documenting essential property details, such as address, size, layout, and amenities. This information serves as a reference for tenants, vendors, and internal team members, ensuring everyone is aligned on property specifications."

Jack emphasized the importance of accuracy and completeness in documenting property details. He recalled a time when detailed property information had expedited maintenance tasks and enhanced tenant satisfaction.

The next slide displayed "Maintenance History and Records." "2. **Maintenance History and Records.** Maintaining detailed maintenance records allows us to track past maintenance activities, identify recurring issues, and plan future maintenance tasks effectively. This includes documenting maintenance schedules, work orders, and invoices for reference and analysis."

Sarah, with her meticulous approach, nodded in agreement. She understood the value of maintaining organized maintenance records to track property performance and inform decision-making.

The third slide depicted "Legal Documentation and Compliance Records." "3. **Legal Documentation and Compliance Records.** Ensuring compliance with local laws, regulations, and leasing agreements requires accurate and up-to-date documentation. This includes lease agreements, property insurance policies, inspection reports, and permits. Documenting compliance records demonstrates our commitment to legal and regulatory standards."

David, always thorough in his approach, recognized the significance of maintaining comprehensive legal documentation to mitigate risks and liabilities. He made a mental note to review existing documentation and update records as needed to ensure compliance.

The next image showed "Tenant Communication and Correspondence." "4. **Tenant Communication and Correspondence.** Documenting tenant communication and correspondence provides a record of interactions, inquiries, and requests. This includes emails, phone calls, and notes from meetings or conversations. Maintaining accurate records enables us to track tenant preferences, address concerns promptly, and ensure transparency."

Lisa, their communication expert, saw the potential in leveraging documented tenant communication to enhance tenant satisfaction and improve service delivery. She began brainstorming ways to streamline communication documentation and analysis processes.

The fifth slide highlighted "Financial Transactions and Accounting Records." "5. **Financial Transactions and Accounting Records.** Tracking financial transactions and maintaining accounting records is essential for financial transparency and compliance. This includes rental income, expenses, invoices, and receipts. Documenting financial records enables us to monitor revenue and expenses, track budget performance, and prepare accurate financial reports."

Jack stressed the importance of maintaining accurate financial records to ensure fiscal responsibility and transparency. He encouraged the team to adhere to accounting best practices and keep detailed financial documentation for auditing and reporting purposes.

The final slide displayed "Data Security and Confidentiality Measures." "6. **Data Security and Confidentiality Measures.** Protecting sensitive property information and tenant data is paramount. We must implement data security measures, such as secure storage systems, access controls, and encryption protocols, to safeguard confidential information and prevent unauthorized access or breaches."

Jack turned off the projector and faced his team, the gravity of their responsibility evident in his expression. "Documenting property information is more than just record-keeping—it's our commitment to organization, compliance, and transparency. By maintaining accurate and comprehensive records, we ensure efficient operations and mitigate risks."

He stepped closer, his voice filled with determination. "Let's approach documentation with diligence and attention to detail, knowing that our efforts will contribute to the success and longevity of our property management endeavors."

The room was silent, each team member absorbing the importance of their role in documenting property information accurately and comprehensively. Jack could see the determination in their eyes—a readiness to apply their expertise and professionalism to ensure property management success.

"Remember," Jack concluded, "documentation is the backbone of efficient property management. Let's embrace our responsibility to maintain accurate records and protect sensitive information, knowing that each document contributes to our overall success."

The session ended with a renewed sense of purpose and a plan to implement robust documentation processes for each property. The team was equipped with the understanding and motivation needed to prioritize organization, compliance, and transparency in their property management approach.

5

Chapter 5: Marketing and Leasing

Developing a Marketing Strategy

Jack Miller gathered his team in the conference room, the anticipation palpable as they prepared to delve into the realm of marketing and leasing. With their properties primed for success, it was time to craft a strategic approach to attract and retain quality tenants.

"Team," Jack began, his voice infused with enthusiasm. "Marketing and leasing are the lifeblood of our property management efforts. It's where we showcase the unique value of our properties and attract tenants who align with our vision. Let's explore the first step: developing a marketing strategy."

He clicked the remote, and the screen illuminated with a checklist titled "Developing a Marketing Strategy." "A robust marketing strategy is essential for maximizing property visibility, attracting prospective tenants, and optimizing rental income."

The first slide highlighted "Target Audience Identification." "1. **Target Audience Identification.** We begin by identifying our target audience—the demographic, psychographic, and behavioral characteristics of prospective tenants who are most likely to be interested in our properties. Understanding our target audience allows us to tailor our marketing efforts and messaging to resonate with their needs and preferences."

Jack emphasized the importance of conducting market research to gain insights into target audience demographics and preferences. He recalled a time when a targeted marketing campaign had resulted in a significant increase in qualified leads and tenant applications.

The next slide displayed "Property Branding and Positioning." "2. **Property Branding and Positioning.** Establishing a strong property brand and positioning is essential for differentiating our properties in the market. This includes defining our unique selling points, crafting compelling property narratives, and creating visually appealing branding materials to communicate our value proposition effectively."

Sarah, with her creative flair, nodded in agreement. She understood the significance of crafting a distinctive property brand that resonated with target audiences and set their properties apart from the competition.

The third slide depicted "Online Presence and Digital Marketing." "3. **Online Presence and Digital Marketing.** In today's digital age, a strong online presence is crucial for property visibility and tenant engagement. This includes creating a user-friendly property website, optimizing for search engines, leveraging social media platforms, and running targeted online advertising campaigns to reach prospective tenants effectively."

David, always analytical in his approach, recognized the power of digital marketing in reaching a wider audience and driving qualified leads. He made a mental note to explore data-driven approaches to optimize their online marketing efforts.

The next image showed "Offline Marketing Channels." "4. **Offline Marketing Channels.** While digital marketing is essential, offline channels also play a significant role in reaching prospective tenants. This includes traditional marketing tactics such as print advertising, direct mail campaigns, signage, and local community outreach events. Combining online and offline channels ensures comprehensive property visibility and engagement."

Lisa, their marketing expert, saw the potential in leveraging a mix of online and offline marketing channels to maximize reach and engagement. She began brainstorming creative offline marketing tactics to complement their digital efforts and enhance property visibility in the local community.

The fifth slide highlighted "Tenant Referral Programs and Incentives." "5. **Tenant Referral Programs and Incentives.** Harnessing the power of tenant referrals can be a highly effective marketing strategy. By incentivizing existing tenants to refer friends, family, or colleagues to our properties, we can generate qualified leads and foster a sense of community. Offering incentives such as rent discounts, gift cards, or exclusive amenities encourages tenant engagement and word-of-mouth marketing."

Jack stressed the importance of leveraging tenant relationships to drive referrals and expand their tenant base. He encouraged the team to explore creative incentive programs that would motivate tenants to become brand ambassadors for their properties.

The final slide displayed "Performance Tracking and Optimization." "6. **Performance Tracking and Optimization.** Monitoring the performance of our marketing efforts allows us to measure success, identify areas for improvement, and optimize our strategies over time. This includes tracking key performance indicators (KPIs), such as website traffic, lead generation, conversion rates, and tenant retention. Regular performance analysis enables us to refine our marketing tactics and maximize return on investment (ROI)."

Jack turned off the projector and faced his team, the excitement of possibility evident in his expression. "Developing a marketing strategy is our opportunity to showcase the unique value of our properties and attract quality tenants who align with our vision."

He stepped closer, his voice filled with determination. "Let's approach our marketing efforts with creativity, strategy, and a commitment to excellence. By crafting compelling narratives, leveraging digital and offline channels, and nurturing tenant relationships, we can maximize property visibility and achieve leasing success."

The room buzzed with energy, each team member eager to apply their skills and creativity to develop a winning marketing strategy. Jack could see the determination in their eyes—a readiness to showcase their properties to the world and attract tenants who would call them home.

"Remember," Jack concluded, "our marketing strategy is more than just promoting properties—it's about connecting with tenants and creating communities. Let's embrace this opportunity with enthusiasm and innovation, knowing that each marketing effort brings us one step closer to leasing success."

The session ended with a renewed sense of purpose and a plan to develop a comprehensive marketing strategy that would elevate their properties in the market. The team was equipped with the understanding and motivation needed to showcase their properties effectively and attract quality tenants who would contribute to their communities' vibrancy and success.

Advertising Channels and Techniques

Jack Miller reconvened his team in the conference room, their focus now shifting to exploring the diverse landscape of advertising channels and techniques. With their marketing strategy taking shape, it was time to identify the most effective avenues to showcase their properties and attract prospective tenants.

"Team," Jack began, his voice brimming with anticipation. "Advertising channels and techniques are the vehicles through which we bring our marketing strategy to life. It's where we amplify our message and capture the attention of prospective tenants. Let's explore the second step: advertising channels and techniques."

He clicked the remote, and the screen illuminated with a checklist titled "Advertising Channels and Techniques." "Choosing the right advertising channels and employing effective techniques are essential for maximizing property visibility and attracting qualified leads."

The first slide highlighted "Digital Advertising Platforms." "1. **Digital Advertising Platforms.** In today's digital age, digital advertising offers a wealth of opportunities to reach prospective tenants online. This includes paid search advertising on search engines like Google, display advertising on relevant websites and platforms, social media advertising on platforms like Facebook and Instagram, and video advertising on platforms like YouTube. Leveraging digital advertising allows us to target specific demographics, interests, and behaviors effectively."

Jack emphasized the power of digital advertising in reaching a highly targeted audience and driving qualified leads. He recalled a successful digital advertising campaign that had resulted in a surge of website traffic and tenant inquiries.

The next slide displayed "Property Listing Websites and Portals." "2. **Property Listing Websites and Portals.** Property listing websites and portals are popular destinations for prospective tenants searching for rental properties. This includes websites like Zillow, Trulia, Apartments.com, and Realtor.com. By listing our properties on these platforms, we increase their visibility to a wide audience of renters actively seeking accommodation."

Sarah, with her attention to detail, nodded in agreement. She understood the importance of leveraging property listing websites to reach a broad audience of prospective tenants and drive traffic to their property listings.

The third slide depicted "Local Advertising and Publications." "3. **Local Advertising and Publications.** Local advertising channels and publications provide opportunities to target tenants within specific geographic areas. This includes local newspapers, magazines, community newsletters, and bulletin boards. By advertising in local publications, we can reach tenants who prefer to search for rental properties within their neighborhood or city."

David, always analytical in his approach, recognized the value of targeting local audiences through geographically relevant advertising channels. He made a mental note to explore local advertising opportunities to enhance their property visibility in key markets.

The next image showed "Outdoor Advertising and Signage."

"4. **Outdoor Advertising and Signage.** Outdoor advertising and signage offer visibility to passersby and commuters in high-traffic areas. This includes billboards, bus stop advertisements, banners, and property signage. Eye-catching outdoor advertising can capture the attention of potential tenants and drive traffic to our properties."

Lisa, their marketing expert, saw the potential in leveraging outdoor advertising to increase property visibility and generate leads. She began brainstorming creative outdoor advertising concepts that would resonate with their target audience and stand out in the local landscape.

The fifth slide highlighted "Email Marketing Campaigns."

"5. **Email Marketing Campaigns.** Email marketing allows us to nurture relationships with prospective tenants and maintain engagement with current tenants. This includes sending regular newsletters, property updates, and promotional offers to subscribers. By leveraging email marketing, we can stay top-of-mind with prospects and encourage them to consider our properties."

Jack stressed the importance of personalized and targeted email marketing campaigns in building relationships with prospective tenants and fostering tenant loyalty. He encouraged the team to segment their email lists and tailor content to meet the needs and interests of different audience segments.

The final slide displayed "Content Marketing and Blogging."

"6. **Content Marketing and Blogging.** Content marketing and blogging allow us to showcase our expertise, provide valuable information to prospective tenants, and enhance our property brand. This includes creating informative blog posts, property guides, virtual tours, and video content that educates and engages our audience. By sharing valuable content, we position ourselves as trusted authorities in the rental market and attract tenants seeking informative resources."

Jack turned off the projector and faced his team, the excitement of possibility evident in his expression. "Advertising channels and techniques offer us a diverse array of opportunities to showcase our properties and connect with prospective tenants."

He stepped closer, his voice filled with determination. "Let's approach our advertising efforts with creativity, strategy, and a commitment to excellence. By leveraging a mix of digital, local, outdoor, and email marketing channels, we can maximize property visibility and attract qualified leads."

The room buzzed with energy, each team member eager to explore the advertising landscape and implement innovative strategies to showcase their properties. Jack could see the determination in their eyes—a readiness to deploy their expertise and creativity to drive leasing success.

"Remember," Jack concluded, "our advertising efforts are the gateway to connecting with prospective tenants and showcasing the unique value of our properties. Let's embrace this opportunity with enthusiasm and innovation, knowing that each advertising initiative brings us closer to leasing success."

The session ended with a renewed sense of purpose and a

plan to explore and implement a diverse mix of advertising channels and techniques to elevate their properties in the market. The team was equipped with the understanding and motivation needed to showcase their properties effectively and attract quality tenants who would contribute to their communities' vibrancy and success.

Crafting Effective Listings

Jack Miller gathered his team once more in the conference room, their attention now focused on the art of crafting compelling property listings. With their advertising channels identified, it was time to ensure that their property listings stood out in a crowded market and captured the interest of prospective tenants.

"Team," Jack began, his voice resonating with purpose. "Crafting effective listings is where our marketing strategy comes to life. It's the first impression we make on prospective tenants, and it's essential that we make it count. Let's explore the third step: crafting effective listings."

He clicked the remote, and the screen illuminated with a checklist titled "Crafting Effective Listings." "Our property listings serve as the gateway to our properties, capturing the attention of prospective tenants and inviting them to explore further."

The first slide highlighted "Compelling Property Descriptions." "1. **Compelling Property Descriptions.** We begin by crafting detailed and engaging property descriptions that highlight the unique features, amenities, and benefits of our properties. This includes using descriptive language, highlighting key selling points, and painting a vivid picture of the lifestyle our properties offer."

Jack emphasized the importance of storytelling in property descriptions, creating an emotional connection with prospective tenants. He recalled a time when a captivating property description had attracted a flood of inquiries and applications.

The next slide displayed "High-Quality Visuals and Media." "2. **High-Quality Visuals and Media.** High-quality visuals are essential for showcasing our properties in the best light. This includes professional photography, virtual tours, and video walkthroughs that provide prospective tenants with a comprehensive view of the property. Stunning visuals capture attention and encourage further exploration."

Sarah, with her keen eye for detail, nodded in agreement. She understood the impact of high-quality visuals in capturing the imagination of prospective tenants and enticing them to schedule a viewing.

The third slide depicted "Clear and Informative Property Details." "3. **Clear and Informative Property Details.** Providing clear and comprehensive property details is essential for transparency and credibility. This includes listing accurate information about the property size, layout, amenities, utilities, and rental terms. Clear and informative property details help prospective tenants make informed decisions and reduce the likelihood of misunderstandings."

David, always thorough in his approach, recognized the importance of accuracy and transparency in property listings. He made a mental note to ensure that all property details were up-to-date and accurately represented in their listings.

The next image showed "Unique Selling Points Highlighted." "4. **Unique Selling Points Highlighted.** Identifying and highlighting the unique selling points of our properties sets them apart in a competitive market. Whether it's a stunning view, state-of-the-art amenities, or a convenient location, showcasing these features prominently in our listings attracts the attention of prospective tenants and differentiates our properties from others."

Lisa, their marketing expert, saw the potential in emphasizing unique selling points to capture the interest of prospective tenants. She began brainstorming creative ways to highlight the distinctive features of their properties in their listings.

The fifth slide highlighted "Call-to-Action (CTA) for Engagement." "5. **Call-to-Action (CTA) for Engagement.** Including a clear call-to-action in our listings encourages prospective tenants to take the next step. Whether it's scheduling a viewing, contacting us for more information, or submitting a rental application, a compelling CTA prompts action and drives engagement with our properties."

Jack stressed the importance of incorporating a strong call-to-action in their listings to guide prospective tenants towards conversion. He encouraged the team to use persuasive language and provide clear instructions to facilitate engagement.

The final slide displayed "Continuous Optimization Based on Feedback." "6. **Continuous Optimization Based on Feedback.** Soliciting feedback from prospective tenants and analyzing listing performance allows us to continuously optimize our listings for effectiveness. This includes refining property descriptions, updating visuals, and adjusting marketing tactics based on insights gathered from tenant interactions and engagement metrics."

Jack turned off the projector and faced his team, the

determination evident in his expression. "Crafting effective listings is our opportunity to showcase the unique value of our properties and capture the attention of prospective tenants."

He stepped closer, his voice filled with determination. "Let's approach our listings with creativity, authenticity, and a commitment to excellence. By crafting compelling narratives, showcasing stunning visuals, and providing clear information, we can maximize engagement and drive leasing success."

The room buzzed with energy, each team member eager to apply their skills and creativity to craft compelling property listings. Jack could see the determination in their eyes—a readiness to showcase their properties effectively and attract quality tenants who would call them home.

"Remember," Jack concluded, "our listings are the first touchpoint with prospective tenants. Let's make every word, every image, and every detail count, knowing that each listing brings us one step closer to leasing success."

The session ended with a renewed sense of purpose and a plan to craft compelling property listings that would capture the imagination of prospective tenants and drive engagement. The team was equipped with the understanding and motivation needed to showcase their properties effectively and attract quality tenants who would contribute to their communities' vibrancy and success.

Conducting Property Showings

Jack Miller gathered his team once again in the conference room, their focus now directed towards the pivotal stage of conducting property showings. With their compelling listings crafted, it was time to bring their properties to life and create memorable experiences for prospective tenants.

"Team," Jack began, his voice infused with energy. "Property showings are where the magic happens. It's our opportunity to showcase the unique features and amenities of our properties and make a lasting impression on prospective tenants. Let's explore the fourth step: conducting property showings."

He clicked the remote, and the screen illuminated with a checklist titled "Conducting Property Showings." "Property showings are our chance to engage with prospective tenants, answer their questions, and guide them through the rental process."

The first slide highlighted "Preparation and Presentation." "1. **Preparation and Presentation.** We begin by ensuring that the property is clean, well-maintained, and staged to highlight its best features. This includes decluttering, freshening up the space with flowers or air fresheners, and arranging furniture to create a welcoming atmosphere. A well-presented property sets the stage for a positive showing experience."

Jack emphasized the importance of attention to detail in preparing the property for showings. He recalled a successful showing where the property's impeccable presentation had left a lasting impression on prospective tenants.

The next slide displayed "Personalized Tours and Engaging Narratives." "2. **Personalized Tours and Engaging Narratives.** During the showing, we personalize the tour to highlight the features and amenities that are most relevant to the prospective tenant's needs and preferences. This includes sharing engaging narratives about the property's history, architecture, and unique selling points to create an emotional connection with the prospective tenant."

Sarah, with her knack for storytelling, nodded in agreement. She understood the power of personalized tours and engaging narratives in capturing the imagination of prospective tenants and fostering a sense of connection with the property.

The third slide depicted "Responsive and Knowledgeable Guidance." "3. **Responsive and Knowledgeable Guidance.** Throughout the showing, we remain responsive to the prospective tenant's questions and provide knowledgeable guidance on various aspects of the property, including its layout, amenities, utilities, and rental terms. Clear and informative communication builds trust and confidence in the property and the leasing process."

David, always meticulous in his approach, recognized the importance of being responsive and knowledgeable during property showings. He made a mental note to brush up on his knowledge of each property's features and amenities to provide comprehensive guidance to prospective tenants.

The next image showed "Encouraging Tenant Interaction and Feedback." "4. **Encouraging Tenant Interaction and Feedback.** We encourage prospective tenants to interact with the property, explore its features, and envision themselves living there. This includes inviting questions, soliciting feedback, and gauging the prospective tenant's level of interest and enthusiasm. Open dialogue fosters engagement and allows us to address any concerns or questions in real-time."

Lisa, their leasing expert, saw the potential in encouraging tenant interaction and feedback to gauge interest and address concerns proactively. She began brainstorming ways to create an interactive and engaging showing experience that would leave a lasting impression on prospective tenants.

The fifth slide highlighted "Follow-Up and Next Steps." "5. **Follow-Up and Next Steps.** After the showing, we follow up with prospective tenants to gather feedback, answer any additional questions, and guide them through the next steps of the leasing process. This includes providing rental applications, scheduling follow-up appointments, and addressing any concerns or hesitations the prospective tenant may have."

Jack stressed the importance of proactive follow-up in nurturing tenant relationships and guiding prospective tenants through the leasing process. He encouraged the team to stay attentive and responsive to prospective tenants' needs and concerns to ensure a positive leasing experience.

The final slide displayed "Continuous Improvement and Feedback Loop." "6. **Continuous Improvement and Feedback Loop.** Soliciting feedback from prospective tenants and analyzing showing performance allows us to continuously improve our showing experience and optimize our leasing process. This includes gathering insights, identifying areas for enhancement, and implementing changes to enhance prospective tenant engagement and satisfaction."

Jack turned off the projector and faced his team, the determination evident in his expression. "Conducting property showings is our opportunity to create memorable experiences for prospective tenants and guide them through the leasing process."

He stepped closer, his voice filled with determination. "Let's approach our showings with enthusiasm, authenticity, and a commitment to excellence. By providing personalized tours, engaging narratives, and responsive guidance, we can create positive impressions and build lasting relationships with prospective tenants."

The room buzzed with energy, each team member eager to apply their skills and creativity to conduct engaging and memorable property showings. Jack could see the determination in their eyes—a readiness to showcase their properties effectively and guide prospective tenants towards leasing success.

"Remember," Jack concluded, "our showings are more than just tours—they're opportunities to create connections and inspire dreams. Let's make every showing count, knowing that each interaction brings us one step closer to leasing success."

The session ended with a renewed sense of purpose and a plan to conduct engaging and personalized property showings that would leave a lasting impression on prospective tenants. The team was equipped with the understanding and motivation needed to showcase their properties effectively and guide prospective tenants towards finding their ideal homes.

Screening Potential Tenants

Jack Miller gathered his team once more in the conference room, the focus now shifting to the critical task of screening potential tenants. With property showings conducted and interest generated, it was time to ensure that only the most qualified tenants were selected to call their properties home.

"Team," Jack began, his voice filled with purpose. "Screening potential tenants is a crucial step in the leasing process. It's where we safeguard the integrity of our properties and ensure a positive living experience for all residents. Let's explore the fifth step: screening potential tenants."

He clicked the remote, and the screen illuminated with a checklist titled "Screening Potential Tenants." "Tenant screening allows us to evaluate the suitability of prospective tenants based on their financial stability, rental history, and background."

The first slide highlighted "Rental Application Review." "1. **Rental Application Review.** We begin by thoroughly reviewing rental applications submitted by prospective tenants. This includes verifying personal information, employment history, income documentation, rental history, and references. A detailed rental application provides valuable insights into the prospective tenant's background and suitability."

Jack emphasized the importance of meticulous application review in identifying qualified tenants and mitigating rental risks. He recalled a time when a thorough application review had prevented a potential lease default and protected the property's integrity.

The next slide displayed "Credit and Background Checks." "2. **Credit and Background Checks.** Conducting credit and background checks allows us to assess the prospective tenant's financial responsibility and identify any red flags or risk factors. This includes reviewing credit reports for outstanding debts, late payments, and bankruptcies, as well as conducting criminal background checks to ensure a safe living environment for all residents."

Sarah, with her attention to detail, nodded in agreement. She understood the importance of credit and background checks in identifying potential rental risks and safeguarding their properties' integrity.

The third slide depicted "Income Verification." "3. **Income Verification.** Verifying the prospective tenant's income ensures their ability to meet rental obligations and maintain financial stability throughout the lease term. This includes requesting pay stubs, employment verification, tax returns, or bank statements to confirm consistent and sufficient income levels."

David, always analytical in his approach, recognized the significance of income verification in assessing the prospective tenant's ability to afford the rent and meet their financial obligations. He made a mental note to review income documentation thoroughly to ensure accuracy and reliability.

The next image showed "Rental References and Past Performance." "4. **Rental References and Past Performance.** Contacting previous landlords or property managers provides valuable insights into the prospective tenant's rental history, behavior, and reliability. This includes verifying rental references, asking about payment history, property care, and adherence to lease terms. Past performance is often indicative of future behavior."

Lisa, their leasing expert, saw the potential in contacting rental references to gain firsthand insights into the prospective tenant's rental behavior and reliability. She began drafting thoughtful reference inquiries to gather comprehensive feedback from previous landlords.

The fifth slide highlighted "Tenant Interview and Assessment." "5. **Tenant Interview and Assessment.** Conducting a face-to-face or virtual interview allows us to assess the prospective tenant's communication skills, demeanor, and compatibility with our property community. This includes discussing rental expectations, lifestyle preferences, and any special considerations to ensure a mutually beneficial leasing relationship."

Jack stressed the importance of conducting tenant interviews to gauge the prospective tenant's personality, communication style, and suitability for their property community. He encouraged the team to ask open-ended questions and actively listen to the prospective tenant's responses to gather valuable insights.

The final slide displayed "Legal Compliance and Fair Housing Practices." "6. **Legal Compliance and Fair Housing Practices.** Ensuring compliance with fair housing laws and regulations is paramount throughout the tenant screening process. This includes treating all applicants equally, avoiding discriminatory practices, and adhering to federal, state, and local housing laws to protect tenants' rights and promote inclusivity."

Jack turned off the projector and faced his team, the gravity of their responsibility evident in his expression. "Screening potential tenants is our duty to protect our properties, our residents, and our communities."

He stepped closer, his voice filled with determination. "Let's approach tenant screening with diligence, fairness, and a commitment to excellence. By conducting thorough background checks, verifying income, and assessing rental history, we can ensure that our properties are occupied by qualified tenants who uphold our standards of excellence."

The room was silent, each team member absorbing the importance of their role in tenant screening and the impact it had on the overall integrity of their properties. Jack could see the determination in their eyes—a readiness to uphold fair housing practices and select tenants who would contribute positively to their property communities.

"Remember," Jack concluded, "tenant screening is more

than just a formality—it's our responsibility to safeguard our properties and promote a safe, inclusive, and thriving community. Let's embrace this responsibility with integrity and professionalism, knowing that each qualified tenant selected strengthens the foundation of our property management endeavors."

The session ended with a renewed sense of purpose and a commitment to conducting thorough and fair tenant screenings that would uphold their standards of excellence and promote a positive living experience for all residents. The team was equipped with the understanding and motivation needed to select qualified tenants who would contribute to their communities' vibrancy and success.

Lease Agreement Essentials

Jack Miller gathered his team once more in the conference room, the focus now shifting to the final stage of the leasing process: ensuring that lease agreements were comprehensive, legally sound, and tailored to meet the needs of both landlords and tenants.

"Team," Jack began, his voice resonating with purpose. "Lease agreements are the foundation of our landlord-tenant relationships. They outline rights, responsibilities, and expectations, providing clarity and protection for both parties. Let's explore the sixth step: lease agreement essentials."

He clicked the remote, and the screen illuminated with a checklist titled "Lease Agreement Essentials." "A well-crafted lease agreement is essential for establishing clear terms and fostering a positive leasing experience for all parties involved."

The first slide highlighted "Property and Tenant Information." "1. **Property and Tenant Information.** We begin by including detailed information about the property and the tenants involved in the lease agreement. This includes the property address, unit number, landlord's contact information, tenant's names, and any additional occupants. Accurate information ensures clarity and accountability for all parties."

Jack emphasized the importance of accurately documenting property and tenant information to avoid confusion and disputes later on. He recalled a time when a meticulously detailed lease agreement had resolved a misunderstanding between a landlord and tenant swiftly and amicably.

The next slide displayed "Lease Term and Rent Details." "2. **Lease Term and Rent Details.** Clearly specifying the lease term, including start and end dates, rent amount, due date, and acceptable payment methods, establishes the financial obligations of the lease. Additionally, outlining any late fees, grace periods, or rent escalation clauses provides transparency and consistency in rent payments."

Sarah, with her attention to detail, nodded in agreement. She understood the importance of clearly defining lease terms and rent details to avoid misunderstandings and ensure timely rent payments.

The third slide depicted "Occupancy and Use Restrictions." "3. **Occupancy and Use Restrictions.** Establishing occupancy limits, pet policies, subletting restrictions, and property use guidelines ensures the property's proper care and maintenance. Additionally, outlining prohibited activities, noise policies, and maintenance responsibilities promotes a harmonious living environment for all residents."

David, always analytical in his approach, recognized the significance of occupancy and use restrictions in maintaining property integrity and fostering a positive community atmosphere. He made a mental note to review and refine their property use guidelines to align with tenant expectations.

The next image showed "Maintenance and Repairs Protocols." "4. **Maintenance and Repairs Protocols.** Clearly defining the landlord's and tenant's responsibilities for maintenance and repairs helps prevent disputes and ensures timely resolution of issues. This includes outlining procedures for reporting maintenance requests, scheduling repairs, and addressing emergency situations to maintain property safety and habitability."

Lisa, their leasing expert, saw the potential in establishing clear maintenance and repairs protocols to streamline communication and promote proactive property care. She began drafting comprehensive guidelines that would empower both landlords and tenants to uphold their responsibilities effectively.

The fifth slide highlighted "Security Deposit and Move-In Procedures." "5. **Security Deposit and Move-In Procedures.** Detailing the amount of the security deposit, its purpose, and the conditions for its refund or deduction protects both parties' interests. Additionally, outlining move-in procedures, inspection protocols, and condition reports establishes accountability and transparency during the lease commencement."

Jack stressed the importance of addressing security deposit and move-in procedures to ensure a smooth transition for tenants and protect the landlord's investment. He encouraged the team to conduct thorough move-in inspections and document property conditions to mitigate disputes at the end of the lease term.

The final slide displayed "Legal Compliance and Governing Laws." "6. **Legal Compliance and Governing Laws.** Ensuring compliance with federal, state, and local housing laws and regulations is paramount in lease agreements. This includes incorporating required disclosures, adhering to fair housing practices, and referencing governing laws to protect tenants' rights and promote legal compliance."

Jack turned off the projector and faced his team, the gravity of their responsibility evident in his expression. "Lease agreement essentials are our commitment to establishing clear, fair, and legally sound terms for our landlord-tenant relationships."

He stepped closer, his voice filled with determination. "Let's approach lease agreements with diligence, fairness, and a commitment to excellence. By crafting comprehensive agreements that address all aspects of the leasing relationship, we can ensure a positive and mutually beneficial experience for all parties involved."

The room was silent, each team member absorbing the importance of their role in lease agreement essentials and the impact it had on the overall integrity of their leasing process. Jack could see the determination in their eyes—a readiness to uphold legal compliance and protect the interests of both landlords and tenants.

"Remember," Jack concluded, "lease agreements are more than just contracts—they're the foundation of trust and accountability in our landlord-tenant relationships. Let's uphold our standards with integrity and professionalism, knowing that each lease agreement strengthens the foundation of our property management endeavors."

The session ended with a renewed sense of purpose and

a commitment to crafting comprehensive lease agreements that would protect the interests of both landlords and tenants and promote a positive leasing experience for all. The team was equipped with the understanding and motivation needed to uphold legal compliance and foster trust and transparency in their leasing process.

6

Chapter 6: Tenant Relations

Building Positive Tenant Relationships

Jack Miller convened his team in the conference room, their focus now directed towards the pivotal aspect of tenant relations. With lease agreements signed and tenants settled into their new homes, it was time to foster positive relationships and create a sense of community within their properties.

"Team," Jack began, his voice filled with enthusiasm. "Building positive tenant relationships is essential for maintaining tenant satisfaction, promoting property retention, and fostering a sense of belonging within our communities. Let's explore the first step: building positive tenant relationships."

He clicked the remote, and the screen illuminated with a checklist titled "Building Positive Tenant Relationships." "Positive tenant relationships are built on trust, communication, and mutual respect. They are the cornerstone of a thriving property community."

The first slide highlighted "Clear Communication and Accessibility." "1. **Clear Communication and Accessibility.** We begin by establishing open lines of communication and being accessible to tenants. This includes promptly responding to inquiries, addressing concerns, and providing timely updates on property-related matters. Clear communication builds trust and fosters a sense of transparency and support."

Jack emphasized the importance of being responsive and accessible to tenants, recognizing that effective communication lay at the heart of positive tenant relationships. He recalled a time when transparent communication had diffused a potentially tense situation and strengthened the landlord-tenant bond.

The next slide displayed "Responsive Maintenance and Service." "2. **Responsive Maintenance and Service.** Providing prompt and reliable maintenance and service enhances tenant satisfaction and promotes a positive living experience. This includes addressing maintenance requests promptly, scheduling repairs efficiently, and ensuring that common areas are well-maintained. Responsive service demonstrates our commitment to tenant comfort and well-being."

Sarah, with her attention to detail, nodded in agreement. She understood the importance of responsive maintenance and service in addressing tenant needs promptly and maintaining property satisfaction levels.

The third slide depicted "Respect for Privacy and Property Rights." "3. **Respect for Privacy and Property Rights.** Respecting tenants' privacy and property rights is paramount in building trust and fostering a positive living environment. This includes providing advance notice for property inspections or entry, respecting quiet hours, and upholding tenant confidentiality. Respectful conduct promotes a sense of security and respect within the community."

David, always analytical in his approach, recognized the significance of respecting privacy and property rights in maintaining tenant trust and satisfaction. He made a mental note to review their property access policies to ensure compliance with tenant privacy rights.

The next image showed "Community Engagement and Events." "4. **Community Engagement and Events.** Creating opportunities for community engagement and hosting events fosters a sense of belonging and camaraderie among tenants. This includes organizing social gatherings, fitness classes, holiday events, and community clean-up days. Community engagement promotes a vibrant and inclusive living environment."

Lisa, their community liaison, saw the potential in organizing community events to bring tenants together and foster a sense of belonging. She began brainstorming creative event ideas that would cater to the diverse interests and preferences of their tenant community.

The fifth slide highlighted "Conflict Resolution and Mediation." "5. **Conflict Resolution and Mediation.** Addressing conflicts and disputes promptly and impartially is essential for maintaining positive tenant relationships. This includes providing a platform for tenants to voice concerns, facilitating constructive dialogue, and mediating disputes when necessary. Effective conflict resolution promotes understanding, cooperation, and mutual respect."

Jack stressed the importance of proactive conflict resolution in preserving tenant satisfaction and promoting a harmonious living environment. He encouraged the team to approach conflicts with empathy and fairness, seeking mutually beneficial solutions that upheld the interests of all parties involved.

The final slide displayed "Continuous Feedback and Improvement." "6. **Continuous Feedback and Improvement.** Soliciting feedback from tenants and using insights to drive continuous improvement initiatives demonstrates our commitment to tenant satisfaction and community enhancement. This includes conducting tenant surveys, holding focus groups, and implementing feedback-driven improvements to property amenities and services."

Jack turned off the projector and faced his team, the determination evident in his expression. "Building positive tenant relationships is our opportunity to create a thriving, supportive, and inclusive community within our properties."

He stepped closer, his voice filled with determination. "Let's approach tenant relations with empathy, responsiveness, and a commitment to excellence. By fostering open communication, providing responsive service, and promoting community engagement, we can create a living environment where tenants feel valued, respected, and connected."

The room buzzed with energy, each team member eager to apply their skills and creativity to build positive tenant relationships and foster a sense of community within their properties. Jack could see the determination in their eyes—a readiness to uphold tenant satisfaction as a cornerstone of their property management endeavors.

"Remember," Jack concluded, "positive tenant relationships are the bedrock of our property communities. Let's cultivate these relationships with care and dedication, knowing that each interaction strengthens the fabric of our community and contributes to our collective success."

The session ended with a renewed sense of purpose and a commitment to building positive tenant relationships that would foster a vibrant and supportive community within their properties. The team was equipped with the understanding and motivation needed to uphold tenant satisfaction as a priority in their property management approach.

Effective Communication Skills

Jack Miller reconvened his team in the conference room, their focus now shifting to the essential aspect of effective communication skills in fostering positive tenant relationships. With the foundation laid for building trust and rapport, it was time to enhance their communication strategies to better serve their tenant community.

"Team," Jack began, his voice projecting confidence. "Effective communication skills are fundamental in nurturing positive tenant relationships. They are the key to understanding tenant needs, addressing concerns, and fostering a sense of community within our properties. Let's explore the second step: effective communication skills."

He clicked the remote, and the screen illuminated with a checklist titled "Effective Communication Skills." "Clear and empathetic communication builds trust, promotes transparency, and enhances tenant satisfaction. It is the cornerstone of successful tenant relations."

The first slide highlighted "Active Listening and Empathy."
"1. **Active Listening and Empathy.** We begin by practicing active listening and demonstrating empathy towards tenants' concerns and inquiries. This includes giving tenants our

full attention, paraphrasing their concerns to ensure understanding, and expressing empathy for their perspectives and experiences. Active listening fosters trust and shows tenants that their voices are heard and valued."

Jack emphasized the importance of active listening and empathy in understanding tenant needs and building rapport. He recalled a time when empathetic listening had de-escalated a tense situation and strengthened the landlord-tenant bond.

The next slide displayed "Clarity and Transparency." "2. **Clarity and Transparency.** Communicating with clarity and transparency ensures that tenants understand property policies, procedures, and expectations. This includes providing clear and concise information, avoiding jargon or technical language, and being transparent about any changes or updates that may affect tenants. Clarity and transparency promote trust and reduce misunderstandings."

Sarah, with her knack for detail, nodded in agreement. She understood the importance of clear and transparent communication in fostering trust and minimizing confusion among tenants.

The third slide depicted "Timeliness and Responsiveness." "3. **Timeliness and Responsiveness.** Responding to tenant inquiries and concerns promptly demonstrates our commitment to their needs and satisfaction. This includes setting realistic response times, acknowledging receipt of inquiries, and providing regular updates on the status of requests or issues. Timeliness and responsiveness show tenants that their concerns are taken seriously and will be addressed promptly."

David, always analytical in his approach, recognized the significance of timeliness and responsiveness in building tenant trust and satisfaction. He made a mental note to streamline their communication channels to ensure prompt responses to tenant inquiries and concerns.

The next image showed "Adaptability and Flexibility." "4. **Adaptability and Flexibility.** Being adaptable and flexible in our communication approach allows us to accommodate diverse tenant preferences and communication styles. This includes offering multiple channels for communication, such as phone, email, or in-person meetings, and adjusting our communication style to suit individual tenant needs. Adaptability fosters understanding and promotes positive interactions with tenants."

Lisa, their communication specialist, saw the potential in adapting their communication approach to cater to diverse tenant preferences. She began exploring new communication tools and techniques that would enhance their ability to connect with tenants effectively.

The fifth slide highlighted "Constructive Feedback and Conflict Resolution." "5. **Constructive Feedback and Conflict Resolution.** Providing constructive feedback and facilitating conflict resolution demonstrates our commitment to addressing tenant concerns and promoting a harmonious living environment. This includes offering constructive criticism with empathy and respect, facilitating open dialogue to resolve conflicts amicably, and seeking mutually beneficial solutions that uphold tenant satisfaction."

Jack stressed the importance of providing constructive feedback and facilitating conflict resolution in maintaining positive tenant relationships. He encouraged the team to approach conflicts with empathy and professionalism, seeking solutions that prioritize tenant satisfaction and community harmony.

The final slide displayed "Continuous Improvement and Learning." "6. **Continuous Improvement and Learning.** Embracing a culture of continuous improvement and learning allows us to refine our communication skills and adapt to evolving tenant needs and preferences. This includes seeking feedback from tenants, participating in communication training or workshops, and staying informed about best practices in tenant relations. Continuous improvement enhances our ability to connect with tenants and strengthen our property communities."

Jack turned off the projector and faced his team, the determination evident in his expression. "Effective communication skills are our gateway to building positive tenant relationships and fostering a sense of community within our properties."

He stepped closer, his voice filled with determination. "Let's approach communication with empathy, clarity, and a commitment to excellence. By practicing active listening, communicating with transparency, and resolving conflicts constructively, we can create an environment where tenants feel heard, valued, and respected."

The room buzzed with energy, each team member eager to enhance their communication skills and strengthen tenant relationships. Jack could see the determination in their eyes—a readiness to embrace effective communication as a catalyst for community-building within their properties.

"Remember," Jack concluded, "effective communication is the cornerstone of successful tenant relations. Let's cultivate our communication skills with care and dedication, knowing that each interaction brings us closer to fostering a thriving and inclusive community within our properties."

The session ended with a renewed sense of purpose and a commitment to enhancing communication skills that would deepen tenant connections and promote a positive living experience for all residents. The team was equipped with the understanding and motivation needed to communicate effectively and build strong tenant relationships within their properties.

Conflict Resolution Strategies

Jack Miller gathered his team once again in the conference room, their attention now directed towards the critical aspect of conflict resolution. As property managers, they understood that conflicts were inevitable, but how they were managed could make all the difference in maintaining positive tenant relationships and fostering a harmonious community.

"Team," Jack began, his voice steady and authoritative. "Conflict resolution is an essential skill in maintaining positive tenant relationships and promoting a peaceful living environment within our properties. Let's explore the third step: conflict resolution strategies."

He clicked the remote, and the screen illuminated with a checklist titled "Conflict Resolution Strategies." "Effective conflict resolution requires empathy, communication, and a commitment to finding mutually beneficial solutions. It is the key to resolving disputes amicably and preserving tenant satisfaction."

The first slide highlighted "Empathy and Active Listening." "1. **Empathy and Active Listening.** We begin by demonstrating empathy towards the concerns and perspectives of all parties involved in the conflict. This includes practicing active listening, acknowledging emotions, and validating feelings to create a supportive and understanding environment. Empathy lays the foundation for constructive dialogue and promotes a collaborative approach to conflict resolution."

Jack emphasized the importance of empathy and active listening in understanding the underlying issues driving the conflict. He recalled a time when empathetic listening had transformed a tense situation into a constructive dialogue, ultimately leading to a mutually beneficial resolution.

The next slide displayed "Open Dialogue and Mediation."

"2. **Open Dialogue and Mediation.** Facilitating open dialogue and mediation allows all parties to express their perspectives, concerns, and needs in a safe and neutral environment. This includes encouraging respectful communication, setting ground rules for the discussion, and facilitating constructive exchanges to identify common ground and potential solutions. Open dialogue promotes understanding and fosters collaboration in resolving conflicts."

Sarah, with her attention to detail, nodded in agreement. She understood the importance of creating a structured and supportive environment for open dialogue and mediation to foster constructive conflict resolution.

The third slide depicted "Problem-Solving and Solution-Oriented Approach." "3. **Problem-Solving and Solution-Oriented Approach.** Adopting a problem-solving and solution-oriented approach focuses on identifying underlying issues and exploring mutually beneficial solutions. This includes brainstorming potential solutions, evaluating their feasibility and impact, and collaboratively selecting the most suitable course of action. A solution-oriented approach promotes creativity and flexibility in resolving conflicts."

David, always analytical in his approach, recognized the significance of problem-solving and solution-oriented approach in addressing conflicts effectively. He made a mental note to encourage brainstorming sessions and collaborative problem-solving techniques to identify innovative solutions to conflicts.

The next image showed "Fairness and Impartiality." "4. **Fairness and Impartiality.** Maintaining fairness and impartiality throughout the conflict resolution process demonstrates our commitment to upholding tenants' rights and promoting a just outcome. This includes treating all parties equally, considering evidence and perspectives objectively, and adhering to established policies and procedures. Fairness and impartiality build trust and confidence in the conflict resolution process."

Lisa, their conflict resolution expert, saw the potential in maintaining fairness and impartiality to ensure the credibility and integrity of the conflict resolution process. She began reviewing their conflict resolution policies and procedures to ensure consistency and fairness in their application.

The fifth slide highlighted "Follow-Up and Resolution Monitoring." "5. **Follow-Up and Resolution Monitoring.** Following up on resolved conflicts and monitoring their outcomes ensures that agreements are upheld and any lingering issues are addressed promptly. This includes checking in with all parties involved to ensure satisfaction with the resolution, addressing any post-resolution concerns or adjustments, and documenting the outcome for future reference. Follow-up and resolution monitoring promote accountability and prevent recurring conflicts."

Jack stressed the importance of follow-up and resolution monitoring in ensuring the long-term effectiveness of conflict resolution efforts. He encouraged the team to stay engaged with all parties involved and address any post-resolution concerns proactively to prevent conflicts from resurfacing.

The final slide displayed "Continuous Improvement and Learning." "6. **Continuous Improvement and Learning.** Embracing a culture of continuous improvement and learning allows us to refine our conflict resolution skills and adapt to evolving tenant needs and preferences. This includes seeking feedback from all parties involved in the conflict resolution process, participating in conflict resolution training or workshops, and reflecting on past experiences to identify areas for improvement. Continuous improvement enhances our ability to resolve conflicts effectively and promote a harmonious living environment."

Jack turned off the projector and faced his team, the determination evident in his expression. "Conflict resolution is our opportunity to demonstrate professionalism, empathy, and commitment to tenant satisfaction."

He stepped closer, his voice filled with determination. "Let's approach conflict resolution with integrity, creativity, and a commitment to finding mutually beneficial solutions. By fostering open dialogue, adopting a solution-oriented approach, and maintaining fairness and impartiality, we can resolve conflicts effectively and promote a peaceful and supportive community within our properties."

The room buzzed with energy, each team member eager to enhance their conflict resolution skills and contribute to a harmonious living environment. Jack could see the determination in their eyes—a readiness to embrace conflict resolution as an opportunity for growth and community-building within their properties.

"Remember," Jack concluded, "conflict resolution is more than just resolving disputes—it's about fostering understanding, promoting collaboration, and building stronger tenant relationships. Let's cultivate our conflict resolution skills with care and dedication, knowing that each resolution brings us one step closer to a thriving and inclusive community within our properties."

The session ended with a renewed sense of purpose and a commitment to applying conflict resolution strategies that would promote harmony and collaboration among tenants. The team was equipped with the understanding and motivation needed to address conflicts effectively and preserve tenant satisfaction within their properties.

Tenant Retention Programs

Jack Miller gathered his team once more in the conference room, their focus now shifting towards the crucial aspect of tenant retention. With conflicts addressed and relationships strengthened, it was time to implement strategies to ensure tenants felt valued and motivated to renew their leases.

"Team," Jack began, his voice filled with determination. "Tenant retention is essential for maintaining a stable occupancy rate, reducing turnover costs, and fostering a sense of community within our properties. Let's explore the fourth step: tenant retention programs."

He clicked the remote, and the screen illuminated with

a checklist titled "Tenant Retention Programs." "Effective tenant retention programs focus on creating positive tenant experiences, fostering tenant loyalty, and incentivizing lease renewals. They are the key to long-term success in property management."

The first slide highlighted "Personalized Tenant Services." "1. **Personalized Tenant Services.** We begin by offering personalized tenant services tailored to meet individual needs and preferences. This includes providing responsive customer support, addressing tenant inquiries promptly, and offering amenities or services that enhance the tenant experience. Personalized services demonstrate our commitment to tenant satisfaction and create a strong bond between tenants and the property."

Jack emphasized the importance of personalized tenant services in creating memorable experiences and strengthening tenant loyalty. He recalled a time when a personalized gesture had made a lasting impression on a tenant, leading to a long-term lease renewal and positive word-of-mouth referrals.

The next slide displayed "Ongoing Tenant Engagement." "2. **Ongoing Tenant Engagement.** Maintaining regular communication and engagement with tenants fosters a sense of belonging and community within our properties. This includes organizing tenant appreciation events, soliciting feedback through surveys or focus groups, and keeping tenants informed about property updates or events. Ongoing engagement strengthens tenant relationships and encourages active participation in property activities."

Sarah, with her attention to detail, nodded in agreement. She understood the importance of ongoing tenant engagement in building a sense of community and fostering tenant loyalty within their properties.

The third slide depicted "Exclusive Tenant Benefits." "3. **Exclusive Tenant Benefits.** Offering exclusive benefits or rewards to long-term tenants incentivizes lease renewals and promotes tenant loyalty. This includes providing discounts on rent renewals, access to exclusive amenities or services, or referral bonuses for recommending new tenants. Exclusive benefits recognize and reward tenant loyalty, encouraging tenants to choose to stay with us."

David, always analytical in his approach, recognized the significance of exclusive tenant benefits in incentivizing lease renewals and reducing turnover rates. He made a mental note to explore creative incentives that would add value to their tenants' living experience and encourage long-term commitment.

The next image showed "Proactive Issue Resolution." "4. **Proactive Issue Resolution.** Addressing tenant concerns and resolving issues promptly demonstrates our commitment to tenant satisfaction and retention. This includes conducting regular property inspections to identify and address maintenance issues proactively, offering solutions to common tenant concerns, and providing assistance or resources to help tenants overcome challenges. Proactive issue resolution fosters trust and confidence in our property management team."

Lisa, their resolution expert, saw the potential in proactive issue resolution to prevent dissatisfaction and encourage lease renewals. She began implementing proactive maintenance programs and addressing recurring tenant concerns to improve overall tenant satisfaction and retention rates.

The fifth slide highlighted "Flexible Lease Options." "5. **Flexible Lease Options.** Offering flexible lease options allows tenants to customize their leasing experience to meet their changing needs and circumstances. This includes offering short-term or month-to-month lease options, flexible lease terms, or lease extension incentives. Flexible lease options provide tenants with greater flexibility and control over their living arrangements, reducing turnover rates and promoting long-term residency."

Jack stressed the importance of offering flexible lease options to accommodate diverse tenant preferences and life situations. He encouraged the team to explore innovative lease structures that would appeal to tenants seeking flexibility and convenience in their housing arrangements.

The final slide displayed "Continuous Feedback and Improvement." "6. **Continuous Feedback and Improvement.** Embracing a culture of continuous feedback and improvement allows us to refine our tenant retention strategies and adapt to evolving tenant needs and preferences. This includes soliciting feedback from tenants about their leasing experience, analyzing retention rates and lease renewal patterns, and implementing feedback-driven improvements to our tenant retention programs. Continuous improvement enhances our ability to retain tenants and strengthen our property communities."

Jack turned off the projector and faced his team, the determination evident in his expression. "Tenant retention is our opportunity to create lasting relationships and build a vibrant and supportive community within our properties."

He stepped closer, his voice filled with determination. "Let's approach tenant retention with creativity, empathy, and a commitment to excellence. By offering personalized services, maintaining ongoing engagement, and providing exclusive benefits, we can create an environment where tenants feel valued, appreciated, and motivated to renew their leases."

The room buzzed with energy, each team member eager to implement tenant retention strategies that would foster loyalty and strengthen community ties within their properties. Jack could see the determination in their eyes—a readiness to prioritize tenant satisfaction and retention as a cornerstone of their property management approach.

"Remember," Jack concluded, "tenant retention is more than just retaining leases—it's about building lasting connections and creating a home where tenants feel welcomed, valued, and supported. Let's cultivate our tenant retention programs with care and dedication, knowing that each retention brings us one step closer to a thriving and inclusive community within our properties."

The session ended with a renewed sense of purpose and a commitment to implementing tenant retention programs that would promote loyalty and enhance tenant satisfaction. The team was equipped with the understanding and motivation needed to prioritize tenant retention as a key driver of success within their properties.

Handling Tenant Complaints

Jack Miller convened his team once again in the conference room, their focus now directed towards the critical aspect of handling tenant complaints. As property managers, they understood that addressing tenant concerns promptly and effectively was vital for maintaining tenant satisfaction and fostering a positive living environment within their properties.

"Team," Jack began, his voice firm yet empathetic. "Handling tenant complaints is an integral part of our role as property managers. It's not just about resolving issues; it's about demonstrating our commitment to tenant satisfaction and ensuring that our properties remain desirable places to live. Let's explore the fifth step: handling tenant complaints."

He clicked the remote, and the screen illuminated with a checklist titled "Handling Tenant Complaints." "Effective handling of tenant complaints requires empathy, communication, and a proactive approach to problem-solving. It is the key to addressing concerns swiftly and preserving tenant trust and satisfaction."

The first slide highlighted "Prompt Response and Acknowledgment." "1. **Prompt Response and Acknowledgment.** We begin by acknowledging tenant complaints promptly and communicating our commitment to addressing their concerns. This includes acknowledging receipt of the complaint, expressing empathy for the tenant's experience, and providing a timeline for resolution. Prompt response and acknowledgment demonstrate our responsiveness and dedication to tenant satisfaction."

Jack emphasized the importance of prompt response and acknowledgment in reassuring tenants that their concerns were being taken seriously. He recalled a time when a swift response had prevented a minor issue from escalating into a major problem, ultimately strengthening the landlord-tenant relationship.

The next slide displayed "Active Listening and Empathetic

Understanding." "2. **Active Listening and Empathetic Understanding.** Actively listening to tenants' concerns and demonstrating empathy towards their experiences is essential for building trust and rapport. This includes giving tenants our full attention, paraphrasing their concerns to ensure understanding, and expressing empathy for their perspectives and emotions. Active listening and empathetic understanding show tenants that their voices are heard and valued."

Sarah, with her attention to detail, nodded in agreement. She understood the importance of active listening and empathetic understanding in validating tenants' experiences and fostering trust and rapport.

The third slide depicted "Transparent Communication and Updates." "3. **Transparent Communication and Updates.** Maintaining transparent communication and providing regular updates on the status of the complaint instills confidence in tenants and demonstrates our commitment to resolution. This includes keeping tenants informed about the progress of the complaint, any challenges or delays encountered, and the proposed timeline for resolution. Transparent communication promotes trust and reduces uncertainty."

David, always analytical in his approach, recognized the significance of transparent communication in keeping tenants informed and reassured throughout the complaint resolution process. He made a mental note to provide regular updates to tenants, even if there were no significant developments to report.

The next image showed "Proactive Problem-Solving and Resolution." "4. **Proactive Problem-Solving and Resolution.** Taking proactive steps to address tenant complaints and resolve issues promptly is essential for maintaining tenant satisfaction. This includes identifying the root cause of the complaint, exploring potential solutions, and implementing corrective actions to prevent recurrence. Proactive problem-solving demonstrates our commitment to resolving issues effectively and preventing future challenges."

Lisa, their resolution expert, saw the potential in proactive problem-solving to address tenant complaints swiftly and prevent dissatisfaction. She began implementing proactive measures to address common issues and improve overall tenant satisfaction levels.

The fifth slide highlighted "Fair and Equitable Resolution." "5. **Fair and Equitable Resolution.** Ensuring that complaints are resolved fairly and equitably demonstrates our commitment to upholding tenant rights and promoting a just outcome. This includes considering all available evidence and perspectives, conducting a thorough investigation if necessary, and implementing a resolution that is fair and satisfactory to all parties involved. Fair and equitable resolution builds trust and confidence in our property management team."

Jack stressed the importance of fairness and equity in resolving tenant complaints to ensure the credibility and integrity of the resolution process. He encouraged the team to approach each complaint with impartiality and professionalism, seeking solutions that prioritized tenant satisfaction and community harmony.

The final slide displayed "Continuous Improvement and Learning." "6. **Continuous Improvement and Learning.** Embracing a culture of continuous improvement and learning allows us to refine our complaint handling processes and adapt to evolving tenant needs and preferences. This includes soliciting feedback from tenants about their complaint resolution experience, analyzing complaint trends and patterns, and implementing feedback-driven improvements to our complaint handling procedures. Continuous improvement enhances our ability to address tenant concerns effectively and preserve tenant satisfaction."

Jack turned off the projector and faced his team, the determination evident in his expression. "Handling tenant complaints is our opportunity to demonstrate professionalism, empathy, and a commitment to tenant satisfaction."

He stepped closer, his voice filled with determination. "Let's approach complaint handling with integrity, transparency, and a commitment to excellence. By responding promptly, listening actively, and resolving issues fairly, we can address tenant concerns effectively and preserve trust and satisfaction within our properties."

The room buzzed with energy, each team member eager to enhance their complaint handling skills and contribute to a positive living experience for their tenants. Jack could see the determination in their eyes—a readiness to prioritize tenant satisfaction and address complaints with care and dedication.

"Remember," Jack concluded, "handling tenant complaints is about more than just resolving issues—it's about building trust, maintaining satisfaction, and fostering a sense of community within our properties. Let's cultivate our complaint handling skills with empathy and professionalism, knowing that each resolution brings us closer to achieving our goal of tenant-centric property management."

The session ended with a renewed sense of purpose and a commitment to implementing complaint handling strategies that would promote trust and satisfaction among tenants.

The team was equipped with the understanding and motivation needed to address tenant complaints effectively and preserve tenant trust within their properties.

Enforcing Lease Terms

Jack Miller convened his team once more in the conference room, their attention now focused on the crucial aspect of enforcing lease terms. As property managers, they understood that upholding lease agreements was essential for maintaining order, protecting property assets, and ensuring a positive living environment within their properties.

"Team," Jack began, his voice firm yet fair. "Enforcing lease terms is a fundamental responsibility that ensures the integrity of our property management operations and promotes a harmonious community environment. Let's explore the sixth step: enforcing lease terms."

He clicked the remote, and the screen illuminated with a checklist titled "Enforcing Lease Terms." "Effective enforcement of lease terms requires consistency, transparency, and adherence to legal regulations. It is the key to upholding property standards and fostering a respectful tenant community."

The first slide highlighted "Clear Communication of Lease Terms." "1. **Clear Communication of Lease Terms.** We begin by ensuring that lease terms are communicated clearly and effectively to all tenants during the leasing process. This includes reviewing lease agreements with tenants, explaining their rights and responsibilities, and providing opportunities for clarification or questions. Clear communication sets expectations and minimizes misunderstandings regarding lease obligations."

Jack emphasized the importance of clear communication in ensuring that tenants understood their contractual obligations. He recalled a time when proactive communication had prevented lease violations and maintained a positive landlord-tenant relationship.

The next slide displayed "Consistent Enforcement Policies." "2. **Consistent Enforcement Policies.** Implementing consistent enforcement policies ensures that all tenants are held to the same standards and expectations outlined in their lease agreements. This includes enforcing lease terms uniformly across all tenants, regardless of tenure or relationship, and applying consequences for lease violations fairly and impartially. Consistent enforcement promotes a sense of fairness and accountability within the tenant community."

Sarah, with her attention to detail, nodded in agreement. She understood the importance of consistent enforcement policies in maintaining order and promoting respect for property rules among tenants.

The third slide depicted "Timely Response to Lease Violations." "3. **Timely Response to Lease Violations.** Addressing lease violations promptly demonstrates our commitment to upholding property standards and ensuring tenant compliance. This includes promptly notifying tenants of lease violations, providing opportunities for remedy or correction, and escalating enforcement actions if necessary. Timely response reinforces the importance of lease compliance and prevents escalation of issues."

David, always analytical in his approach, recognized the significance of timely response in preventing lease violations from becoming chronic problems. He made a mental note to streamline their response procedures to ensure swift action when addressing lease violations.

The next image showed "Documentation and Record-Keeping." "4. **Documentation and Record-Keeping.** Maintaining thorough documentation of lease violations and enforcement actions taken ensures accountability and transparency in the enforcement process. This includes documenting all communications with tenants regarding lease violations, keeping records of enforcement actions taken, and storing documentation in a secure and accessible manner. Documentation provides a clear record of lease compliance efforts and supports enforcement decisions if challenged."

Lisa, their documentation expert, saw the potential in meticulous record-keeping to strengthen their enforcement efforts and ensure compliance with legal requirements. She began implementing standardized documentation procedures to capture all lease-related communications and enforcement actions.

The fifth slide highlighted "Legal Compliance and Due Process." "5. **Legal Compliance and Due Process.** Ensuring that all enforcement actions comply with legal regulations and due process rights protects tenants' rights and prevents potential legal challenges. This includes familiarizing ourselves with relevant landlord-tenant laws and regulations, providing tenants with notice of lease violations and opportunities for remedy, and adhering to established legal procedures for eviction or lease termination if necessary. Legal compliance safeguards tenant rights and preserves the integrity of the enforcement process."

Jack stressed the importance of legal compliance and due process in enforcing lease terms and protecting tenant rights.

He encouraged the team to stay informed about relevant legal regulations and seek legal guidance when necessary to ensure compliance with legal requirements.

The final slide displayed "Continuous Improvement and Training." "6. **Continuous Improvement and Training.** Embracing a culture of continuous improvement and training allows us to refine our enforcement processes and adapt to evolving legal requirements and tenant needs. This includes conducting regular training sessions for staff on lease enforcement procedures and legal compliance, soliciting feedback from tenants about their leasing experience, and implementing feedback-driven improvements to our enforcement policies and practices. Continuous improvement enhances our ability to enforce lease terms effectively and maintain a respectful tenant community."

Jack turned off the projector and faced his team, the determination evident in his expression. "Enforcing lease terms is our responsibility to uphold property standards and protect the rights and interests of all tenants."

He stepped closer, his voice filled with determination. "Let's approach lease enforcement with consistency, fairness, and a commitment to legal compliance. By communicating lease terms clearly, enforcing policies consistently, and responding to violations promptly, we can maintain order and promote a respectful tenant community within our properties."

The room buzzed with energy, each team member eager to enhance their lease enforcement efforts and contribute to a positive living environment for their tenants. Jack could see the determination in their eyes—a readiness to uphold property standards and enforce lease terms with care and dedication.

"Remember," Jack concluded, "enforcing lease terms is about maintaining a safe, orderly, and respectful living environment for all tenants. Let's cultivate our enforcement practices with professionalism and integrity, knowing that each enforcement action contributes to the well-being and satisfaction of our tenant community."

The session ended with a renewed sense of purpose and a commitment to implementing lease enforcement strategies that would uphold property standards and foster a positive tenant experience. The team was equipped with the understanding and motivation needed to enforce lease terms effectively and promote a harmonious community environment within their properties.

Chapter 7: Financial Management

Budgeting and Financial Planning

Jack Miller gathered his team once again in the conference room, their focus now shifting to the critical aspect of financial management. As property managers, they understood that effective budgeting and financial planning were essential for ensuring the financial health and sustainability of their properties.

"Team," Jack began, his voice projecting confidence. "Financial management is a cornerstone of successful property management. It's not just about balancing the books; it's about making strategic decisions that optimize revenue, minimize expenses, and ensure long-term financial stability. Let's explore the first step: budgeting and financial planning."

He clicked the remote, and the screen illuminated with a checklist titled "Budgeting and Financial Planning." "Effective budgeting and financial planning require foresight, attention to detail, and a commitment to fiscal responsibility. They are the key to achieving our financial goals and maintaining the financial health of our properties."

The first slide highlighted "Establishing a Comprehensive Budget." "1. **Establishing a Comprehensive Budget.** We begin by developing a comprehensive budget that outlines projected revenues, expenses, and cash flow for the upcoming fiscal period. This includes conducting a thorough analysis of historical financial data, identifying revenue sources, and estimating expenses for operations, maintenance, and capital improvements. A comprehensive budget serves as a roadmap for financial decision-making and ensures that resources are allocated effectively to support property operations."

Jack emphasized the importance of establishing a comprehensive budget to guide financial decision-making and ensure the prudent allocation of resources. He recalled a time when a well-planned budget had enabled them to undertake necessary property improvements without compromising financial stability.

The next slide displayed "Forecasting Revenue and Expenses." "2. **Forecasting Revenue and Expenses.** Accurately forecasting revenue and expenses allows us to anticipate financial trends and make informed decisions about resource allocation. This includes analyzing historical revenue and expense data, considering market trends and economic indicators, and adjusting projections based on current conditions and future expectations. Forecasting revenue and expenses provides valuable insights for budget planning and risk management."

Sarah, with her knack for detail, nodded in agreement. She understood the importance of forecasting revenue and expenses in identifying potential financial opportunities and challenges and adjusting budget plans accordingly.

The third slide depicted "Risk Assessment and Contingency Planning." "3. **Risk Assessment and Contingency Planning.** Conducting a risk assessment and developing contingency plans helps mitigate financial risks and ensure business continuity in the face of unforeseen challenges. This includes identifying potential risks, such as vacancy rates, economic downturns, or unexpected maintenance expenses, and developing strategies to minimize their impact. Risk assessment and contingency planning enable us to prepare for the unexpected and maintain financial resilience."

David, always analytical in his approach, recognized the significance of risk assessment and contingency planning in safeguarding financial stability. He made a mental note to review their contingency plans and update them as needed to address emerging risks and challenges.

The next image showed "Expense Management and Cost Control." "4. **Expense Management and Cost Control.** Implementing effective expense management and cost control measures helps optimize financial performance and maximize profitability. This includes scrutinizing expenses for efficiency and necessity, negotiating favorable terms with vendors and service providers, and implementing cost-saving initiatives where possible. Expense management and cost control minimize waste and ensure that resources are utilized efficiently to support property operations."

Lisa, their cost control expert, saw the potential in implementing cost-saving initiatives to improve their financial performance and profitability. She began exploring opportunities to renegotiate vendor contracts and streamline operational processes to reduce expenses without sacrificing quality.

The fifth slide highlighted "Monitoring and Performance Evaluation." "5. **Monitoring and Performance Evaluation.** Regular monitoring and performance evaluation allow us to track financial performance against budget projections and identify areas for improvement or adjustment. This includes reviewing financial reports and statements regularly, analyzing variances between budgeted and actual revenue and expenses, and identifying trends or patterns that may require corrective action. Monitoring and performance evaluation provide valuable feedback for refining budget plans and optimizing financial outcomes."

Jack stressed the importance of monitoring and performance evaluation in maintaining financial accountability and transparency. He encouraged the team to conduct regular financial reviews and identify opportunities for improvement to ensure the ongoing financial health of their properties.

The final slide displayed "Continuous Improvement and Adaptation." "6. **Continuous Improvement and Adaptation.** Embracing a culture of continuous improvement and adaptation allows us to refine our budgeting and financial planning processes and adapt to evolving market conditions and financial trends. This includes seeking feedback from stakeholders about financial performance and budget plans, staying informed about industry best practices and emerging technologies, and implementing feedback-driven improvements to our financial management practices. Continuous improvement ensures that our budgeting and financial planning efforts remain responsive and effective in achieving our financial goals."

Jack turned off the projector and faced his team, the

determination evident in his expression. "Budgeting and financial planning are not just administrative tasks—they are strategic initiatives that shape the financial future of our properties."

He stepped closer, his voice filled with determination. "Let's approach budgeting and financial planning with diligence, foresight, and a commitment to fiscal responsibility. By establishing comprehensive budgets, forecasting revenue and expenses, and implementing effective expense management strategies, we can optimize financial performance and ensure the long-term success of our properties."

The room buzzed with energy, each team member eager to enhance their budgeting and financial planning efforts and contribute to the financial health and sustainability of their properties.

Rent Collection Processes

Jack Miller reconvened his team in the conference room, their focus now shifting to the critical aspect of rent collection processes. As property managers, they understood that timely and efficient rent collection was essential for maintaining cash flow and ensuring the financial stability of their properties.

"Team," Jack began, his voice projecting authority. "Rent collection is the lifeblood of our financial operations. It's not just about collecting payments; it's about establishing streamlined processes that promote consistency, reliability, and transparency. Let's explore the second step: rent collection processes."

He clicked the remote, and the screen illuminated with a

checklist titled "Rent Collection Processes." "Effective rent collection processes require diligence, organization, and a commitment to tenant communication. They are the key to ensuring that rent payments are received on time and in full."

The first slide highlighted "Clear Rent Payment Policies." "1. **Clear Rent Payment Policies.** We begin by establishing clear and transparent rent payment policies that outline the terms, methods, and deadlines for rent payment. This includes communicating rent payment policies to tenants at lease signing, providing multiple payment options to accommodate tenant preferences, and setting clear expectations regarding late fees and consequences for non-payment. Clear rent payment policies promote consistency and accountability in rent collection."

Jack emphasized the importance of clear rent payment policies in setting expectations and minimizing confusion among tenants. He recalled a time when well-communicated policies had reduced late payments and improved overall rent collection rates.

The next slide displayed "Convenient Payment Options." "2. **Convenient Payment Options.** Offering convenient and flexible payment options makes it easier for tenants to submit rent payments on time. This includes accepting multiple payment methods, such as online payments, automatic bank transfers, credit card payments, and traditional methods like checks or money orders. Providing convenient payment options increases tenant satisfaction and reduces barriers to timely rent payment."

Sarah, with her attention to detail, nodded in agreement. She understood the importance of offering convenient payment options to accommodate diverse tenant preferences and lifestyles, ultimately improving rent collection efficiency.

The third slide depicted "Automated Rent Collection Systems." "3. **Automated Rent Collection Systems.** Implementing automated rent collection systems streamlines the payment process and reduces administrative burden for both tenants and property management staff. This includes setting up automated recurring payments, issuing electronic invoices or reminders, and integrating rent collection software with property management systems for seamless tracking and reporting. Automated rent collection systems improve efficiency and accuracy in rent collection."

David, always analytical in his approach, recognized the efficiency gains of automated rent collection systems in reducing manual tasks and minimizing errors. He made a mental note to explore software solutions that would automate rent collection processes and streamline their operations.

The next image showed "Proactive Rent Monitoring and Follow-Up." "4. **Proactive Rent Monitoring and Follow-Up.** Monitoring rent payments proactively and following up on late or missed payments ensures prompt resolution of payment issues. This includes monitoring rent payment deadlines, sending timely reminders or notifications to tenants with outstanding balances, and initiating follow-up communications to address payment discrepancies or concerns. Proactive rent monitoring reduces delinquencies and improves overall rent collection efficiency."

Lisa, their follow-up expert, saw the potential in proactive rent monitoring to reduce late payments and improve cash flow predictability. She began implementing a proactive follow-up system to track rent payments and address payment issues promptly.

The fifth slide highlighted "Consistent Enforcement of Rent Policies." "5. **Consistent Enforcement of Rent Policies.** Enforcing rent policies consistently and impartially ensures that all tenants are held to the same standards regarding rent payment. This includes applying late fees or penalties consistently for late payments, following established procedures for addressing payment disputes or non-compliance, and communicating enforcement actions clearly and respectfully to tenants. Consistent enforcement promotes accountability and maintains the integrity of rent collection processes."

Jack stressed the importance of consistent enforcement of rent policies in maintaining fairness and transparency in rent collection. He encouraged the team to apply policies impartially and communicate enforcement actions with empathy and professionalism.

The final slide displayed "Continuous Improvement and Adaptation." "6. **Continuous Improvement and Adaptation.** Embracing a culture of continuous improvement and adaptation allows us to refine our rent collection processes and adapt to evolving tenant needs and preferences. This includes soliciting feedback from tenants about their rent payment experience, evaluating rent collection performance regularly, and implementing feedback-driven improvements to our rent collection procedures. Continuous improvement ensures that our rent collection processes remain responsive and effective in maximizing revenue and ensuring financial stability."

Jack turned off the projector and faced his team, the determination evident in his expression. "Rent collection is not just about collecting payments—it's about fostering positive tenant relationships and maintaining financial stability."

He stepped closer, his voice filled with determination. "Let's approach rent collection with diligence, empathy, and a commitment to efficiency. By establishing clear policies, offering convenient payment options, and implementing proactive monitoring systems, we can optimize rent collection processes and ensure the financial health of our properties."

The room buzzed with energy, each team member eager to enhance their rent collection processes and contribute to the financial success of their properties. Jack could see the determination in their eyes—a readiness to prioritize rent collection efficiency and effectiveness.

Managing Operating Expenses

Jack Miller reconvened his team once more in the conference room, their focus now shifting to the crucial aspect of managing operating expenses. As property managers, they understood that effective expense management was essential for maximizing profitability and ensuring the financial sustainability of their properties.

"Team," Jack began, his voice resonating with authority. "Managing operating expenses is a fundamental aspect of our financial responsibilities. It's not just about cutting costs; it's about optimizing spending to achieve the best possible return on investment. Let's explore the third step: managing operating expenses."

He clicked the remote, and the screen illuminated with a checklist titled "Managing Operating Expenses." "Effective management of operating expenses requires diligence, analysis, and a commitment to efficiency. It is the key to maintaining financial health and maximizing profitability."

The first slide highlighted "Expense Analysis and Budget Allocation." "1. **Expense Analysis and Budget Allocation.** We begin by conducting a thorough analysis of our operating expenses to identify areas for optimization and improvement. This includes reviewing expense reports and statements, categorizing expenses by type and frequency, and comparing actual expenses to budgeted allocations. Expense analysis enables us to identify opportunities for cost reduction and reallocation of resources to higher-priority areas."

Jack emphasized the importance of expense analysis in identifying inefficiencies and opportunities for improvement. He recalled a time when strategic budget allocation had enabled them to redirect funds towards property maintenance, resulting in improved tenant satisfaction and reduced long-term expenses.

The next slide displayed "Vendor Negotiation and Contract Management." "2. **Vendor Negotiation and Contract Management.** Negotiating favorable terms with vendors and service providers helps minimize operating expenses and maximize value for money. This includes soliciting competitive bids from multiple vendors, negotiating pricing and contract terms, and establishing clear performance metrics and service level agreements. Effective vendor negotiation and contract management ensure that we receive quality services at competitive rates."

Sarah, with her meticulous approach, nodded in agreement. She understood the importance of vendor negotiation in reducing costs without sacrificing service quality, ultimately improving the bottom line for their properties.

The third slide depicted "Expense Reduction Strategies." "3. **Expense Reduction Strategies.** Implementing cost-saving initiatives and efficiency measures helps reduce operating expenses and improve overall profitability. This includes identifying areas of waste or inefficiency, implementing energy-saving measures to reduce utility costs, and exploring alternative sourcing options for supplies or materials. Expense reduction strategies optimize spending and maximize the financial performance of our properties."

David, always analytical in his approach, recognized the potential for expense reduction strategies to improve their properties' financial performance. He made a mental note to explore energy-saving initiatives and evaluate their potential impact on operating expenses.

The next image showed "Preventive Maintenance and Asset Management." "4. **Preventive Maintenance and Asset Management.** Prioritizing preventive maintenance and asset management practices helps minimize unexpected repair costs and prolong the lifespan of property assets. This includes implementing regular maintenance schedules, conducting property inspections to identify maintenance needs proactively, and investing in capital improvements to prevent deterioration and obsolescence. Preventive maintenance and asset management reduce long-term operating expenses and ensure the reliability and value of our properties."

Lisa, their maintenance expert, saw the value of preventive maintenance in reducing repair costs and preserving property value. She began implementing a proactive maintenance program to address maintenance needs before they escalated into costly repairs.

The fifth slide highlighted "Expense Tracking and Performance Evaluation." "5. **Expense Tracking and Performance Evaluation.** Regular tracking and evaluation of operating expenses allow us to monitor financial performance and identify trends or patterns that may require corrective action. This includes tracking expenses against budget allocations, analyzing variances and deviations, and identifying opportunities for improvement or adjustment. Expense tracking and performance evaluation provide valuable insights for optimizing expense management strategies and maximizing profitability."

Jack stressed the importance of expense tracking in maintaining financial accountability and transparency. He encouraged the team to review expense reports regularly and identify opportunities for improvement to ensure the ongoing financial health of their properties.

The final slide displayed "Continuous Improvement and Adaptation." "6. **Continuous Improvement and Adaptation.** Embracing a culture of continuous improvement and adaptation allows us to refine our expense management strategies and adapt to evolving market conditions and financial trends. This includes soliciting feedback from stakeholders about expense management practices, evaluating performance metrics and benchmarks, and implementing feedback-driven improvements to our expense management procedures. Continuous improvement ensures that our expense management efforts remain responsive and effective in optimizing financial outcomes."

Jack turned off the projector and faced his team, the determination evident in his expression. "Managing operating expenses is not just about cutting costs—it's about optimizing spending to achieve the best possible outcomes for our properties."

He stepped closer, his voice filled with determination. "Let's approach expense management with diligence, creativity, and a commitment to efficiency. By analyzing expenses, negotiating with vendors, and implementing cost-saving initiatives, we can maximize profitability and ensure the financial sustainability of our properties."

The room buzzed with energy, each team member eager to enhance their expense management efforts and contribute to the financial success of their properties. Jack could see the determination in their eyes—a readiness to prioritize expense management efficiency and effectiveness to achieve their financial goals.

Financial Reporting and Analysis

Jack Miller gathered his team once again in the conference room, their focus now directed towards the crucial aspect of financial reporting and analysis. As property managers, they understood that accurate and insightful financial reporting was essential for making informed decisions and ensuring the financial health of their properties.

"Team," Jack began, his voice carrying authority. "Financial reporting and analysis are the backbone of our financial management efforts. It's not just about crunching numbers; it's about extracting meaningful insights that drive strategic decision-making. Let's explore the fourth step: financial reporting and analysis."

He clicked the remote, and the screen illuminated with a checklist titled "Financial Reporting and Analysis." "Effective financial reporting and analysis require attention to detail, analytical skills, and a commitment to transparency. They are the key to understanding our financial performance and identifying opportunities for improvement."

The first slide highlighted "Accurate Financial Record-Keeping." "1. **Accurate Financial Record-Keeping.** We begin by maintaining accurate and up-to-date financial records that capture all income, expenses, and transactions related to property operations. This includes documenting rent payments, vendor invoices, maintenance expenses, and other financial transactions in a systematic and organized manner. Accurate financial record-keeping forms the foundation for reliable financial reporting and analysis."

Jack emphasized the importance of accurate financial record-keeping in ensuring the integrity and reliability of financial data. He recalled a time when meticulous record-keeping had enabled them to identify discrepancies and address financial issues promptly, ultimately improving financial performance.

The next slide displayed "Regular Financial Reporting." "2. **Regular Financial Reporting.** Generating regular financial reports allows us to track financial performance over time and assess progress towards our financial goals. This includes preparing monthly, quarterly, and annual financial statements, such as income statements, balance sheets, and cash flow statements, and distributing reports to stakeholders, such as property owners, investors, and management teams. Regular financial reporting provides stakeholders with timely insights into our financial performance and informs decision-making."

Sarah, with her meticulous approach, nodded in agreement. She understood the importance of regular financial reporting in keeping stakeholders informed and fostering transparency and accountability in financial management.

The third slide depicted "Variance Analysis and Performance Metrics." "3. **Variance Analysis and Performance Metrics.** Conducting variance analysis and monitoring key performance metrics allows us to assess financial performance against budgeted expectations and identify areas for improvement or optimization. This includes analyzing variances between budgeted and actual revenues and expenses, calculating financial ratios and benchmarks, and identifying trends or patterns that may require corrective action. Variance analysis and performance metrics provide valuable insights for optimizing financial performance and achieving financial goals."

David, always analytical in his approach, recognized the value of variance analysis in identifying trends and deviations from expected financial performance. He made a mental note to conduct regular variance analysis to identify opportunities for improvement and optimization.

The next image showed "Trend Analysis and Forecasting." "4. **Trend Analysis and Forecasting.** Performing trend analysis and forecasting helps us anticipate future financial trends and plan for potential opportunities or challenges. This includes analyzing historical financial data to identify trends and patterns, extrapolating trends to forecast future financial performance, and incorporating external factors, such as market conditions and economic indicators, into financial projections. Trend analysis and forecasting provide valuable insights for strategic planning and decision-making."

Lisa, their forecasting expert, saw the potential in trend analysis and forecasting to anticipate future financial trends and adapt their strategies accordingly. She began incorporating trend analysis into their financial reporting process to provide stakeholders with forward-looking insights into financial performance.

The fifth slide highlighted "Data Visualization and Communication." "5. **Data Visualization and Communication.** Presenting financial data in a clear and accessible format facilitates understanding and decision-making among stakeholders. This includes using data visualization techniques, such as charts, graphs, and dashboards, to present financial information visually, and communicating financial insights effectively to stakeholders through written reports or presentations. Data visualization and communication enhance the accessibility and impact of financial reporting and analysis."

Jack stressed the importance of data visualization and communication in making financial insights accessible and actionable for stakeholders. He encouraged the team to use visual aids and clear language to communicate financial information effectively and engage stakeholders in decision-making processes.

The final slide displayed "Continuous Improvement and Adaptation." "6. **Continuous Improvement and Adaptation.** Embracing a culture of continuous improvement and adaptation allows us to refine our financial reporting and analysis processes and adapt to evolving market conditions and stakeholder needs. This includes soliciting feedback from stakeholders about financial reporting practices, evaluating the effectiveness of performance metrics and benchmarks, and implementing feedback-driven improvements to our reporting and analysis procedures. Continuous improvement ensures that our financial reporting and analysis efforts remain responsive and effective in supporting strategic decision-making."

Jack turned off the projector and faced his team, the determination evident in his expression. "Financial reporting and analysis are not just about numbers—they're about providing insights that drive strategic decision-making and ensure the financial health of our properties."

He stepped closer, his voice filled with determination. "Let's approach financial reporting and analysis with diligence, transparency, and a commitment to continuous improvement. By maintaining accurate records, analyzing performance metrics, and communicating insights effectively, we can optimize financial performance and achieve our financial goals."

The room buzzed with energy, each team member eager to enhance their financial reporting and analysis efforts and contribute to the financial success of their properties. Jack could see the determination in their eyes—a readiness to prioritize financial transparency and accountability to achieve their shared goals.

Handling Delinquencies and Evictions

Jack Miller gathered his team once again in the conference room, their focus now directed towards the challenging aspect of handling delinquencies and evictions. As property managers, they understood that dealing with late payments and potential evictions required sensitivity, legality, and firmness.

"Team," Jack began, his tone serious yet empathetic. "Handling delinquencies and evictions is one of the toughest parts of our job. It's not just about collecting rent—it's about navigating complex legal processes while maintaining respect and dignity for our tenants. Let's explore the fifth step: handling delinquencies and evictions."

He clicked the remote, and the screen illuminated with a checklist titled "Handling Delinquencies and Evictions." "Effective management of delinquencies and evictions requires compassion, legal knowledge, and a commitment to fairness. They are the key to protecting our financial interests while upholding the rights of our tenants."

The first slide highlighted "Early Intervention and Communication." "1. **Early Intervention and Communication.** We begin by establishing clear communication channels with tenants and intervening early at the first sign of payment difficulties. This includes reaching out to delinquent tenants promptly, offering support and understanding, and discussing payment options or assistance programs that may be available. Early intervention demonstrates our commitment to helping tenants resolve payment issues and prevents situations from escalating to eviction."

Jack emphasized the importance of early intervention in addressing payment difficulties before they became insurmountable. He recalled a time when compassionate communication had enabled them to work with struggling tenants and prevent evictions through mutual agreement.

The next slide displayed "Rent Reminder Notices and Late Fees." "2. **Rent Reminder Notices and Late Fees.** Sending rent reminder notices and applying late fees for overdue payments reinforces the importance of timely rent payment and encourages compliance with lease terms. This includes sending reminder notices to tenants with outstanding balances, clearly outlining the amount owed and the consequences of continued non-payment, and applying late fees as specified in the lease agreement. Rent reminder notices and late fees provide incentives for prompt payment and deter future delinquencies."

Sarah, with her meticulous approach, nodded in agreement. She understood the importance of enforcing lease terms consistently and applying late fees as a deterrent to late payments, ultimately promoting timely rent payment behavior among tenants.

The third slide depicted "Payment Plans and Arrangements." "3. **Payment Plans and Arrangements.** Offering payment plans or arrangements to delinquent tenants provides a structured approach to resolving payment issues and avoiding eviction. This includes working with tenants to develop personalized payment plans based on their financial situation and ability to pay, establishing clear terms and timelines for repayment, and documenting agreements in writing to ensure mutual understanding and accountability. Payment plans and arrangements offer flexibility and support to tenants facing temporary financial difficulties."

David, always analytical in his approach, recognized the importance of offering payment plans to tenants experiencing financial hardship. He made a mental note to review their existing policies and ensure that payment arrangements were fair and sustainable for both parties.

The next image showed "Legal Notices and Eviction Proceedings." "4. **Legal Notices and Eviction Proceedings.** Initiating legal notices and eviction proceedings is a last resort when all other efforts to resolve payment issues have been exhausted. This includes serving tenants with formal eviction notices in compliance with state and local laws, initiating legal proceedings through the court system if necessary, and following established eviction procedures to ensure compliance with legal requirements. Legal notices and eviction proceedings protect our rights as property owners while providing tenants with due process and legal recourse."

Lisa, their legal expert, understood the complexities of eviction proceedings and the importance of adhering to legal requirements. She began reviewing their eviction procedures to ensure compliance with state and local laws and protect both the rights of the property owners and the tenants.

The fifth slide highlighted "Tenant Support Services and Resources." "5. **Tenant Support Services and Resources.** Connecting delinquent tenants with support services and resources can help address underlying issues contributing to payment difficulties and prevent future delinquencies. This includes providing information about financial assistance programs, community resources, and tenant advocacy services that may be available to tenants facing financial hardship, and offering support and guidance throughout the process. Tenant support services and resources demonstrate our commitment to tenant well-being and facilitate positive outcomes for all parties involved."

Jack stressed the importance of providing support to tenants facing financial difficulties and connecting them with available resources. He encouraged the team to approach each situation with empathy and compassion, recognizing that behind every late payment was a tenant facing challenges.

The final slide displayed "Continuous Improvement and Adaptation." "6. **Continuous Improvement and Adaptation.** Embracing a culture of continuous improvement and adaptation allows us to refine our approach to handling delinquencies and evictions and adapt to evolving tenant needs and legal requirements. This includes soliciting feedback from tenants about their experiences with the eviction process, evaluating the effectiveness of support services and resources, and implementing feedback-driven improvements to our procedures. Continuous improvement ensures that our approach remains responsive and effective in supporting tenants and protecting our financial interests."

Jack turned off the projector and faced his team, the determination evident in his expression. "Handling delinquencies and evictions is one of the toughest challenges we face, but it's also an opportunity to demonstrate compassion and integrity in our work."

He stepped closer, his voice filled with determination. "Let's approach delinquencies and evictions with empathy, fairness, and a commitment to finding positive solutions. By intervening early, offering support, and adhering to legal requirements, we can navigate these challenges while upholding the rights and dignity of our tenants."

The room buzzed with a sense of purpose, each team member ready to approach delinquencies and evictions with compassion and professionalism. Jack could see the determination in their eyes—a readiness to handle these tough situations with integrity and empathy, ensuring the best possible outcomes for all involved.

Tax Considerations for Property Managers

Jack Miller gathered his team once more in the conference room, their attention now shifting to the complex yet vital aspect of tax considerations for property managers. As property managers, they understood that navigating tax obligations was crucial for maintaining compliance and optimizing financial outcomes.

"Team," Jack began, his tone serious yet focused. "Understanding tax considerations is essential for our financial management efforts. It's not just about filing paperwork—it's about maximizing deductions, minimizing liabilities, and ensuring compliance with tax laws. Let's explore the sixth step: tax considerations for property managers."

He clicked the remote, and the screen illuminated with a checklist titled "Tax Considerations for Property Managers." "Effective management of tax considerations requires knowledge, attention to detail, and a commitment to compliance. They are the key to optimizing financial outcomes and minimizing tax liabilities."

The first slide highlighted "Income and Expense Tracking." "1. **Income and Expense Tracking.** We begin by accurately tracking income and expenses related to property operations throughout the fiscal year. This includes documenting rental income, vendor invoices, maintenance expenses, and other financial transactions, and maintaining organized records for tax reporting purposes. Accurate income and expense tracking ensure that we can claim all eligible deductions and credits while minimizing the risk of audit."

Jack emphasized the importance of meticulous income and expense tracking in maximizing deductions and minimizing tax liabilities. He recalled a time when detailed record-keeping had enabled them to claim significant deductions and reduce their tax burden effectively.

The next slide displayed "Property Depreciation and Capitalization." "2. **Property Depreciation and Capitalization.** Understanding the principles of property depreciation and capitalization allows us to maximize tax benefits and optimize financial planning strategies. This includes calculating depreciation expenses for eligible property assets over their useful life, identifying capital expenditures that qualify for immediate deduction or capitalization, and utilizing tax planning techniques to optimize depreciation schedules and minimize tax liabilities. Property depreciation and capitalization strategies enhance tax efficiency and improve cash flow management."

Sarah, with her attention to detail, nodded in agreement. She understood the importance of leveraging property depreciation and capitalization strategies to reduce taxable income and enhance cash flow, ultimately improving overall financial performance for their properties.

The third slide depicted "Tax Deductions and Credits." "3. **Tax Deductions and Credits.** Identifying eligible tax deductions and credits allows us to reduce taxable income and maximize tax savings. This includes claiming deductions for expenses such as property maintenance, repairs, insurance premiums, and property management fees, as well as utilizing tax credits for energy-efficient improvements, low-income housing investments, and other eligible activities. Maximizing tax deductions and credits optimizes financial outcomes and enhances overall profitability."

David, always analytical in his approach, recognized the

importance of identifying and claiming eligible tax deductions and credits to reduce tax liabilities effectively. He made a mental note to review their expenses and identify opportunities for additional deductions and credits.

The next image showed "Tax Compliance and Reporting."
"4. **Tax Compliance and Reporting.** Ensuring compliance with tax laws and regulations is essential for avoiding penalties and maintaining financial integrity. This includes staying informed about changes to tax laws and regulations that may affect property management operations, filing accurate and timely tax returns, and retaining documentation to support tax reporting and deductions. Tax compliance and reporting demonstrate our commitment to transparency and accountability in financial management."

Lisa, their compliance expert, understood the importance of adhering to tax laws and regulations to avoid penalties and maintain trust with stakeholders. She began reviewing their tax reporting procedures to ensure accuracy and compliance with current tax requirements.

The fifth slide highlighted "Tax Planning and Strategy."
"5. **Tax Planning and Strategy.** Developing proactive tax planning strategies helps us optimize financial outcomes and minimize tax liabilities over the long term. This includes collaborating with tax professionals to identify tax-saving opportunities, such as entity structuring, like-kind exchanges, and tax-deferred investments, and implementing strategies to maximize tax efficiency while achieving financial goals. Tax planning and strategy enable us to anticipate tax implications and make informed decisions that support our overall financial objectives."

Jack stressed the importance of proactive tax planning in

optimizing financial outcomes and minimizing tax liabilities. He encouraged the team to work closely with tax professionals to develop tailored strategies that aligned with their financial goals and priorities.

The final slide displayed "Continuous Improvement and Adaptation." "6. **Continuous Improvement and Adaptation.** Embracing a culture of continuous improvement and adaptation allows us to refine our tax planning strategies and adapt to changes in tax laws and regulations. This includes staying informed about developments in tax legislation, soliciting advice from tax professionals, and implementing feedback-driven improvements to our tax planning processes. Continuous improvement ensures that our tax strategies remain responsive and effective in optimizing financial outcomes."

Jack turned off the projector and faced his team, the determination evident in his expression. "Tax considerations are a critical aspect of our financial management efforts, and they require diligence, knowledge, and collaboration to navigate effectively."

He stepped closer, his voice filled with determination. "Let's approach tax considerations with attention to detail, proactive planning, and a commitment to compliance. By leveraging tax-saving opportunities and staying informed about changes in tax laws, we can optimize financial outcomes and ensure the long-term success of our properties."

The room buzzed with a sense of purpose, each team member ready to approach tax considerations with diligence and expertise. Jack could see the determination in their eyes—a readiness to navigate the complexities of tax management and maximize financial benefits for their properties.

8

Chapter 8: Maintenance and Repairs

Preventive Maintenance Planning

Jack Miller called his team together, their focus now on the critical aspect of preventive maintenance planning. As property managers, they understood that proactive maintenance was essential for preserving property value and minimizing costly repairs.

"Team," Jack began, his voice projecting authority. "Preventive maintenance planning is the cornerstone of property management. It's not just about fixing things when they break—it's about identifying potential issues before they escalate. Let's explore the first step: preventive maintenance planning."

He clicked the remote, and the screen illuminated with a checklist titled "Preventive Maintenance Planning." "Effective preventive maintenance planning requires foresight, organization, and a commitment to property preservation. It is the key to maximizing property value and minimizing costly repairs."

The first slide highlighted "Property Inspection and Assessment." "1. **Property Inspection and Assessment.** We begin by conducting thorough inspections of our properties to identify potential maintenance issues and assess the condition of key components. This includes inspecting structural elements, mechanical systems, and common areas, and documenting findings to inform preventive maintenance planning. Property inspections provide valuable insights into maintenance needs and priorities."

Jack emphasized the importance of regular property inspections in identifying maintenance needs proactively. He recalled a time when a routine inspection had revealed minor water damage, allowing them to address the issue before it escalated into a costly repair.

The next slide displayed "Maintenance Schedule Development." "2. **Maintenance Schedule Development.** Developing a comprehensive maintenance schedule helps us prioritize tasks and allocate resources effectively. This includes creating a calendar of routine maintenance activities, such as HVAC servicing, plumbing inspections, and landscaping, and scheduling recurring tasks based on seasonal needs and manufacturer recommendations. Maintenance schedules ensure that preventive maintenance tasks are performed on time and according to established guidelines."

Sarah, with her meticulous approach, nodded in agreement. She understood the importance of scheduling routine maintenance tasks to ensure that critical systems and components were inspected and serviced regularly, ultimately extending their lifespan and reducing the risk of unexpected failures.

The third slide depicted "Equipment and Parts Inventory

Management." "3. **Equipment and Parts Inventory Management.** Maintaining an inventory of equipment and parts allows us to streamline maintenance operations and ensure timely repairs. This includes cataloging essential equipment and spare parts, tracking usage and replacement schedules, and replenishing inventory as needed to avoid delays in maintenance activities. Equipment and parts inventory management improves efficiency and reduces downtime for maintenance tasks."

David, always analytical in his approach, recognized the value of efficient inventory management in minimizing disruptions to maintenance operations. He made a mental note to review their inventory systems and identify opportunities for optimization.

The next image showed "Vendor and Contractor Relationships." "4. **Vendor and Contractor Relationships.** Cultivating strong relationships with vendors and contractors enables us to access specialized expertise and resources for maintenance and repairs. This includes vetting vendors and contractors based on qualifications and experience, negotiating favorable terms and pricing for services, and maintaining open communication channels for scheduling and coordination. Strong vendor and contractor relationships ensure prompt and reliable support for maintenance activities."

Lisa, their vendor liaison, saw the potential in nurturing vendor relationships to ensure timely and high-quality maintenance services. She began reaching out to preferred vendors to discuss upcoming maintenance needs and ensure availability for scheduled tasks.

The fifth slide highlighted "Budget Allocation for Maintenance." "5. **Budget Allocation for Maintenance.** Allocating sufficient funds for maintenance activities ensures that we can address maintenance needs promptly and prevent deferred maintenance issues. This includes budgeting for routine maintenance expenses, setting aside funds for unexpected repairs or emergencies, and prioritizing maintenance investments based on property condition and strategic priorities. Budget allocation for maintenance supports proactive property management and preserves property value over time."

Jack stressed the importance of budgeting for maintenance as a proactive investment in property preservation. He encouraged the team to prioritize maintenance funding and allocate resources strategically to address critical maintenance needs and prevent costly repairs down the line.

The final slide displayed "Continuous Improvement and Adaptation." "6. **Continuous Improvement and Adaptation.** Embracing a culture of continuous improvement and adaptation allows us to refine our preventive maintenance planning processes and adapt to evolving property needs and industry standards. This includes soliciting feedback from maintenance staff and tenants about maintenance effectiveness, evaluating the performance of maintenance schedules and procedures, and implementing feedback-driven improvements to our preventive maintenance planning. Continuous improvement ensures that our maintenance efforts remain responsive and effective in preserving property value and enhancing tenant satisfaction."

Jack turned off the projector and faced his team, the determination evident in his expression. "Preventive maintenance planning is not just about fixing things—it's about protecting our investments and ensuring the long-term success of our properties."

He stepped closer, his voice filled with determination. "Let's approach preventive maintenance planning with foresight, diligence, and a commitment to excellence. By conducting thorough inspections, developing comprehensive maintenance schedules, and nurturing strong vendor relationships, we can maximize property value and enhance tenant satisfaction."

The room buzzed with energy, each team member eager to enhance their preventive maintenance planning efforts and contribute to the success of their properties. Jack could see the determination in their eyes—a readiness to prioritize proactive maintenance and preserve property value for the long term.

Routine Maintenance Tasks

With the foundation of preventive maintenance planning laid out, Jack Miller shifted the focus of the meeting to the essential aspect of routine maintenance tasks. As property managers, they understood that consistent upkeep was crucial for preserving property value and ensuring tenant satisfaction.

"Team," Jack began, his voice carrying a sense of purpose. "Routine maintenance tasks are the lifeblood of property management. They're not just chores—they're investments in the long-term health of our properties. Let's explore the second step: routine maintenance tasks."

He clicked the remote, and the screen illuminated with a checklist titled "Routine Maintenance Tasks." "Effective management of routine maintenance tasks requires organization, attention to detail, and a commitment to proactive upkeep. They are the key to preserving property value and maintaining tenant satisfaction."

The first slide highlighted "HVAC System Inspection and Servicing." "1. **HVAC System Inspection and Servicing.** We begin by scheduling regular inspections and servicing for HVAC systems to ensure optimal performance and energy efficiency. This includes inspecting air filters, ductwork, and outdoor units, cleaning or replacing filters as needed, and performing routine maintenance tasks, such as lubricating moving parts and checking refrigerant levels. HVAC system inspection and servicing improve comfort for tenants and reduce the risk of costly repairs."

Jack emphasized the importance of HVAC system maintenance in maintaining indoor air quality and preventing system failures. He recalled a time when proactive HVAC servicing had prevented a breakdown during extreme weather conditions, ensuring tenant comfort and satisfaction.

The next slide displayed "Plumbing System Checks and Maintenance." "2. **Plumbing System Checks and Maintenance.** Regular checks and maintenance of plumbing systems help identify leaks, clogs, and other issues before they escalate into costly water damage or plumbing emergencies. This includes inspecting fixtures, pipes, and connections for signs of wear or damage, repairing leaks and replacing worn components, and clearing clogged drains or pipes as needed. Plumbing system checks and maintenance prevent water damage and ensure reliable water supply for tenants."

Sarah, with her attention to detail, nodded in agreement. She understood the importance of proactive plumbing maintenance in preventing water damage and ensuring the functionality of essential systems for tenant comfort and convenience.

The third slide depicted "Electrical System Inspections and Testing." "3. **Electrical System Inspections and Testing.** Regular inspections and testing of electrical systems help identify potential hazards and ensure compliance with safety standards. This includes inspecting wiring, outlets, and electrical panels for signs of wear or damage, testing circuit breakers and GFCI outlets for proper functioning, and addressing any issues promptly to prevent electrical fires or shocks. Electrical system inspections and testing promote tenant safety and reduce the risk of electrical failures."

David, always analytical in his approach, recognized the importance of electrical system maintenance in preventing safety hazards and ensuring compliance with regulations. He made a mental note to review their electrical inspection procedures and update them as needed to align with industry standards.

The next image showed "Exterior Maintenance and Landscaping." "4. **Exterior Maintenance and Landscaping.** Regular exterior maintenance and landscaping enhance curb appeal, promote tenant satisfaction, and protect property value. This includes mowing lawns, trimming bushes, and removing debris from common areas, as well as inspecting and repairing exterior surfaces, such as siding, roofs, and walkways. Exterior maintenance and landscaping create a welcoming environment for tenants and visitors and contribute to the overall attractiveness of the property."

Lisa, their landscaping expert, saw the value in maintaining attractive outdoor spaces to enhance tenant satisfaction and promote a sense of community. She began coordinating with landscaping crews to ensure that routine maintenance tasks were completed in a timely manner, enhancing the property's curb appeal.

The fifth slide highlighted "Appliance Checks and Servicing." "5. **Appliance Checks and Servicing.** Regular checks and servicing of appliances ensure their proper functioning and longevity. This includes inspecting and cleaning appliances, such as refrigerators, stoves, and dishwashers, checking for signs of wear or malfunction, and performing routine maintenance tasks, such as replacing filters or lubricating moving parts. Appliance checks and servicing prevent breakdowns and extend the lifespan of appliances, reducing the need for costly replacements."

Jack stressed the importance of appliance maintenance in ensuring tenant comfort and satisfaction. He encouraged the team to schedule regular appliance checks and servicing to address issues proactively and minimize disruptions for tenants.

The final slide displayed "Continuous Improvement and Adaptation." "6. **Continuous Improvement and Adaptation.** Embracing a culture of continuous improvement and adaptation allows us to refine our routine maintenance tasks and adapt to evolving property needs and industry best practices. This includes soliciting feedback from maintenance staff and tenants about maintenance effectiveness, evaluating the performance of routine maintenance schedules and procedures, and implementing feedback-driven improvements to our routine maintenance processes. Continuous improvement ensures that our maintenance efforts remain responsive and effective in preserving property value and enhancing tenant satisfaction."

Jack turned off the projector and faced his team, the determination evident in his expression. "Routine maintenance tasks are the foundation of property management, and they require diligence, attention to detail, and a commitment to excellence."

He stepped closer, his voice filled with determination. "Let's approach routine maintenance with dedication, efficiency, and a focus on continuous improvement. By scheduling regular checks and addressing maintenance needs promptly, we can preserve property value and ensure tenant satisfaction for years to come."

Managing Emergency Repairs

With routine maintenance tasks discussed, Jack Miller shifted the team's focus to the critical aspect of managing emergency repairs. As property managers, they understood that quick and effective response to emergencies was crucial for tenant safety and satisfaction.

"Team," Jack began, his voice steady yet urgent. "Managing emergency repairs is one of the most challenging aspects of property management. It's not just about fixing problems—it's about responding swiftly to protect our tenants and assets. Let's explore the third step: managing emergency repairs."

He clicked the remote, and the screen illuminated with a checklist titled "Managing Emergency Repairs." "Effective management of emergency repairs requires readiness, coordination, and a commitment to tenant safety. They are the key to minimizing damage and ensuring tenant satisfaction during crises."

The first slide highlighted "Emergency Response Protocol." "1. **Emergency Response Protocol.** We begin by establishing clear protocols and procedures for responding to emergencies, such as fires, floods, or severe weather events. This includes designating emergency contacts and escalation procedures, providing training for staff on emergency response protocols, and communicating emergency procedures to tenants through signage and written materials. A well-defined emergency response protocol ensures a swift and coordinated response to emergencies, minimizing damage and ensuring tenant safety."

Jack emphasized the importance of having a clear and concise emergency response protocol in place. He recalled a time when their prompt response to a burst pipe had prevented extensive water damage and ensured the safety of their tenants.

The next slide displayed "24/7 Availability and Contact Information." "2. **24/7 Availability and Contact Information.** Maintaining 24/7 availability and providing tenants with emergency contact information enables them to report urgent maintenance issues promptly. This includes establishing an emergency hotline or contact number that tenants can call outside of regular business hours, ensuring that emergency contacts are responsive and accessible at all times, and providing tenants with clear instructions on when and how to report emergency repairs. 24/7 availability and contact information ensure that tenants can receive assistance quickly in case of emergencies."

Sarah, with her meticulous approach, nodded in agreement. She understood the importance of being accessible to tenants at all times to address emergency repair needs promptly and ensure their safety and well-being.

The third slide depicted "Emergency Repair Prioritization." "3. **Emergency Repair Prioritization.** Prioritizing emergency repairs based on severity and potential impact helps us allocate resources effectively and address urgent issues first. This includes triaging emergency repair requests to assess their urgency and potential impact on tenant safety and property integrity, dispatching maintenance staff or contractors to address immediate threats, and communicating with affected tenants about repair timelines and expectations. Emergency repair prioritization ensures that urgent issues are addressed promptly, minimizing disruption and ensuring tenant satisfaction."

David, always analytical in his approach, recognized the importance of prioritizing emergency repairs to address the most pressing issues first. He made a mental note to review their prioritization criteria and ensure that emergency repairs were handled efficiently and effectively.

The next image showed "Coordination with Vendors and Contractors." "4. **Coordination with Vendors and Contractors.** Establishing relationships with reliable vendors and contractors enables us to access specialized expertise and resources for emergency repairs. This includes maintaining a list of pre-qualified vendors and contractors for emergency response, communicating emergency repair needs promptly and clearly, and coordinating with vendors to ensure timely arrival and completion of emergency repairs. Coordination with vendors and contractors facilitates swift resolution of emergency issues and minimizes downtime for tenants."

Lisa, their vendor liaison, understood the importance of coordinating with vendors and contractors to ensure prompt resolution of emergency repairs. She began reaching out to their network of trusted partners to reinforce their readiness to respond to urgent maintenance needs.

The fifth slide highlighted "Documentation and Follow-Up." "5. **Documentation and Follow-Up.** Documenting emergency repair requests and follow-up actions taken helps us track resolution progress and identify opportunities for improvement. This includes logging emergency repair requests, documenting actions taken to address urgent issues, and following up with tenants to ensure that repairs were completed satisfactorily. Documentation and follow-up provide accountability and transparency in emergency repair management and support continuous improvement efforts."

Jack stressed the importance of documenting emergency repair requests and follow-up actions to ensure accountability and transparency in their response efforts. He encouraged the team to maintain detailed records of emergency repairs to identify trends and areas for improvement.

The final slide displayed "Continuous Improvement and Adaptation." "6. **Continuous Improvement and Adaptation.** Embracing a culture of continuous improvement and adaptation allows us to refine our emergency repair procedures and adapt to evolving property needs and industry best practices. This includes conducting post-emergency debriefings to review response effectiveness, soliciting feedback from tenants about their emergency repair experiences, and implementing feedback-driven improvements to our emergency repair protocols. Continuous improvement ensures that our emergency repair efforts remain responsive and effective in protecting tenant safety and satisfaction."

Jack turned off the projector and faced his team, the urgency evident in his expression. "Managing emergency repairs is a critical aspect of property management, and it requires readiness, coordination, and a commitment to tenant safety."

He stepped closer, his voice filled with determination. "Let's approach emergency repairs with urgency, efficiency, and a focus on continuous improvement. By establishing clear protocols, prioritizing repairs effectively, and coordinating with vendors, we can ensure swift resolution of emergency issues and safeguard the well-being of our tenants."

The room buzzed with a sense of purpose, each team member ready to enhance their emergency repair management efforts and uphold their commitment to tenant safety and satisfaction. Jack could see the determination in their eyes—a readiness to respond swiftly and effectively to emergencies and ensure the well-being of their tenants.

Hiring and Managing Contractors

With emergency repair management discussed, Jack Miller turned the team's attention to another crucial aspect: hiring and managing contractors. As property managers, they understood that outsourcing certain maintenance tasks to qualified professionals was essential for ensuring quality work and efficient property upkeep.

"Team," Jack began, his voice carrying a sense of purpose. "Hiring and managing contractors is integral to our maintenance and repair efforts. It's not just about finding someone to do the job—it's about building partnerships with reliable professionals who share our commitment to excellence. Let's explore the fourth step: hiring and managing contractors."

He clicked the remote, and the screen illuminated with a

checklist titled "Hiring and Managing Contractors." "Effective management of contractors requires diligence, communication, and a commitment to quality. They are the key to ensuring timely and satisfactory completion of maintenance tasks."

The first slide highlighted "Vendor Selection Criteria." "1. **Vendor Selection Criteria.** We begin by establishing clear criteria for selecting vendors and contractors to ensure they meet our standards for quality, reliability, and professionalism. This includes conducting background checks and verifying credentials, checking references and reviews from previous clients, and assessing their experience and expertise in relevant maintenance areas. Vendor selection criteria ensure that we partner with qualified professionals who can deliver exceptional service."

Jack emphasized the importance of thoroughly vetting vendors and contractors to ensure they met their standards for quality and reliability. He recalled a time when rigorous vendor selection had resulted in a successful partnership with a skilled contractor who consistently delivered high-quality work.

The next slide displayed "Contract Negotiation and Agreement." "2. **Contract Negotiation and Agreement.** Establishing clear expectations and terms in contracts helps prevent misunderstandings and ensures that both parties are aligned on scope, schedule, and budget. This includes outlining project specifications and deliverables, defining payment terms and schedules, and specifying dispute resolution procedures and liability provisions. Contract negotiation and agreement provide clarity and accountability in contractor relationships."

Sarah, with her attention to detail, nodded in agreement. She understood the importance of negotiating clear and comprehensive contracts to protect their interests and ensure that contractors delivered as promised.

The third slide depicted "Communication and Coordination." "3. **Communication and Coordination.** Maintaining open communication channels and coordinating effectively with contractors is essential for ensuring smooth project execution and timely completion of maintenance tasks. This includes establishing regular check-ins and progress updates, addressing any issues or concerns promptly, and providing clear instructions and feedback throughout the project lifecycle. Communication and coordination foster collaboration and ensure that projects stay on track."

David, always analytical in his approach, recognized the importance of clear communication and coordination in managing contractor relationships. He made a mental note to establish regular communication channels with contractors and provide them with the support and guidance they needed to succeed.

The next image showed "Quality Assurance and Performance Monitoring." "4. **Quality Assurance and Performance Monitoring.** Monitoring contractor performance and ensuring quality workmanship is essential for maintaining standards and achieving satisfactory outcomes. This includes conducting periodic inspections and quality checks, reviewing work progress against project milestones and specifications, and addressing any deviations or deficiencies promptly to ensure corrective action. Quality assurance and performance monitoring uphold standards of excellence and accountability in contractor relationships."

Lisa, their quality assurance expert, understood the importance of monitoring contractor performance to ensure that maintenance tasks were completed to their satisfaction. She began implementing procedures to track contractor progress and quality of work, ensuring that their standards were consistently met.

The fifth slide highlighted "Payment Processing and Invoicing." "5. **Payment Processing and Invoicing.** Streamlining payment processing and invoicing procedures helps ensure timely and accurate payment for contractor services. This includes establishing clear invoicing guidelines and procedures, verifying completed work against contractual agreements and specifications, and processing payments promptly upon satisfactory completion of work. Efficient payment processing and invoicing facilitate positive contractor relationships and support timely project completion."

Jack stressed the importance of prompt and accurate payment processing to maintain positive relationships with contractors. He encouraged the team to streamline their invoicing procedures and ensure that payments were processed promptly to avoid delays and disputes.

The final slide displayed "Continuous Feedback and Improvement." "6. **Continuous Feedback and Improvement.** Embracing a culture of continuous feedback and improvement allows us to refine our contractor management processes and adapt to evolving needs and challenges. This includes soliciting feedback from contractors about their experiences and performance, evaluating the effectiveness of contractor management procedures, and implementing feedback-driven improvements to enhance contractor relationships and project outcomes. Continuous feedback and improvement support our commitment to excellence in contractor management."

Jack turned off the projector and faced his team, the determination evident in his expression. "Hiring and managing contractors is essential for maintaining property value and ensuring efficient maintenance and repair operations. It requires diligence, communication, and a commitment to quality."

He stepped closer, his voice filled with determination. "Let's approach contractor management with professionalism, transparency, and a focus on continuous improvement. By selecting qualified vendors, establishing clear expectations, and maintaining open communication channels, we can build successful partnerships that contribute to the overall success of our properties."

The room buzzed with a sense of purpose, each team member ready to enhance their contractor management efforts and uphold their commitment to excellence in maintenance and repair operations. Jack could see the determination in their eyes—a readiness to forge strong partnerships with contractors and ensure the continued success of their properties.

Implementing a Maintenance Request System

With contractor management discussed, Jack Miller redirected the team's focus to another critical aspect: implementing a maintenance request system. As property managers, they understood that streamlining maintenance requests was essential for ensuring timely resolution of tenant issues and efficient allocation of resources.

"Team," Jack began, his voice resonating with purpose.

"Implementing a maintenance request system is vital for our maintenance and repair operations. It's not just about receiving requests—it's about empowering tenants, optimizing resource allocation, and enhancing overall tenant satisfaction. Let's explore the fifth step: implementing a maintenance request system."

He clicked the remote, and the screen illuminated with a checklist titled "Implementing a Maintenance Request System." "Effective implementation of a maintenance request system requires organization, communication, and a commitment to responsiveness. It is the key to ensuring prompt resolution of tenant issues and maintaining high levels of tenant satisfaction."

The first slide highlighted "System Selection and Setup." "1. **System Selection and Setup.** We begin by selecting a maintenance request system that meets our needs and preferences for functionality, ease of use, and integration with existing management software. This includes researching available options, evaluating features and pricing, and setting up the selected system to align with our maintenance workflow and tenant communication channels. System selection and setup lay the foundation for efficient maintenance request management."

Jack emphasized the importance of choosing the right maintenance request system to streamline their operations effectively. He recalled a time when they had struggled with an outdated system, resulting in delays and frustration among tenants.

The next slide displayed "Tenant Education and Communication." "2. **Tenant Education and Communication.** Educating tenants about the maintenance request system and communicating clear guidelines for submitting requests helps streamline the process and ensure that issues are reported promptly and accurately. This includes providing written instructions and tutorials on how to submit maintenance requests, specifying acceptable request types and response times, and encouraging tenants to report issues as soon as they arise. Tenant education and communication facilitate proactive issue reporting and timely resolution."

Sarah, with her attention to detail, nodded in agreement. She understood the importance of educating tenants about the maintenance request system to empower them to report issues efficiently and effectively.

The third slide depicted "Internal Training and Procedures."

"3. **Internal Training and Procedures.** Providing training for staff on using the maintenance request system and establishing clear procedures for processing and resolving requests ensures consistency and efficiency in maintenance operations. This includes conducting training sessions or workshops to familiarize staff with system functionality and workflows, defining roles and responsibilities for handling maintenance requests, and implementing protocols for prioritizing and assigning tasks based on urgency and severity. Internal training and procedures support smooth operation of the maintenance request system and facilitate timely resolution of tenant issues."

David, always analytical in his approach, recognized the importance of internal training and procedures in ensuring that their team could effectively utilize the maintenance request system. He made a mental note to schedule training sessions for staff and document procedures for handling maintenance requests.

The next image showed "Monitoring and Performance Tracking." "4. **Monitoring and Performance Tracking.** Monitoring system performance and tracking key metrics help identify areas for improvement and ensure that the maintenance request system meets our goals for responsiveness and efficiency. This includes tracking metrics such as response times, resolution rates, and tenant satisfaction scores, analyzing data to identify trends and patterns in maintenance requests, and making adjustments to workflows or system settings as needed to improve performance. Monitoring and performance tracking enable us to continuously optimize the maintenance request system and enhance tenant satisfaction."

Lisa, their performance tracker, understood the importance of monitoring system performance to identify areas for improvement and ensure that tenant issues were resolved promptly. She began analyzing data from the maintenance request system to identify trends and patterns and make recommendations for process improvements.

The fifth slide highlighted "Feedback Collection and Analysis." "5. **Feedback Collection and Analysis.** Soliciting feedback from tenants about their experiences with the maintenance request system and analyzing responses helps identify opportunities for improvement and ensure that the system meets tenant needs and expectations. This includes conducting surveys or feedback sessions to gather input on system usability and effectiveness, reviewing feedback to identify common issues or pain points, and implementing changes or enhancements based on tenant suggestions. Feedback collection and analysis support continuous improvement of the maintenance request system and enhance overall tenant satisfaction."

Jack stressed the importance of soliciting feedback from tenants to ensure that the maintenance request system met their needs and expectations. He encouraged the team to actively seek input from tenants and use their feedback to make adjustments and improvements to the system.

The final slide displayed "Continuous Improvement and Adaptation." "6. **Continuous Improvement and Adaptation.** Embracing a culture of continuous improvement and adaptation allows us to refine our maintenance request system and adapt to evolving tenant needs and preferences. This includes regularly reviewing system performance and feedback, soliciting input from staff and tenants about potential enhancements or changes, and implementing feedback-driven improvements to optimize system functionality and user experience. Continuous improvement ensures that our maintenance request system remains responsive and effective in addressing tenant issues and maintaining high levels of satisfaction."

Ensuring Compliance with Safety Standards

With the implementation of the maintenance request system discussed, Jack Miller turned the team's focus to another critical aspect: ensuring compliance with safety standards. As property managers, they understood that adhering to safety regulations was paramount for protecting both tenants and property assets.

"Team," Jack began, his voice carrying a tone of urgency. "Ensuring compliance with safety standards is non-negotiable in our line of work. It's not just about following rules—it's about safeguarding lives and properties. Let's explore the sixth step: ensuring compliance with safety standards."

He clicked the remote, and the screen illuminated with a checklist titled "Ensuring Compliance with Safety Standards." "Effective compliance with safety standards requires vigilance, attention to detail, and a commitment to prioritizing safety above all else. It is the key to protecting our tenants and properties from harm."

The first slide highlighted "Regulatory Familiarity and Updates." "1. **Regulatory Familiarity and Updates.** We begin by staying informed about relevant safety regulations and updates at the local, state, and federal levels. This includes regularly reviewing safety codes and standards applicable to our properties, attending training sessions or workshops to stay abreast of regulatory changes, and implementing procedures to ensure compliance with current safety requirements. Regulatory familiarity and updates provide the foundation for effective safety management."

Jack emphasized the importance of staying up-to-date with safety regulations to ensure their properties met the necessary standards. He recalled a time when their thorough knowledge of fire safety regulations had allowed them to address potential hazards before an inspection, preventing fines and ensuring tenant safety.

The next slide displayed "Regular Inspections and Audits." "2. **Regular Inspections and Audits.** Conducting regular inspections and audits of our properties helps identify potential safety hazards and ensure compliance with safety standards. This includes scheduling routine inspections of building systems and common areas, conducting audits of safety equipment and emergency procedures, and addressing any deficiencies or non-compliance issues promptly. Regular inspections and audits promote a proactive approach to safety management and minimize risks to tenants and properties."

Sarah, with her meticulous approach, nodded in agreement. She understood the importance of regular inspections in identifying and addressing safety hazards before they posed a threat to tenants or property assets.

The third slide depicted "Maintenance of Safety Equipment and Systems." "3. **Maintenance of Safety Equipment and Systems.** Maintaining safety equipment and systems in proper working condition is essential for ensuring effective response to emergencies and compliance with safety standards. This includes scheduling regular maintenance for fire alarm systems, sprinkler systems, emergency lighting, and other safety equipment, testing equipment functionality according to manufacturer guidelines, and promptly addressing any maintenance issues or malfunctions. Maintenance of safety equipment and systems enhances tenant safety and ensures compliance with regulatory requirements."

David, always analytical in his approach, recognized the importance of maintaining safety equipment to ensure their properties were prepared to respond to emergencies effectively. He made a mental note to schedule routine maintenance for their safety systems and equipment and verify their functionality regularly.

The next image showed "Tenant Education and Training." "4. **Tenant Education and Training.** Educating tenants about safety procedures and providing training on emergency preparedness promotes a culture of safety and ensures that tenants are equipped to respond effectively to emergencies. This includes distributing safety manuals or guidelines to tenants, conducting training sessions or drills on evacuation procedures and emergency protocols, and providing information about local emergency services and resources. Tenant education and training empower tenants to take an active role in their safety and contribute to overall property safety."

Lisa, their safety advocate, understood the importance of educating tenants about safety procedures to empower them to respond effectively to emergencies. She began organizing safety workshops and drills for tenants to ensure they were prepared for various scenarios.

The fifth slide highlighted "Documentation and Record-Keeping." "5. **Documentation and Record-Keeping.** Maintaining thorough documentation of safety inspections, maintenance activities, and training sessions helps demonstrate compliance with safety standards and provides a record of safety-related efforts. This includes documenting inspection findings and corrective actions taken, keeping records of maintenance activities and equipment testing results, and maintaining logs of tenant education and training sessions. Documentation and record-keeping support transparency and accountability in safety management and provide valuable evidence in case of audits or inspections."

Jack stressed the importance of maintaining detailed records of safety-related activities to demonstrate compliance with safety standards. He encouraged the team to keep meticulous records of inspections, maintenance, and training sessions to ensure they were prepared for audits or inspections.

The final slide displayed "Continuous Improvement and Adaptation." "6. **Continuous Improvement and Adaptation.** Embracing a culture of continuous improvement and adaptation allows us to refine our safety management practices and adapt to evolving regulatory requirements and industry best practices. This includes soliciting feedback from staff and tenants about safety procedures and protocols, conducting post-incident reviews to identify areas for improvement, and implementing feedback-driven changes to enhance safety management efforts. Continuous improvement ensures that our properties remain safe and compliant with safety standards."

Jack turned off the projector and faced his team, the determination evident in his expression. "Ensuring compliance with safety standards is not negotiable—it's our responsibility as property managers. Let's approach safety management with vigilance, attention to detail, and a commitment to prioritizing the well-being of

9

Chapter 9: Legal Aspects of Property Management

Understanding Landlord-Tenant Laws

As the team gathered for their next discussion, Jack Miller took a moment to emphasize the importance of understanding the legal aspects of property management. He knew that navigating landlord-tenant laws was crucial for protecting both tenants' rights and property owner interests.

"Team," Jack began, his voice carrying a tone of seriousness. "In our line of work, compliance with landlord-tenant laws is paramount. It's not just about avoiding legal trouble—it's about fostering positive landlord-tenant relationships and ensuring fair treatment for all parties involved. Let's delve into the first subpoint: understanding landlord-tenant laws."

He clicked the remote, and the screen illuminated with a checklist titled "Understanding Landlord-Tenant Laws." "Comprehensive knowledge of landlord-tenant laws requires diligence, attention to detail, and a commitment to upholding legal standards. It is the cornerstone of effective property management."

The first slide highlighted "Research and Familiarity." "1. **Research and Familiarity.** We begin by conducting thorough research into landlord-tenant laws at the local, state, and federal levels to ensure a comprehensive understanding of legal requirements and obligations. This includes reviewing relevant statutes, regulations, and case law, consulting legal resources and experts as needed, and staying updated on changes or developments in landlord-tenant legislation. Research and familiarity provide the foundation for compliance with legal standards and informed decision-making."

Jack emphasized the importance of staying informed about landlord-tenant laws to ensure their practices aligned with legal requirements. He recalled a time when their knowledge of eviction procedures had enabled them to navigate a challenging tenant dispute successfully.

The next slide displayed "Lease Agreement Compliance." "2. **Lease Agreement Compliance.** Ensuring that lease agreements comply with applicable landlord-tenant laws is essential for protecting the rights of both landlords and tenants. This includes drafting lease agreements that clearly outline the rights and responsibilities of both parties, avoiding provisions that may conflict with legal requirements or tenant rights, and periodically reviewing lease agreements to ensure compliance with updated laws or regulations. Lease agreement compliance fosters transparency and fairness in landlord-tenant relationships."

Sarah, with her meticulous approach, nodded in agreement. She understood the importance of drafting lease agreements that adhered to legal standards to protect both landlords and tenants' interests.

The third slide depicted "Tenant Screening and Fair Housing Laws." "3. **Tenant Screening and Fair Housing Laws.** Conducting tenant screening in accordance with fair housing laws is critical for preventing discrimination and ensuring equal housing opportunities for all applicants. This includes familiarizing ourselves with fair housing laws and protected classes, establishing consistent screening criteria based on objective factors relevant to tenancy, and applying screening criteria uniformly to all applicants. Tenant screening compliance promotes fair and equitable treatment of all prospective tenants."

David, always analytical in his approach, recognized the importance of fair housing laws in ensuring equal access to housing opportunities. He made a mental note to review their tenant screening criteria to ensure compliance with fair housing regulations.

The next image showed "Property Maintenance and Habitability Standards." "4. **Property Maintenance and Habitability Standards.** Maintaining rental properties in compliance with habitability standards is essential for fulfilling landlords' obligations and ensuring tenant well-being. This includes addressing maintenance issues promptly to maintain habitable living conditions, adhering to health and safety codes applicable to rental properties, and providing essential services such as heat, water, and sanitation as required by law. Property maintenance and habitability standards protect tenant health and safety and mitigate legal risks for landlords."

Lisa, their property maintenance expert, understood the importance of maintaining rental properties to comply with habitability standards. She began conducting regular inspections to identify and address maintenance issues promptly, ensuring their properties met legal requirements.

The fifth slide highlighted "Rent Collection and Eviction Procedures." "5. **Rent Collection and Eviction Procedures.** Implementing rent collection policies and eviction procedures in compliance with landlord-tenant laws is crucial for protecting landlords' financial interests while respecting tenants' rights. This includes establishing clear rent payment terms and deadlines in lease agreements, adhering to legal requirements for rent increase notices and eviction notices, and following proper procedures for filing eviction actions in court if necessary. Rent collection and eviction procedure compliance ensures fair and lawful treatment of tenants and protects landlords from legal liabilities."

Jack stressed the importance of following proper procedures for rent collection and evictions to avoid legal complications and maintain positive landlord-tenant relationships. He encouraged the team to review their policies and procedures regularly to ensure compliance with legal standards.

The final slide displayed "Dispute Resolution and Mediation." "6. **Dispute Resolution and Mediation.** Resolving disputes with tenants through informal negotiation or mediation can help avoid costly and time-consuming legal proceedings. This includes establishing open lines of communication with tenants to address concerns or grievances promptly, offering mediation services or alternative dispute resolution mechanisms to resolve conflicts amicably, and seeking legal guidance or representation when necessary to protect landlords' interests. Dispute resolution and mediation promote peaceful resolution of conflicts and preserve landlord-tenant relationships."

Jack turned off the projector and faced his team, the determination evident in his expression. "Understanding landlord-tenant laws is not just about compliance—it's about promoting fairness, equality, and respect in our interactions with tenants. Let's approach legal compliance with diligence, integrity, and a commitment to upholding the rights and responsibilities outlined in landlord-tenant laws."

The room buzzed with a renewed sense of purpose, each team member ready to apply their knowledge of landlord-tenant laws to enhance their property management practices and foster positive landlord-tenant relationships. Jack could see the determination in their eyes—a readiness to uphold legal standards and ensure the well-being of both tenants and property owners.

Lease Agreements and Contracts

As the team delved deeper into the legal aspects of property management, Jack Miller shifted their focus to the critical topic of lease agreements and contracts. He knew that having legally sound contracts was essential for protecting both landlords' and tenants' rights and ensuring smooth property management operations.

"Team," Jack began, his tone serious yet engaging. "Lease agreements and contracts are the backbone of our property management operations. They're not just pieces of paper—they're legally binding agreements that govern our relationships with tenants and protect our interests as property managers. Let's explore the second subpoint: lease agreements and contracts."

He clicked the remote, and the screen illuminated with a checklist titled "Lease Agreements and Contracts." "Creating and managing lease agreements and contracts requires attention to detail, legal expertise, and a commitment to fairness. It is the cornerstone of effective property management."

The first slide highlighted "Drafting and Reviewing Lease Agreements." "1. **Drafting and Reviewing Lease Agreements.** We begin by drafting lease agreements that clearly outline the rights and responsibilities of both landlords and tenants in compliance with local, state, and federal laws. This includes specifying key terms such as rent amount, lease duration, security deposit requirements, and maintenance responsibilities, and reviewing lease agreements carefully to ensure clarity, completeness, and legal compliance. Drafting and reviewing lease agreements protect the interests of both parties and minimize the risk of disputes."

Jack emphasized the importance of drafting comprehensive lease agreements that addressed all pertinent details to avoid misunderstandings or disputes later on. He recalled a time when a well-drafted lease agreement had helped them resolve a tenant dispute swiftly and amicably.

The next slide displayed "Negotiation and Modification." "2. **Negotiation and Modification.** Flexibility in negotiating lease terms and making modifications to accommodate specific tenant needs or preferences can help foster positive landlord-tenant relationships and reduce the risk of lease violations. This includes engaging in open and transparent communication with tenants to address concerns or requests for modifications, considering reasonable requests for changes to lease terms, and documenting any agreed-upon modifications in writing to ensure clarity and enforceability.

Negotiation and modification promote mutual understanding and cooperation between landlords and tenants."

Sarah, with her knack for communication, nodded in agreement. She understood the importance of flexibility in lease negotiations to accommodate tenants' needs while still protecting the landlord's interests.

The third slide depicted "Compliance with Legal Requirements." "3. **Compliance with Legal Requirements.** Ensuring that lease agreements comply with applicable landlord-tenant laws and regulations is essential for protecting the rights of both parties and avoiding legal disputes. This includes familiarizing ourselves with legal requirements for lease agreements in our jurisdiction, incorporating mandatory lease provisions and disclosures as required by law, and periodically reviewing lease agreements to ensure compliance with updated regulations. Compliance with legal requirements upholds the integrity of lease agreements and minimizes legal risks for landlords."

David, always thorough in his approach, recognized the importance of legal compliance in lease agreements to avoid potential legal pitfalls. He made a mental note to review their lease agreements regularly to ensure they remained compliant with current regulations.

The next image showed "Enforcement and Remedies." "4. **Enforcement and Remedies.** Establishing procedures for enforcing lease terms and addressing lease violations promptly is crucial for maintaining order and resolving disputes effectively. This includes clearly outlining consequences for lease violations in lease agreements, enforcing lease terms consistently and fairly, and pursuing legal remedies such as eviction proceedings or lease termination when necessary to address persistent violations. Enforcement and remedies uphold the integrity of lease agreements and protect landlords' interests."

Lisa, their enforcement expert, understood the importance of enforcing lease terms to maintain order and protect the landlord's interests. She began implementing procedures for addressing lease violations promptly to ensure tenants understood the consequences of non-compliance.

The fifth slide highlighted "Renewal and Termination Procedures." "5. **Renewal and Termination Procedures.** Establishing clear procedures for lease renewal and termination helps ensure smooth transitions between lease periods and reduces the risk of disputes at the end of the lease term. This includes providing advance notice to tenants regarding lease renewal options and deadlines, offering lease renewal incentives to encourage tenant retention, and following legal requirements for lease termination notices and procedures if a tenant decides not to renew or breaches the lease agreement. Renewal and termination procedures facilitate transparent and orderly lease management."

Jack stressed the importance of clear renewal and termination procedures to maintain positive landlord-tenant relationships and avoid misunderstandings at the end of the lease term. He encouraged the team to communicate effectively with tenants regarding their lease options and obligations.

The final slide displayed "Record-Keeping and Documentation." "6. **Record-Keeping and Documentation.** Maintaining thorough records of lease agreements and related communications helps protect landlords' interests and provides valuable evidence in case of disputes or legal proceedings.

This includes keeping copies of signed lease agreements, documenting any modifications or amendments to lease terms, and maintaining records of communications with tenants regarding lease-related matters. Record-keeping and documentation support transparency and accountability in lease management."

Jack turned off the projector and faced his team, the determination evident in his expression. "Lease agreements and contracts are the foundation of our landlord-tenant relationships. Let's approach their creation and management with diligence, fairness, and a commitment to upholding legal standards. By drafting clear and comprehensive agreements and adhering to legal requirements, we can protect both our interests and those of our tenants."

The room buzzed with a renewed sense of purpose, each team member ready to apply their knowledge of lease agreements and contracts to enhance their property management practices and foster positive landlord-tenant relationships. Jack could see the determination in their eyes—a readiness to uphold legal standards and ensure the smooth operation of their properties.

Handling Evictions Legally

As the team delved deeper into the legal intricacies of property management, Jack Miller shifted their focus to the sensitive yet crucial topic of handling evictions legally. He understood that navigating the eviction process with care and compliance was essential for protecting both landlords' rights and tenants' interests.

"Team," Jack began, his tone measured yet compassionate.

"Handling evictions legally is one of the toughest challenges we face as property managers. It's not just about reclaiming property—it's about upholding the rights of both landlords and tenants while adhering to legal procedures. Let's explore the third subpoint: handling evictions legally."

He clicked the remote, and the screen illuminated with a checklist titled "Handling Evictions Legally." "Navigating the eviction process requires empathy, expertise, and a commitment to fairness. It is the ultimate test of our legal and ethical responsibilities as property managers."

The first slide highlighted "Legal Grounds for Eviction." "1. **Legal Grounds for Eviction.** We begin by understanding the legal grounds for eviction as outlined in landlord-tenant laws. This includes familiarizing ourselves with permissible reasons for eviction, such as nonpayment of rent, lease violations, or criminal activity, and ensuring that any eviction proceedings are initiated in accordance with the specific grounds specified in applicable laws. Understanding legal grounds for eviction ensures that our actions are lawful and justified."

Jack emphasized the importance of grounding eviction proceedings in valid legal reasons to ensure they held up in court and protected both landlords' and tenants' rights. He recalled a time when their thorough understanding of eviction laws had helped them resolve a difficult tenant situation without escalating into a legal battle.

The next slide displayed "Notice Requirements." "2. **Notice Requirements.** Providing proper notice to tenants prior to initiating eviction proceedings is a fundamental legal requirement. This includes adhering to state-specific notice periods and requirements for different eviction grounds, serving notices in accordance with legal procedures, and documenting the delivery of notices to tenants. Fulfilling notice requirements is essential for ensuring that tenants are informed of the reasons for eviction and have an opportunity to address any issues before legal action is taken."

Sarah, with her attention to detail, nodded in agreement. She understood the importance of following proper notice procedures to ensure that tenants were informed of eviction proceedings and had an opportunity to respond.

The third slide depicted "Legal Documentation and Paperwork." "3. **Legal Documentation and Paperwork.** Maintaining accurate and complete documentation of eviction-related communications and actions is essential for supporting legal proceedings and protecting landlords' interests. This includes keeping copies of eviction notices, lease agreements, rental payment records, and any correspondence with tenants regarding eviction matters, and ensuring that all paperwork is properly formatted and filed according to legal requirements. Legal documentation and paperwork provide crucial evidence in case of disputes or legal challenges."

David, always thorough in his approach, recognized the importance of maintaining meticulous records of eviction proceedings to ensure their legality and enforceability. He made a mental note to review their documentation procedures to ensure compliance with legal standards.

The next image showed "Court Proceedings and Representation." "4. **Court Proceedings and Representation.** If eviction proceedings escalate to court, seeking legal representation and preparing thoroughly for hearings or trials is essential for protecting landlords' interests and ensuring fair treatment under the law. This includes hiring qualified legal counsel with expertise in landlord-tenant law, gathering evidence and documentation to support the eviction case, and presenting arguments and evidence effectively in court proceedings. Court proceedings and representation uphold the integrity of eviction proceedings and protect landlords' rights."

Lisa, their legal liaison, understood the importance of seeking legal representation to navigate court proceedings effectively. She began researching qualified legal counsel to ensure they were prepared for any potential legal challenges.

The fifth slide highlighted "Tenant Rights and Due Process." "5. **Tenant Rights and Due Process.** Respecting tenants' rights and ensuring due process throughout the eviction process is essential for upholding legal standards and avoiding allegations of unfair treatment or discrimination. This includes providing tenants with the opportunity to respond to eviction notices and present their case in court, adhering to legal procedures for serving notices and filing eviction actions, and avoiding actions that may be construed as retaliatory or discriminatory. Respecting tenant rights and due process promotes fairness and equity in eviction proceedings."

Jack stressed the importance of respecting tenants' rights and ensuring due process throughout the eviction process to maintain trust and fairness in their landlord-tenant relationships. He encouraged the team to approach eviction proceedings with empathy and professionalism, always keeping tenants' well-being in mind.

The final slide displayed "Alternative Dispute Resolution." "6. **Alternative Dispute Resolution.** Exploring alternative dispute resolution mechanisms, such as mediation or settlement negotiations, can help resolve eviction-related conflicts amicably and avoid the need for costly and time-consuming court proceedings. This includes engaging in open and constructive communication with tenants to explore mutually agreeable solutions, seeking the assistance of neutral third parties to facilitate discussions, and considering compromises or concessions that address both parties' interests. Alternative dispute resolution fosters collaborative problem-solving and reduces the adversarial nature of eviction proceedings."

Jack turned off the projector and faced his team, the determination evident in his expression. "Handling evictions legally is one of the toughest challenges we face, but it's also an opportunity to demonstrate our commitment to fairness and integrity in property management. Let's approach eviction proceedings with empathy, professionalism, and a commitment to upholding legal standards. By navigating evictions legally and ethically, we can protect both our interests and those of our tenants."

The room buzzed with a renewed sense of purpose, each team member ready to apply their knowledge of eviction procedures to ensure they upheld legal standards and protected the rights of both landlords and tenants. Jack could see the determination in their eyes—a readiness to navigate eviction proceedings with compassion and integrity, even in the face of difficult circumstances.

Dealing with Disputes and Litigation

As the team continued their exploration of the legal intricacies of property management, Jack Miller turned their attention to the challenging yet inevitable aspect of dealing with disputes and litigation. He knew that resolving conflicts effectively and navigating legal proceedings with care were essential for maintaining positive landlord-tenant relationships and protecting property owner interests.

"Team," Jack began, his voice steady yet empathetic. "Dealing with disputes and litigation is an unavoidable part of property management. It's not just about resolving conflicts—it's about upholding legal standards and protecting the interests of both landlords and tenants. Let's explore the fourth subpoint: dealing with disputes and litigation."

He clicked the remote, and the screen illuminated with a checklist titled "Dealing with Disputes and Litigation." "Navigating disputes and litigation requires patience, diplomacy, and a commitment to fairness. It is the ultimate test of our ability to uphold legal standards and preserve landlord-tenant relationships."

The first slide highlighted "Early Resolution Attempts." "1. **Early Resolution Attempts.** We begin by attempting to resolve disputes through informal means, such as open dialogue and mediation, before escalating to formal legal proceedings. This includes engaging in constructive communication with tenants to address concerns or grievances, exploring mutually agreeable solutions to resolve conflicts, and seeking the assistance of neutral third parties, such as mediators or arbitrators, to facilitate discussions. Early resolution attempts promote collaborative problem-solving and may prevent the need for costly and time-consuming litigation."

Jack emphasized the importance of attempting to resolve disputes amicably before resorting to formal legal action. He recalled a time when their willingness to engage in open dialogue had helped them resolve a tenant dispute without escalating to court proceedings.

The next slide displayed "Legal Representation and Consultation." "2. **Legal Representation and Consultation.** If disputes escalate to the point where legal action is necessary, seeking qualified legal representation or consultation is essential for protecting landlords' interests and ensuring compliance with legal procedures. This includes hiring experienced legal counsel with expertise in landlord-tenant law, seeking legal advice or opinions on the merits of the case, and following legal counsel's guidance throughout the litigation process. Legal representation and consultation uphold the integrity of legal proceedings and protect landlords from potential liabilities."

Sarah, with her keen sense of strategy, nodded in agreement. She understood the importance of seeking legal advice to navigate complex legal disputes effectively and mitigate risks for property owners.

The third slide depicted "Evidence Gathering and Documentation." "3. **Evidence Gathering and Documentation.** Collecting and maintaining thorough documentation of relevant facts and evidence is crucial for supporting legal claims or defenses in litigation. This includes gathering documents, records, and communication logs related to the dispute, documenting any incidents or interactions relevant to the case, and organizing evidence in a clear and organized manner for presentation in court. Evidence gathering and documentation provide critical support for legal arguments and enhance the credibility of landlords' positions in litigation."

David, always meticulous in his approach, recognized the importance of gathering compelling evidence to support their legal claims. He made a mental note to organize their documentation systematically to ensure it was readily accessible for litigation purposes.

The next image showed "Court Proceedings and Representation." "4. **Court Proceedings and Representation.** If disputes cannot be resolved through alternative means and litigation becomes necessary, engaging in court proceedings with qualified legal representation is essential for protecting landlords' interests and ensuring fair treatment under the law. This includes preparing thoroughly for court hearings or trials, presenting evidence and arguments effectively in court, and complying with legal procedures and deadlines throughout the litigation process. Court proceedings and representation uphold the integrity of the legal system and protect landlords' rights."

Lisa, their legal liaison, understood the importance of presenting a strong case in court to achieve a favorable outcome for their clients. She began preparing diligently for upcoming court proceedings, ensuring they were well-equipped to navigate the litigation process effectively.

The fifth slide highlighted "Settlement Negotiations and Agreements." "5. **Settlement Negotiations and Agreements.** Exploring settlement negotiations and agreements as an alternative to trial can help resolve disputes efficiently and cost-effectively while preserving relationships between landlords and tenants. This includes engaging in constructive negotiations with opposing parties to reach mutually agreeable resolutions, drafting settlement agreements that outline terms and conditions for resolving the dispute, and obtaining legal advice or review of settlement agreements to ensure their enforceability. Settlement negotiations and agreements provide a means for resolving disputes amicably and avoiding the uncertainties of trial."

Jack stressed the importance of considering settlement negotiations as a viable option for resolving disputes without resorting to trial. He encouraged the team to approach negotiations with an open mind and a willingness to compromise when necessary.

The final slide displayed "Post-Litigation Follow-Up." "6. **Post-Litigation Follow-Up.** After the conclusion of litigation, conducting post-litigation follow-up to assess outcomes and address any lingering issues is essential for achieving closure and moving forward. This includes reviewing the outcome of court proceedings and any settlement agreements reached, evaluating lessons learned from the litigation experience, and implementing measures to prevent similar disputes in the future. Post-litigation follow-up promotes continuous improvement in dispute resolution processes and strengthens landlords' capabilities to handle future legal challenges."

Jack turned off the projector and faced his team, the determination evident in his expression. "Dealing with disputes and litigation is never easy, but it's an opportunity for us to demonstrate our commitment to upholding legal standards and protecting our clients' interests. Let's approach disputes and litigation with professionalism, integrity, and a commitment to fairness. By navigating legal challenges effectively, we can safeguard our clients' interests and preserve positive landlord-tenant relationships."

The room buzzed with a renewed sense of purpose, each team member ready to apply their knowledge of dispute resolution and litigation to ensure they upheld legal standards and protected the interests of their clients. Jack could see the determination in their eyes—a readiness to navigate legal challenges with resilience and integrity, even in the face of adversity.

Ensuring Fair Housing Compliance

As the team delved further into the legal complexities of property management, Jack Miller turned their attention to the critical aspect of ensuring fair housing compliance. He knew that upholding fair housing laws was not only a legal obligation but also a moral imperative to promote equality and prevent discrimination in housing.

"Team," Jack began, his tone firm yet empathetic. "Ensuring fair housing compliance is at the core of our responsibilities as property managers. It's not just about following the law—it's about promoting equal opportunities and fostering inclusive communities. Let's explore the fifth subpoint: ensuring fair housing compliance."

He clicked the remote, and the screen illuminated with a checklist titled "Ensuring Fair Housing Compliance." "Upholding fair housing laws requires vigilance, sensitivity, and a commitment to equality. It is the foundation of our efforts to create diverse and inclusive living environments."

The first slide highlighted "Familiarity with Fair Housing Laws." "1. **Familiarity with Fair Housing Laws.** We begin by familiarizing ourselves with federal, state, and local fair housing laws and regulations to ensure compliance with legal requirements. This includes understanding protected classes under fair housing laws, such as race, color, national origin, religion, sex, familial status, and disability, and familiarizing ourselves with prohibited discriminatory practices in housing. Familiarity with fair housing laws provides the knowledge base necessary to prevent discrimination and ensure equal housing opportunities for all individuals."

Jack emphasized the importance of understanding fair housing laws to prevent discrimination and promote inclusivity in their property management practices. He recalled a time when their adherence to fair housing regulations had helped them create a welcoming environment for diverse tenants.

The next slide displayed "Non-Discrimination Policies and Practices." "2. **Non-Discrimination Policies and Practices.** Implementing non-discrimination policies and practices in all aspects of property management is essential for upholding fair housing principles and preventing discriminatory practices. This includes adopting written policies that explicitly prohibit discrimination based on protected characteristics, training staff members on fair housing laws and diversity awareness, and applying consistent and objective criteria in tenant screening, leasing, and property maintenance processes. Non-discrimination policies and practices promote fairness and equality in housing."

Sarah, with her commitment to inclusivity, nodded in agreement. She understood the importance of implementing non-discrimination policies to create a welcoming environment for all tenants, regardless of background or identity.

The third slide depicted "Equal Treatment of Applicants and Tenants." "3. **Equal Treatment of Applicants and Tenants.** Providing equal treatment to all applicants and tenants, regardless of protected characteristics, is paramount for fair housing compliance. This includes offering the same rental terms, conditions, and services to all applicants and tenants, avoiding discriminatory statements or preferences in advertising or leasing practices, and treating all individuals with respect and dignity throughout the housing process. Equal treatment promotes a culture of inclusivity and respect in housing."

David, always analytical in his approach, recognized the importance of treating all applicants and tenants with fairness and dignity to prevent discrimination and uphold fair housing principles. He made a mental note to review their leasing practices to ensure they were consistent and nondiscriminatory.

The next image showed "Reasonable Accommodations and Modifications." "4. **Reasonable Accommodations and Modifications.** Providing reasonable accommodations and modifications to individuals with disabilities is required under fair housing laws to ensure equal access to housing opportunities. This includes making reasonable modifications to rental properties to accommodate tenants with disabilities, such as installing grab bars or ramps, and providing reasonable accommodations to enable tenants with disabilities to enjoy full use and enjoyment of their rental units, such as allowing service animals or assigning accessible parking spaces. Providing reasonable accommodations and modifications promotes accessibility and inclusivity in housing."

Lisa, their accessibility advocate, understood the importance of providing reasonable accommodations to tenants with disabilities to ensure equal access to housing opportunities. She began exploring ways to make their rental properties more accessible and accommodating for individuals with disabilities.

The fifth slide highlighted "Fair Advertising and Marketing Practices." "5. **Fair Advertising and Marketing Practices.** Ensuring fair advertising and marketing practices is essential for preventing discriminatory practices and promoting equal housing opportunities. This includes avoiding discriminatory language or imagery in advertising materials, using inclusive language that welcomes individuals from diverse backgrounds, and reaching out to diverse communities to encourage equal access to housing opportunities. Fair advertising and marketing practices promote diversity and inclusivity in housing."

Jack stressed the importance of fair advertising and marketing practices to attract a diverse pool of applicants and promote inclusivity in their rental properties. He encouraged the team to review their advertising materials to ensure they were inclusive and non-discriminatory.

The final slide displayed "Training and Education." "6. **Training and Education.** Providing ongoing training and education on fair housing laws and diversity awareness to staff members is essential for maintaining compliance and promoting a culture of inclusivity. This includes conducting regular training sessions on fair housing principles and prohibited discriminatory practices, providing resources and materials to staff members on fair housing compliance, and fostering a culture of diversity and inclusion within the organization. Training and education empower staff members to uphold fair housing principles and prevent discrimination in housing."

Jack turned off the projector and faced his team, the determination evident in his expression. "Ensuring fair housing compliance is not just a legal obligation—it's a moral imperative to promote equality and inclusivity in housing. Let's approach fair housing with vigilance, sensitivity, and a commitment to equality. By upholding fair housing principles, we can create welcoming and inclusive communities where everyone has the opportunity to thrive."

The room buzzed with a renewed sense of purpose, each team member ready to apply their knowledge of fair housing laws to ensure they upheld legal standards and promoted inclusivity in their property management practices. Jack could see the determination in their eyes—a readiness to embrace diversity and foster equality, even in the face of challenges.

Risk Management and Liability

As the team delved deeper into the legal intricacies of property management, Jack Miller shifted their focus to the crucial aspect of risk management and liability. He knew that identifying and mitigating potential risks was essential for protecting property owner interests and minimizing legal exposure.

"Team," Jack began, his tone serious yet pragmatic. "Risk management and liability are integral parts of our role as property managers. It's not just about preventing legal issues—it's about safeguarding our clients' investments and ensuring peace of mind. Let's explore the sixth subpoint: risk management and liability."

He clicked the remote, and the screen illuminated with a checklist titled "Risk Management and Liability." "Effective risk management requires foresight, diligence, and a proactive approach to identify and address potential liabilities. It is the cornerstone of our efforts to protect property owner interests and maintain compliance with legal standards."

The first slide highlighted "Identifying Potential Risks." "1. **Identifying Potential Risks.** We begin by conducting a thorough assessment of potential risks and liabilities associated with property management operations. This includes identifying common sources of risk, such as property damage, tenant disputes, or regulatory violations, and evaluating the likelihood and potential impact of each risk on property owner interests. Identifying potential risks allows us to develop proactive strategies to mitigate or manage risks effectively."

Jack emphasized the importance of conducting a comprehensive risk assessment to identify potential vulnerabilities and liabilities. He recalled a time when their proactive approach to risk management had helped them avoid costly legal disputes and protect their clients' investments.

The next slide displayed "Insurance Coverage and Policies." "2. **Insurance Coverage and Policies.** Maintaining appropriate insurance coverage and policies is essential for protecting property owner interests and mitigating financial risks. This includes securing insurance policies such as property insurance, liability insurance, and umbrella insurance to provide coverage for potential losses or liabilities, and reviewing insurance policies regularly to ensure adequate coverage levels and compliance with legal requirements. Insurance coverage and policies provide a safety net against unforeseen risks and liabilities."

Sarah, with her financial acumen, nodded in agreement. She understood the importance of securing comprehensive insurance coverage to protect property owner interests and minimize financial risks. She made a mental note to review their insurance policies to ensure they provided adequate protection.

The third slide depicted "Contractual Risk Allocation." "3. **Contractual Risk Allocation.** Allocating risks and liabilities effectively through contractual agreements is crucial for protecting property owner interests and clarifying responsibilities among parties involved in property management operations. This includes drafting clear and comprehensive contracts with vendors, contractors, and tenants that outline liability limitations, indemnification clauses, and dispute resolution mechanisms, and reviewing contractual agreements regularly to ensure compliance with legal standards. Contractual risk allocation provides clarity and protection against potential liabilities."

David, always thorough in his approach, recognized the importance of drafting clear and enforceable contracts to allocate risks effectively and protect property owner interests. He made a mental note to review their contractual agreements to ensure they provided adequate protection against potential liabilities.

The next image showed "Compliance with Regulations and Standards." "4. **Compliance with Regulations and Standards.** Ensuring compliance with applicable regulations and industry standards is essential for minimizing legal exposure and protecting property owner interests. This includes staying informed about changes in local, state, and federal regulations affecting property management operations, implementing policies and procedures to ensure compliance with legal requirements, and conducting regular audits or inspections to identify and address potential compliance issues. Compliance with regulations and standards reduces the risk of legal disputes and liabilities."

Lisa, their compliance expert, understood the importance of staying abreast of regulatory changes to ensure their property management practices remained compliant. She began conducting regular audits to identify and address any potential compliance issues proactively.

The fifth slide highlighted "Emergency Preparedness and Response Plans." "5. **Emergency Preparedness and Response Plans.** Developing and implementing emergency preparedness and response plans is essential for mitigating risks and protecting property owner interests in the event of unforeseen emergencies or disasters. This includes identifying potential emergency scenarios, developing protocols and procedures for responding to emergencies, such as natural disasters or property damage, and training staff members on emergency response procedures to ensure swift and effective action. Emergency preparedness and response plans minimize the impact of emergencies on property owner interests and promote business continuity."

Jack stressed the importance of being prepared for emergencies to minimize risks and protect property owner interests. He encouraged the team to develop comprehensive emergency response plans and conduct regular training sessions to ensure readiness for any eventuality.

The final slide displayed "Documentation and Record-Keeping." "6. **Documentation and Record-Keeping.** Maintaining accurate and comprehensive documentation of property management activities and communications is essential for mitigating risks and liabilities and providing evidence in case of disputes or legal proceedings. This includes keeping records of property inspections, maintenance activities, tenant communications, and contractual agreements, and organizing documentation in a secure and accessible manner for easy reference. Documentation and record-keeping support transparency and accountability in property management operations."

Jack turned off the projector and faced his team, the determination evident in his expression. "Risk management and liability are ongoing responsibilities that require diligence and foresight. Let's approach them with a proactive mindset and a commitment to protecting property owner interests. By identifying and mitigating potential risks, we can safeguard our clients' investments and ensure peace of mind."

The room buzzed with a renewed sense of purpose, each team member ready to apply their knowledge of risk management to protect property owner interests and minimize legal exposure. Jack could see the determination in their eyes—a readiness to embrace proactive risk mitigation strategies and uphold their commitment to excellence in property management.

10

Chapter 10: Technology in Property Management

Property Management Software

As the team delved into the evolving landscape of property management, Jack Miller shifted their focus to the transformative role of technology, beginning with the exploration of property management software. He knew that embracing technological innovations was essential for streamlining operations, enhancing efficiency, and delivering superior service to clients.

"Team," Jack began, his voice brimming with enthusiasm. "Technology is revolutionizing the way we approach property management, and at the heart of this transformation is property management software. It's not just about adopting new tools—it's about leveraging technology to drive innovation and excellence in our operations. Let's explore the first subpoint: property management software."

He clicked the remote, and the screen illuminated with a

presentation titled "Property Management Software." "Embracing property management software requires adaptability, creativity, and a commitment to staying ahead of the curve. It is the foundation of our efforts to modernize our operations and deliver exceptional results for our clients."

The first slide highlighted "Centralized Property Management Systems." "1. **Centralized Property Management Systems.** Property management software provides a centralized platform for managing all aspects of property operations, from leasing and tenant management to maintenance and financial reporting. This includes features such as property listings, tenant portals, maintenance request tracking, and accounting tools, all accessible from a single interface. Centralized property management systems streamline workflows, enhance communication, and improve efficiency across the board."

Jack emphasized the transformative power of centralized property management systems to streamline operations and improve collaboration among team members. He recalled a time when implementing property management software had revolutionized their workflow, enabling them to manage properties more effectively and deliver superior service to clients.

The next slide displayed "Automated Processes and Workflows." "2. **Automated Processes and Workflows.** Property management software automates routine tasks and workflows, such as rental payments, lease renewals, and maintenance scheduling, to improve efficiency and reduce manual workload. This includes setting up automated reminders for lease expirations or maintenance inspections, generating automated rent invoices and payment reminders, and tracking maintenance requests and work orders in real-time. Automated processes and workflows save time, minimize errors, and enhance productivity in property management operations."

Sarah, with her focus on efficiency, nodded in agreement. She understood the value of automation in streamlining repetitive tasks and freeing up time for strategic decision-making. She made a mental note to explore the automation features of their property management software to optimize their workflow.

The third slide depicted "Tenant Self-Service Portals." "3. **Tenant Self-Service Portals.** Property management software includes tenant self-service portals that empower tenants to access information and perform tasks conveniently online. This includes features such as online rent payments, maintenance request submission, lease document access, and communication with property managers—all accessible through a secure online portal. Tenant self-service portals enhance tenant satisfaction, improve communication, and reduce administrative burden for property managers."

David, always keen on enhancing tenant experience, recognized the importance of providing convenient self-service options to tenants. He made a mental note to promote the use of tenant self-service portals to improve communication and streamline interactions with tenants.

The next image showed "Real-Time Data Analytics and Reporting." "4. **Real-Time Data Analytics and Reporting.** Property management software provides real-time data analytics and reporting capabilities that enable property managers to track key performance metrics and make data-driven decisions. This includes generating customizable reports on rental income, occupancy rates, maintenance costs, and leasing trends, and accessing real-time dashboards to monitor property performance and identify areas for improvement. Real-time data analytics and reporting empower property managers to optimize operations and maximize returns on investment."

Lisa, their analytics expert, understood the value of real-time data analytics in gaining insights into property performance and trends. She began exploring the reporting features of their property management software to track key metrics and identify opportunities for optimization.

The fifth slide highlighted "Integration with Other Tools and Platforms." "5. **Integration with Other Tools and Platforms.** Property management software integrates seamlessly with other tools and platforms, such as accounting software, marketing platforms, and customer relationship management (CRM) systems, to create a unified ecosystem for property management operations. This includes syncing data between different software applications, automating workflows across multiple platforms, and streamlining communication and collaboration among team members. Integration with other tools and platforms enhances efficiency, improves data accuracy, and facilitates seamless operations."

Jack stressed the importance of integration in creating a seamless and efficient workflow across different software applications. He encouraged the team to explore integration options with their existing tools and platforms to maximize the benefits of their property management software.

The final slide displayed "Scalability and Flexibility." "6. **Scalability and Flexibility.** Property management software is scalable and flexible, allowing property managers to adapt to changing needs and scale operations as their portfolio grows. This includes customizable features and settings that can be tailored to meet specific requirements, scalability to accommodate properties of various sizes and types, and cloud-based accessibility that enables remote management from anywhere, at any time. Scalability and flexibility ensure that property management software can grow with the business and adapt to evolving industry trends."

Jack turned off the projector and faced his team, a sense of excitement palpable in the air. "Property management software is not just a tool—it's a game-changer that empowers us to modernize our operations, enhance efficiency, and deliver exceptional service to our clients. Let's embrace technology with enthusiasm and creativity, leveraging property management software to drive innovation and excellence in our industry."

The room buzzed with energy, each team member eager to explore the possibilities of property management software and harness its potential to elevate their performance. Jack could see the enthusiasm in their eyes—a readiness to embrace technology and embrace the future of property management.

Online Marketing Tools

As the team continued their exploration of technology in property management, Jack Miller shifted their focus to the dynamic world of online marketing tools. He knew that leveraging digital platforms was essential for reaching prospective tenants, maximizing property exposure, and driving leasing success.

"Team," Jack began, his voice brimming with anticipation. "In today's digital age, online marketing tools play a pivotal role in property management success. It's not just about promoting listings—it's about engaging with prospective tenants and creating compelling online experiences. Let's explore the second subpoint: online marketing tools."

He clicked the remote, and the screen illuminated with a presentation titled "Online Marketing Tools." "Embracing online marketing tools requires creativity, adaptability, and a deep understanding of digital trends. It is the key to maximizing property exposure and attracting high-quality tenants in a competitive market."

The first slide highlighted "Property Listing Platforms." "1. **Property Listing Platforms.** Online marketing tools include property listing platforms such as websites, listing aggregators, and real estate marketplaces, where property managers can showcase available units to a wide audience of prospective tenants. This includes platforms like Zillow, Apartments.com, and Craigslist, which offer extensive reach and visibility for property listings, as well as property management websites with customizable listing pages. Property listing platforms increase property exposure, attract qualified leads, and facilitate efficient leasing."

Jack emphasized the importance of leveraging property listing platforms to maximize property exposure and attract qualified leads. He recalled a time when their strategic use of listing platforms had helped them reach a broader audience and accelerate leasing efforts.

The next slide displayed "Virtual Tours and Video Marketing." "2. **Virtual Tours and Video Marketing.** Online marketing tools enable property managers to create immersive virtual tours and engaging video content to showcase properties to prospective tenants remotely. This includes 360-degree virtual tours that provide interactive experiences of property interiors and exteriors, as well as video walkthroughs that highlight key features and amenities. Virtual tours and video marketing captivate prospective tenants, increase engagement, and accelerate leasing by providing a realistic preview of properties."

Sarah, with her focus on innovation, nodded in agreement. She understood the value of virtual tours and video marketing in providing prospective tenants with a comprehensive view of properties from the comfort of their own homes. She made a mental note to explore the implementation of virtual tours for their property listings.

The third slide depicted "Social Media Advertising." "3. **Social Media Advertising.** Online marketing tools include social media advertising platforms such as Facebook, Instagram, and LinkedIn, which enable property managers to target specific demographics and interests with tailored advertising campaigns. This includes creating targeted ads that showcase property listings to relevant audiences, engaging with followers through organic content and community building, and leveraging social media analytics to optimize advertising performance. Social media advertising increases brand visibility, generates leads, and fosters community engagement with prospective tenants."

David, always keen on connecting with audiences, recognized the power of social media advertising in reaching prospective tenants where they spend their time online. He made a mental note to explore the possibilities of social media advertising to amplify their property marketing efforts.

The next image showed "Search Engine Optimization (SEO) Strategies." "4. **Search Engine Optimization (SEO) Strategies.** Online marketing tools include search engine optimization (SEO) strategies that optimize property listings and websites for higher visibility in search engine results. This includes optimizing property descriptions and metadata with relevant keywords, improving website performance and user experience for better search rankings, and generating high-quality backlinks from reputable sources. SEO strategies increase organic traffic, enhance online visibility, and improve search engine rankings for property listings."

Lisa, their SEO expert, understood the importance of optimizing property listings and websites for search engine visibility. She began reviewing their SEO strategies to ensure they were maximizing their online presence and attracting organic traffic to their property listings.

The fifth slide highlighted "Email Marketing Campaigns." "5. **Email Marketing Campaigns.** Online marketing tools include email marketing campaigns that enable property managers to engage with prospective tenants through personalized email communications. This includes creating targeted email campaigns that promote property listings, share leasing incentives or updates, and provide valuable content to subscribers, such as neighborhood guides or moving tips. Email marketing campaigns nurture leads, maintain engagement, and drive conversions by delivering relevant content directly to prospective tenants' inboxes."

Jack stressed the importance of email marketing campaigns in nurturing leads and maintaining engagement throughout the leasing process. He encouraged the team to develop targeted email campaigns that provided value to subscribers and incentivized them to take action.

The final slide displayed "Analytics and Performance Tracking." "6. **Analytics and Performance Tracking.** Online marketing tools provide analytics and performance tracking features that enable property managers to measure the effectiveness of their marketing efforts and optimize strategies for better results. This includes tracking key metrics such as website traffic, lead generation, and conversion rates, analyzing marketing campaign performance with detailed reports and dashboards, and using data insights to refine targeting, messaging, and budget allocation. Analytics and performance tracking empower property managers to make informed decisions and maximize the impact of their marketing investments."

Jack turned off the projector and faced his team, a sense of excitement evident in his expression. "Online marketing tools are not just about promoting listings—they're about creating meaningful connections with prospective tenants and driving leasing success. Let's embrace the power of digital marketing with creativity and innovation, leveraging online tools to maximize property exposure and attract high-quality tenants."

The room buzzed with energy, each team member eager to explore the possibilities of online marketing tools and harness their potential to elevate their property management efforts. Jack could see the enthusiasm in their eyes—a readiness to embrace technology and revolutionize their approach to marketing in the digital age.

Digital Communication Platforms

As the team delved deeper into the realm of technology in property management, Jack Miller redirected their attention to the pivotal role of digital communication platforms. He knew that effective communication was essential for fostering tenant satisfaction, resolving issues promptly, and maintaining positive relationships with clients.

"Team," Jack began, his voice infused with determination. "In our ever-evolving industry, digital communication platforms are the cornerstone of efficient property management. It's not just about exchanging messages—it's about building strong connections with tenants and clients alike. Let's explore the third subpoint: digital communication platforms."

He clicked the remote, and the screen illuminated with a presentation titled "Digital Communication Platforms." "Harnessing digital communication platforms requires agility, responsiveness, and a commitment to meaningful interactions. It is the key to fostering tenant satisfaction and delivering exceptional service in a digital age."

The first slide highlighted "Property Management Portals."
"1. **Property Management Portals.** Digital communication platforms include property management portals that provide tenants with convenient access to important information and services. This includes features such as online rent payment portals, maintenance request submission forms, lease document access, and community forums for tenant interaction. Property management portals enhance tenant satisfaction, streamline communication, and facilitate self-service options for tenants."

Jack emphasized the importance of property management

portals in providing tenants with convenient access to essential services and information. He recalled a time when implementing property management portals had transformed their tenant experience, enabling them to address issues promptly and maintain high levels of tenant satisfaction.

The next slide displayed "Mobile Apps for Property Management." "2. **Mobile Apps for Property Management.** Digital communication platforms include mobile apps designed specifically for property management tasks, allowing property managers and tenants to access information and perform tasks on the go. This includes features such as mobile rent payment capabilities, real-time maintenance request tracking, push notifications for important updates, and secure messaging functionality. Mobile apps for property management increase accessibility, improve responsiveness, and enhance convenience for both property managers and tenants."

Sarah, with her focus on innovation, nodded in agreement. She understood the value of mobile apps in providing property managers and tenants with flexibility and convenience in managing property-related tasks. She made a mental note to explore the implementation of mobile apps for their property management operations.

The third slide depicted "Virtual Communication Tools." "3. **Virtual Communication Tools.** Digital communication platforms include virtual communication tools such as video conferencing software, instant messaging applications, and online collaboration platforms, which enable property managers to communicate effectively with tenants and team members remotely. This includes conducting virtual meetings with tenants to address concerns or provide updates, using instant messaging for quick communication and issue resolution, and collaborating on projects or documents in real time. Virtual communication tools facilitate seamless communication, improve responsiveness, and enable remote collaboration in property management operations."

David, always keen on fostering connections, recognized the importance of virtual communication tools in maintaining meaningful interactions with tenants and team members, regardless of location. He made a mental note to leverage virtual communication tools to enhance their responsiveness and efficiency in property management.

The next image showed "Email and Newsletter Campaigns." "4. **Email and Newsletter Campaigns.** Digital communication platforms include email and newsletter campaigns that enable property managers to engage with tenants and clients through targeted communications. This includes sending regular newsletters with updates on property news or events, sharing valuable resources or tips through email campaigns, and soliciting feedback or reviews from tenants to improve service quality. Email and newsletter campaigns nurture relationships, maintain engagement, and foster community among tenants and clients."

Lisa, their communication expert, understood the value of email and newsletter campaigns in nurturing relationships and maintaining engagement with tenants and clients. She began planning email campaigns that provided valuable content and encouraged interaction to strengthen their connections.

The fifth slide highlighted "Social Media Messaging Platforms." "5. **Social Media Messaging Platforms.** Digital communication platforms include social media messaging platforms such as Facebook Messenger, WhatsApp, and Instagram Direct, which enable property managers to communicate with tenants and clients through private messages on social media. This includes responding to inquiries or concerns from tenants through social media messaging, providing timely updates or announcements about property news or events, and fostering community engagement through direct interactions. Social media messaging platforms enhance accessibility, improve responsiveness, and facilitate informal communication with tenants and clients."

Jack stressed the importance of leveraging social media messaging platforms to connect with tenants and clients in a more informal and accessible manner. He encouraged the team to embrace social media messaging as a way to enhance communication and foster community engagement in their property management efforts.

The final slide displayed "Customer Relationship Management (CRM) Systems." "6. **Customer Relationship Management (CRM) Systems.** Digital communication platforms include customer relationship management (CRM) systems that enable property managers to organize and track interactions with tenants and clients efficiently. This includes managing contact information and communication history for tenants and clients, tracking inquiries or requests through a centralized platform, and segmenting contacts for targeted outreach or marketing campaigns. CRM systems improve organization, enhance communication, and enable personalized interactions with tenants and clients."

Jack turned off the projector and faced his team, a sense of purpose evident in his expression. "Digital communication platforms are not just tools—they're pathways to meaningful connections with tenants and clients. Let's embrace the power of digital communication with responsiveness and empathy, leveraging these platforms to foster tenant satisfaction and deliver exceptional service in our property management operations."

The room buzzed with energy, each team member eager to explore the possibilities of digital communication platforms and harness their potential to enhance tenant satisfaction and client relationships. Jack could see the determination in their eyes—a readiness to embrace technology and elevate their communication efforts in the digital age.

Smart Home Technologies

As the team delved deeper into the realm of technology in property management, Jack Miller redirected their attention to the transformative potential of smart home technologies. He knew that embracing smart home innovations was essential for enhancing tenant experience, optimizing energy efficiency, and staying competitive in the market.

"Team," Jack began, his voice resonating with excitement. "In our quest for excellence in property management, smart home technologies stand at the forefront of innovation. It's not just about modernizing properties—it's about creating smarter, more connected living spaces. Let's explore the fourth subpoint: smart home technologies."

He clicked the remote, and the screen illuminated with a presentation titled "Smart Home Technologies." "Embracing smart home technologies requires vision, adaptability, and a commitment to enhancing tenant experience. It is the key to revolutionizing our properties and staying ahead of the curve in a rapidly evolving market."

The first slide highlighted "Smart Thermostats and Climate Control Systems." "1. **Smart Thermostats and Climate Control Systems.** Smart home technologies include thermostats and climate control systems equipped with sensors and automation capabilities, allowing tenants to regulate indoor temperatures and energy usage remotely. This includes features such as programmable schedules, temperature sensors, and energy usage monitoring, all accessible through smartphone apps or voice assistants. Smart thermostats and climate control systems optimize energy efficiency, reduce utility costs, and enhance tenant comfort and convenience."

Jack emphasized the transformative impact of smart thermostats and climate control systems in optimizing energy usage and enhancing tenant comfort. He recalled a time when implementing smart thermostats had led to significant energy savings and improved tenant satisfaction in their properties.

The next slide displayed "Smart Lighting and Dimming Systems." "2. **Smart Lighting and Dimming Systems.** Smart home technologies include lighting and dimming systems equipped with sensors and automation features, allowing tenants to control lighting levels and ambiance remotely. This includes features such as motion sensors, customizable lighting schedules, and voice-activated controls, all accessible through smartphone apps or smart home hubs. Smart lighting and dimming systems improve energy efficiency, enhance security, and create customizable lighting experiences for tenants."

Sarah, with her focus on sustainability, nodded in agreement. She understood the value of smart lighting systems in reducing energy consumption and creating a more eco-friendly living environment. She made a mental note to explore the implementation of smart lighting solutions in their properties.

The third slide depicted "Smart Locks and Access Control Systems." "3. **Smart Locks and Access Control Systems.** Smart home technologies include smart locks and access control systems that provide tenants with keyless entry and remote access capabilities. This includes features such as digital key access, remote lock/unlock functionality, and activity monitoring, all accessible through smartphone apps or centralized management platforms. Smart locks and access control systems enhance security, improve convenience, and streamline property access for tenants and property managers."

David, always focused on security, recognized the importance of smart locks and access control systems in enhancing property security and streamlining access management. He made a mental note to explore the implementation of smart lock solutions in their properties.

The next image showed "Smart Home Appliances and Devices." "4. **Smart Home Appliances and Devices.** Smart home technologies include appliances and devices equipped with connectivity and automation features, allowing tenants to control and monitor home functions remotely. This includes smart refrigerators, ovens, washers/dryers, and entertainment systems, all accessible through smartphone apps or voice assistants. Smart home appliances and devices increase efficiency, improve convenience, and enhance the overall living experience for tenants."

Lisa, their tech-savvy team member, understood the potential of smart home appliances and devices in creating a more connected and efficient living environment for tenants. She began researching the latest smart home gadgets to integrate into their properties.

The fifth slide highlighted "Integration with Virtual Assistants and Home Automation Platforms." "5. **Integration with Virtual Assistants and Home Automation Platforms.** Smart home technologies integrate seamlessly with virtual assistants and home automation platforms, allowing tenants to control and monitor home functions using voice commands or centralized management interfaces. This includes integration with popular virtual assistants such as Amazon Alexa, Google Assistant, and Apple HomeKit, as well as compatibility with home automation platforms like SmartThings or HomeKit. Integration with virtual assistants and home automation platforms enhances accessibility, improves usability, and fosters a more connected living experience for tenants."

Jack stressed the importance of integrating smart home technologies with virtual assistants and home automation platforms to create a more seamless and intuitive living experience for tenants. He encouraged the team to explore integration options that would enhance usability and convenience for their tenants.

The final slide displayed "Data Analytics and Insights." "6. **Data Analytics and Insights.** Smart home technologies provide data analytics and insights that enable property managers to monitor and optimize property performance. This includes collecting data on energy usage, occupancy patterns, and tenant preferences, and analyzing insights to identify opportunities for efficiency improvements or service enhancements. Data analytics and insights empower property managers to make informed decisions and deliver personalized experiences for tenants."

Jack turned off the projector and faced his team, a sense of anticipation evident in his expression. "Smart home technologies are not just about modernizing properties—they're about creating smarter, more connected living spaces that enhance tenant experience and drive value for our clients. Let's embrace the power of smart home innovations with creativity and enthusiasm, leveraging these technologies to revolutionize our properties and set new standards in the industry."

The room buzzed with excitement, each team member eager to explore the possibilities of smart home technologies and harness their potential to enhance tenant experience and property performance. Jack could see the determination in their eyes—a readiness to embrace innovation and transform their properties into smart, connected living spaces.

Data Security and Privacy

As the team ventured further into the landscape of technology in property management, Jack Miller redirected their focus to the critical aspect of data security and privacy. He knew that safeguarding sensitive information was paramount in maintaining trust with tenants and clients while navigating the complexities of digital operations.

"Team," Jack began, his tone conveying a sense of gravity. "In our pursuit of innovation, we must not overlook the importance of data security and privacy. It's not just about embracing technology—it's about safeguarding the trust and confidence of our tenants and clients. Let's explore the fifth subpoint: data security and privacy."

He clicked the remote, and the screen illuminated with a presentation titled "Data Security and Privacy." "Ensuring data security and privacy requires vigilance, integrity, and a commitment to compliance. It is the cornerstone of our responsibility as stewards of sensitive information in the digital age."

The first slide highlighted "Encryption and Secure Communication Protocols." "1. **Encryption and Secure Communication Protocols.** Data security measures include encryption and secure communication protocols that protect sensitive information from unauthorized access or interception. This includes encrypting data in transit and at rest, implementing secure socket layer (SSL) encryption for website communication, and using virtual private networks (VPNs) for secure remote access. Encryption and secure communication protocols safeguard sensitive data, mitigate the risk of data breaches, and ensure compliance with privacy regulations."

Jack emphasized the importance of encryption and secure communication protocols in safeguarding sensitive information and preventing unauthorized access. He recalled a time when implementing encryption measures had helped them strengthen their data security posture and maintain compliance with privacy regulations.

The next slide displayed "Access Control and User Permissions." "2. **Access Control and User Permissions.** Data security practices include access control mechanisms and user permissions that restrict access to sensitive information based on user roles and responsibilities. This includes implementing role-based access controls (RBAC), multifactor authentication (MFA), and least privilege principles to limit access to confidential data. Access control and user permissions enhance data security, minimize the risk of insider threats, and ensure accountability in data handling processes."

Sarah, with her focus on accountability, nodded in agreement. She understood the importance of access control and user permissions in limiting the exposure of sensitive information and reducing the risk of unauthorized access. She made a mental note to review their access control mechanisms to ensure they were aligned with best practices.

The third slide depicted "Regular Data Audits and Vulnerability Assessments." "3. **Regular Data Audits and Vulnerability Assessments.** Data security protocols include regular data audits and vulnerability assessments to identify and mitigate potential security risks or vulnerabilities. This includes conducting periodic audits of data storage and processing practices, performing vulnerability assessments to identify potential security weaknesses, and implementing remediation measures to address identified risks. Regular data audits and vulnerability assessments enhance proactive security measures, reduce the risk of data breaches, and ensure ongoing compliance with security standards."

David, always focused on risk management, recognized the importance of regular data audits and vulnerability assessments in identifying and addressing potential security risks. He made a mental note to schedule periodic audits and assessments to strengthen their data security posture.

The next image showed "Data Breach Response and Incident Management Plans." "4. **Data Breach Response and Incident Management Plans.** Data security protocols include data breach response and incident management plans that outline procedures for detecting, responding to, and mitigating data breaches or security incidents. This includes establishing incident response teams, defining escalation procedures, and implementing communication protocols for notifying affected parties. Data breach response and incident management plans enable swift and effective responses to security incidents, minimize the impact of data breaches, and protect the reputation of the organization."

Lisa, their crisis management expert, understood the importance of having robust data breach response and incident management plans in place. She began reviewing their existing plans to ensure they were prepared to respond effectively to any security incidents.

The fifth slide highlighted "Compliance with Data Protection Regulations." "5. **Compliance with Data Protection Regulations.** Data security protocols include compliance with data protection regulations such as the General Data Protection Regulation (GDPR) or the California Consumer Privacy Act (CCPA), which outline requirements for protecting personal data and ensuring individual privacy rights. This includes implementing measures to secure personal data, obtaining explicit consent for data collection and processing, and providing individuals with control over their data. Compliance with data protection regulations demonstrates commitment to data security and privacy, builds trust with tenants and clients, and mitigates legal and financial risks associated with non-compliance."

Jack stressed the importance of compliance with data protection regulations in maintaining trust with tenants and clients and mitigating legal and financial risks. He encouraged the team to stay informed about evolving privacy regulations and ensure their data security practices remained compliant with applicable laws.

The final slide displayed "Employee Training and Awareness Programs." "6. **Employee Training and Awareness Programs.** Data security protocols include employee training and awareness programs that educate staff on data handling best practices, security policies, and procedures for safeguarding sensitive information. This includes providing regular training sessions on data security principles, conducting phishing awareness exercises, and promoting a culture of security awareness and accountability throughout the organization. Employee training and awareness programs empower staff to recognize and respond to security threats effectively, reducing the risk of data breaches and insider threats."

Jack turned off the projector and faced his team, a sense of determination evident in his expression. "Data security and privacy are not just checkboxes—they're fundamental principles that underpin our commitment to integrity and trust. Let's embrace the responsibility of protecting sensitive information with diligence and vigilance, ensuring that our data security practices reflect the highest standards of excellence in property management."

The room fell silent, each team member reflecting on their role in safeguarding sensitive information and upholding the trust of tenants and clients. Jack could see the determination in their eyes—a shared commitment to prioritizing data security and privacy in their property management operations.

Emerging Tech Trends

As the team delved deeper into the realm of technology in property management, Jack Miller redirected their focus to the horizon of emerging tech trends. He knew that staying abreast of innovative technologies was essential for driving efficiency, optimizing operations, and future-proofing their business in an ever-evolving industry.

"Team," Jack began, his voice tinged with anticipation. "In our journey towards excellence, we must embrace the frontier of emerging tech trends. It's not just about keeping up—it's about leading the way in innovation and shaping the future of property management. Let's explore the sixth subpoint: emerging tech trends."

He clicked the remote, and the screen illuminated with a presentation titled "Emerging Tech Trends." "Embracing emerging tech trends requires foresight, adaptability, and a willingness to explore uncharted territories. It is the key to unlocking new opportunities and driving sustainable growth in our industry."

The first slide highlighted "Artificial Intelligence and Machine Learning." "1. **Artificial Intelligence and Machine Learning.** Emerging tech trends include artificial intelligence (AI) and machine learning (ML) technologies that enable property managers to automate routine tasks, analyze large datasets, and gain actionable insights. This includes AI-powered chatbots for tenant inquiries, ML algorithms for predictive maintenance, and data analytics platforms for optimizing property performance. Artificial intelligence and machine learning revolutionize property management by enhancing efficiency, reducing costs, and enabling data-driven decision-making."

Jack emphasized the transformative potential of artificial intelligence and machine learning in revolutionizing property management operations. He recalled a time when implementing AI-driven solutions had helped them streamline processes and optimize resource allocation in their properties.

The next slide displayed "Internet of Things (IoT) Devices and Sensors." "2. **Internet of Things (IoT) Devices and Sensors.** Emerging tech trends include Internet of Things (IoT) devices and sensors that connect physical objects and assets to the internet, enabling real-time monitoring and control. This includes IoT sensors for environmental monitoring, smart meters for utility usage tracking, and connected devices for home automation. Internet of Things devices and sensors enhance visibility, optimize resource usage, and improve tenant experience through personalized services and automated processes."

Sarah, with her focus on sustainability, nodded in agreement. She understood the value of IoT devices and sensors in optimizing resource usage and creating more sustainable living environments. She made a mental note to explore the implementation of IoT solutions in their properties.

The third slide depicted "Augmented Reality (AR) and Virtual Reality (VR) Experiences." "3. **Augmented Reality (AR) and Virtual Reality (VR) Experiences.** Emerging tech trends include augmented reality (AR) and virtual reality (VR) technologies that provide immersive experiences for property tours, interior design visualization, and tenant engagement. This includes AR applications for interactive property tours, VR simulations for interior design planning, and virtual staging for vacant units. Augmented reality and virtual reality experiences enhance marketing efforts, increase tenant engagement, and provide innovative solutions for property showcasing and design."

David, always focused on customer experience, recognized the potential of AR and VR experiences in enhancing tenant engagement and marketing efforts. He made a mental note to explore the implementation of AR and VR solutions to create more immersive property experiences for their tenants.

The next image showed "Blockchain Technology for Property Transactions." "4. **Blockchain Technology for Property Transactions.** Emerging tech trends include blockchain technology that enables secure and transparent property transactions through decentralized ledgers and smart contracts. This includes blockchain-based platforms for property listings, smart contracts for rental agreements, and tokenization of property assets. Blockchain technology enhances transparency, reduces transaction costs, and streamlines property transactions by eliminating intermediaries and ensuring data integrity."

Lisa, their blockchain enthusiast, understood the potential of blockchain technology in revolutionizing property transactions and enhancing trust in the real estate market. She began researching blockchain-based solutions to streamline their property transaction processes.

The fifth slide highlighted "Predictive Analytics and Risk Management Solutions." "5. **Predictive Analytics and Risk Management Solutions.** Emerging tech trends include predictive analytics and risk management solutions that enable property managers to anticipate trends, identify risks, and mitigate potential threats proactively. This includes predictive analytics models for forecasting market trends, risk management platforms for assessing property vulnerabilities, and scenario planning tools for mitigating potential risks. Predictive analytics and risk management solutions empower property managers to make informed decisions, mitigate risks, and capitalize on opportunities in a dynamic market environment."

Jack stressed the importance of predictive analytics and risk management solutions in enabling proactive decision-making and mitigating potential threats. He encouraged the team to leverage predictive analytics to anticipate market trends and identify opportunities for growth.

The final slide displayed "Biometric Access Control Systems." "6. **Biometric Access Control Systems.** Emerging tech trends include biometric access control systems that use unique biological traits such as fingerprints or facial recognition for secure property access. This includes biometric authentication for building entry, visitor management systems with biometric identification, and biometric time and attendance tracking for staff. Biometric access control systems enhance security, improve access control, and provide a seamless and secure experience for tenants and staff."

Jack turned off the projector and faced his team, a sense of excitement evident in his expression. "Emerging tech trends are not just buzzwords—they're blueprints for the future of property management. Let's embrace the potential of innovation with curiosity and determination, exploring new horizons and shaping the future of our industry."

The room buzzed with excitement, each team member eager to explore the possibilities of emerging tech trends and harness their potential to drive innovation in property management. Jack could see the determination in their eyes—a shared commitment to leading the way in embracing technology and shaping the future of their industry.

11

Chapter 11: Managing Commercial Properties

Differences Between Residential and Commercial Management

As the team transitioned their focus to managing commercial properties, Jack Miller redirected their attention to understanding the fundamental differences between residential and commercial property management. He knew that navigating the nuances of commercial real estate required a unique approach and a keen understanding of market dynamics.

"Team," Jack began, his voice resonating with authority. "In our exploration of commercial property management, it's essential to recognize the distinct differences between residential and commercial management. It's not just about managing buildings—it's about understanding the unique needs and dynamics of commercial tenants and properties. Let's explore the first subpoint: differences between residential and commercial management."

He clicked the remote, and the screen illuminated with a presentation titled "Differences Between Residential and Commercial Management." "Differentiating between residential and commercial management requires insight, adaptability, and a deep understanding of market dynamics. It is the key to unlocking success in the commercial real estate sector."

The first slide highlighted "Lease Structures and Terms." "1. **Lease Structures and Terms.** One of the primary differences between residential and commercial management lies in lease structures and terms. Residential leases are typically shorter in duration, with terms ranging from six months to a year, and involve standard agreements with fixed rental amounts. In contrast, commercial leases tend to be longer-term commitments, often spanning multiple years, and involve more complex agreements with variable rental rates, operating expenses, and additional provisions such as rent escalations, renewal options, and tenant improvements."

Jack emphasized the importance of understanding lease structures and terms in commercial property management, noting that the longer-term commitments and complexity of commercial leases required a thorough understanding of contractual agreements and negotiation skills.

The next slide displayed "Tenant Profiles and Needs." "2. **Tenant Profiles and Needs.** Another key difference between residential and commercial management is the tenant profiles and needs. Residential tenants are typically individuals or families seeking living accommodations, with relatively standardized needs such as housing amenities, safety, and community features. In contrast, commercial tenants are businesses or organizations with diverse requirements based on their industry, operations, and customer base. Commercial tenants may require specialized facilities, infrastructure, or zoning considerations to support their business activities."

Sarah, with her focus on tenant satisfaction, nodded in agreement. She understood the importance of tailoring property management services to meet the diverse needs of commercial tenants, ranging from retail businesses to office spaces, industrial facilities, and specialized properties.

The third slide depicted "Property Maintenance and Operations." "3. **Property Maintenance and Operations.** The approach to property maintenance and operations differs between residential and commercial management. Residential properties often require routine maintenance and repairs focused on individual units, common areas, and landscaping to ensure tenant satisfaction and retention. In contrast, commercial properties may have more extensive maintenance needs, including specialized systems, equipment, and infrastructure tailored to specific business activities. Commercial property managers must prioritize safety, accessibility, and compliance with industry standards to meet the operational needs of commercial tenants."

David, always focused on operational efficiency, recognized the importance of prioritizing maintenance and operations to meet the unique needs of commercial properties. He made a mental note to develop tailored maintenance plans and protocols for their commercial properties to ensure they met industry standards and tenant expectations.

The next image showed "Financial Considerations and Investment Strategies." "4. **Financial Considerations and Investment Strategies.** Residential and commercial management also differ in terms of financial considerations and investment strategies. Residential properties are often valued based on rental income and comparable sales in the local housing market, with investment strategies focused on rental yield and capital appreciation. In contrast, commercial properties are valued based on income generated by tenants, potential for future cash flow growth, and overall market demand for specific property types. Investment strategies for commercial properties may involve considerations such as lease negotiations, tenant retention, property improvements, and market trends impacting demand and rental rates."

Lisa, their financial expert, understood the importance of adopting different investment strategies for residential and commercial properties based on their unique financial considerations and market dynamics. She began analyzing market trends and investment opportunities to develop tailored strategies for their commercial properties.

The fifth slide highlighted "Regulatory Compliance and Legal Considerations." "5. **Regulatory Compliance and Legal Considerations.** Regulatory compliance and legal considerations vary between residential and commercial management. Residential properties are subject to housing regulations, tenant rights laws, and fair housing practices aimed at protecting tenants from discrimination and ensuring safe living conditions. Commercial properties, on the other hand, are governed by commercial leasing laws, zoning ordinances, building codes, and industry-specific regulations that impact property use, occupancy, and operations. Commercial property managers must stay informed about regulatory changes, building codes, and legal requirements to ensure compliance and mitigate legal risks."

Jack stressed the importance of staying abreast of regulatory compliance and legal considerations in commercial property management, noting that adherence to zoning ordinances, building codes, and industry regulations was essential for maintaining operational integrity and minimizing legal risks.

The final slide displayed "Marketing and Tenant Acquisition Strategies." "6. **Marketing and Tenant Acquisition Strategies.** Marketing and tenant acquisition strategies differ between residential and commercial management. Residential properties often rely on traditional marketing channels such as online listings, real estate agents, and property management companies to attract tenants. In contrast, commercial properties may require targeted marketing efforts tailored to specific tenant industries, such as networking with commercial brokers, attending industry events, and showcasing property features and amenities relevant to business operations. Commercial property managers must adopt proactive marketing strategies to attract and retain tenants in competitive markets."

Jack turned off the projector and faced his team, a sense of satisfaction evident in his expression. "Understanding the differences between residential and commercial management is the foundation of success in the commercial real estate sector. Let's embrace these differences with insight and adaptability, tailoring our approach to meet the unique needs of commercial tenants and properties."

The room fell silent, each team member reflecting on the distinct challenges and opportunities presented by commercial property management. Jack could see the determination in their eyes—a shared commitment to mastering the intricacies of commercial real estate and delivering exceptional results for their clients.

Leasing Commercial Spaces

As the team continued their exploration of commercial property management, Jack Miller redirected their focus to the intricacies of leasing commercial spaces. He knew that leasing commercial properties required a strategic approach and a deep understanding of market dynamics to attract and retain tenants effectively.

"Team," Jack began, his voice projecting confidence. "In our quest for excellence in commercial property management, leasing commercial spaces plays a pivotal role. It's not just about filling vacancies—it's about cultivating relationships with tenants and maximizing the value of our properties. Let's explore the second subpoint: leasing commercial spaces."

He clicked the remote, and the screen illuminated with a presentation titled "Leasing Commercial Spaces." "Mastering the art of leasing commercial spaces demands creativity, negotiation skills, and a keen understanding of tenant needs. It is the cornerstone of success in the commercial real estate sector."

The first slide highlighted "Understanding Tenant Needs and Preferences." "1. **Understanding Tenant Needs and Preferences.** Leasing commercial spaces begins with understanding the needs and preferences of potential tenants. Commercial tenants have diverse requirements based on their industry, operations, and customer base. This includes considerations such as location, space layout, infrastructure, amenities, and lease terms. Commercial property managers must conduct thorough market research and engage in active dialogue with prospective tenants to identify opportunities and tailor leasing solutions to meet their needs."

Jack emphasized the importance of understanding tenant needs and preferences in leasing commercial spaces, noting that a deep understanding of tenant requirements was essential for attracting and retaining high-quality tenants.

The next slide displayed "Positioning and Marketing Commercial Properties." "2. **Positioning and Marketing Commercial Properties.** Effectively leasing commercial spaces requires strategic positioning and targeted marketing efforts to attract prospective tenants. This includes showcasing property features, amenities, and unique selling points that align with tenant needs and market demand. Commercial property managers must develop comprehensive marketing strategies tailored to target tenant industries, utilize various marketing channels such as online listings, signage, brochures, and networking events, and leverage digital marketing tools to reach a wider audience of potential tenants."

Sarah, with her focus on tenant satisfaction, nodded in agreement. She understood the importance of strategic positioning and targeted marketing in attracting high-quality tenants to their commercial properties. She made a mental note to develop tailored marketing strategies to showcase their properties effectively.

The third slide depicted "Negotiating Lease Agreements." "3. **Negotiating Lease Agreements.** The leasing process involves negotiating lease agreements that meet the needs of both landlords and tenants while protecting the interests of all parties involved. This includes negotiating lease terms such as rental rates, lease duration, renewal options, tenant improvements, operating expenses, and lease incentives. Commercial property managers must possess strong negotiation skills, an understanding of market conditions, and knowledge of industry standards to negotiate favorable lease agreements that maximize rental income and minimize risks."

David, always focused on maximizing returns, recognized the importance of negotiating lease agreements that balanced the needs of landlords and tenants while optimizing property performance. He made a mental note to refine his negotiation skills and stay informed about market trends to negotiate favorable terms for their properties.

The next image showed "Tenant Screening and Due Diligence." "4. **Tenant Screening and Due Diligence.** Once prospective tenants express interest in leasing a commercial space, commercial property managers must conduct thorough tenant screening and due diligence to assess their financial stability, creditworthiness, business history, and suitability as tenants. This includes reviewing financial statements, conducting background checks, verifying references, and evaluating the tenant's business model and growth potential. Tenant screening and due diligence help mitigate the risk of leasing to unreliable or high-risk tenants and ensure a stable and sustainable tenant base."

Lisa, their due diligence expert, understood the importance of conducting thorough tenant screening to minimize risks and protect the interests of their properties. She began reviewing their tenant screening processes to ensure they were comprehensive and aligned with best practices.

The fifth slide highlighted "Lease Administration and Tenant Relations." "5. **Lease Administration and Tenant**

Relations. Once lease agreements are signed, commercial property managers must oversee lease administration tasks and maintain positive tenant relations throughout the lease term. This includes managing lease documentation, processing rental payments, addressing tenant inquiries and concerns, coordinating property maintenance and repairs, and facilitating lease renewals or terminations. Effective lease administration and tenant relations are essential for fostering tenant satisfaction, minimizing vacancies, and maximizing property performance."

Jack stressed the importance of lease administration and tenant relations in maintaining positive relationships with tenants and ensuring smooth operations throughout the lease term. He encouraged the team to prioritize tenant satisfaction and responsiveness to tenant needs to build long-term tenant loyalty.

The final slide displayed "Monitoring Market Trends and Adjusting Strategies." "6. **Monitoring Market Trends and Adjusting Strategies.** Leasing commercial spaces requires vigilance and adaptability to changing market conditions and tenant preferences. Commercial property managers must continuously monitor market trends, vacancy rates, rental rates, and tenant demand to adjust leasing strategies accordingly. This includes staying informed about industry developments, competitor activities, and economic indicators that may impact property performance. Monitoring market trends and adjusting leasing strategies proactively ensure that commercial properties remain competitive and attractive to potential tenants."

Jack turned off the projector and faced his team, a sense of determination evident in his expression. "Leasing commercial spaces is not just about filling vacancies—it's about building lasting relationships with tenants and maximizing the value of our properties. Let's approach leasing with creativity, diligence, and a commitment to delivering exceptional results for our clients."

The room fell silent, each team member reflecting on the strategic importance of leasing commercial spaces and their role in driving property performance. Jack could see the determination in their eyes—a shared commitment to mastering the art of leasing and achieving excellence in commercial property management.

Managing Commercial Tenant Relationships

As the team delved deeper into the complexities of commercial property management, Jack Miller redirected their attention to the critical aspect of managing commercial tenant relationships. He knew that fostering positive relationships with tenants was essential for tenant satisfaction, lease renewal, and overall property performance.

"Team," Jack began, his voice carrying a sense of urgency. "In our pursuit of excellence in commercial property management, managing commercial tenant relationships is paramount. It's not just about leasing spaces—it's about nurturing partnerships with our tenants and ensuring their success. Let's explore the third subpoint: managing commercial tenant relationships."

He clicked the remote, and the screen illuminated with a presentation titled "Managing Commercial Tenant Relationships." "Building and maintaining strong relationships with commercial tenants requires empathy, communication, and a commitment to meeting their needs. It is the foundation of tenant satisfaction and long-term property success."

The first slide highlighted "Proactive Communication and Accessibility." "1. **Proactive Communication and Accessibility.** Effective management of commercial tenant relationships begins with proactive communication and accessibility. Commercial property managers must establish open lines of communication with tenants, providing regular updates on property matters, responding promptly to inquiries and concerns, and being accessible to address tenant needs. Proactive communication fosters transparency, trust, and tenant satisfaction, enhancing the overall tenant experience."

Jack emphasized the importance of proactive communication and accessibility in building trust and fostering positive relationships with tenants. He recalled instances where timely communication had helped resolve tenant issues and strengthen tenant loyalty.

The next slide displayed "Understanding Tenant Business Needs." "2. **Understanding Tenant Business Needs.** Managing commercial tenant relationships requires a deep understanding of tenant business needs and objectives. Commercial property managers must take the time to understand each tenant's business model, operations, and goals, and tailor property management services to support their success. This includes offering customized solutions, anticipating tenant needs, and collaborating with tenants to address challenges and opportunities in their business operations."

Sarah, with her focus on tenant satisfaction, nodded in agreement. She understood the importance of aligning property management services with tenant business needs to foster positive relationships and tenant retention. She made a mental note to schedule meetings with their commercial tenants to discuss their business goals and how they could support them.

The third slide depicted "Proactive Issue Resolution and Conflict Management." "3. **Proactive Issue Resolution and Conflict Management.** Despite best efforts, conflicts and issues may arise during the course of the lease term. Commercial property managers must be proactive in addressing tenant concerns, resolving disputes, and managing conflicts in a timely and fair manner. This includes listening to tenant feedback, seeking mutually beneficial solutions, and maintaining professionalism and impartiality in conflict resolution efforts. Proactive issue resolution and conflict management demonstrate commitment to tenant satisfaction and can help preserve tenant relationships and minimize tenant turnover."

David, always focused on operational efficiency, recognized the importance of proactive issue resolution and conflict management in maintaining positive tenant relationships. He made a mental note to develop a protocol for addressing tenant concerns and conflicts promptly and effectively.

The next image showed "Value-Added Services and Tenant Engagement." "4. **Value-Added Services and Tenant Engagement.** Commercial property managers can enhance tenant relationships by offering value-added services and fostering tenant engagement. This includes organizing tenant appreciation events, providing educational workshops or networking opportunities, and offering additional amenities or services that enhance the tenant experience. Value-added services and tenant engagement initiatives strengthen tenant loyalty, increase tenant satisfaction, and contribute to a vibrant and cohesive tenant community."

Lisa, their community engagement expert, understood the importance of offering value-added services and fostering tenant engagement to create a sense of belonging and community among tenants. She began brainstorming ideas for tenant appreciation events and educational workshops to enhance tenant satisfaction and retention.

The fifth slide highlighted "Regular Property Inspections and Maintenance." "5. **Regular Property Inspections and Maintenance.** Maintaining the physical condition of the property is essential for tenant satisfaction and retention. Commercial property managers must conduct regular property inspections to identify maintenance issues or safety concerns, address maintenance requests promptly, and ensure that the property meets the needs and expectations of tenants. Proactive property maintenance demonstrates commitment to tenant comfort, safety, and overall property quality, fostering positive tenant relationships."

Jack stressed the importance of regular property inspections and maintenance in maintaining tenant satisfaction and preserving property value. He encouraged the team to prioritize property upkeep and address maintenance issues promptly to meet tenant expectations.

The final slide displayed "Lease Renewal and Tenant Retention Strategies." "6. **Lease Renewal and Tenant Retention Strategies.** Securing lease renewals and retaining tenants is essential for maintaining property stability and maximizing long-term revenue. Commercial property managers must develop proactive lease renewal strategies, engage with tenants early in the lease term to discuss renewal options, and provide incentives or concessions to encourage lease extensions. Additionally, implementing tenant retention programs, such as loyalty incentives or personalized services, can help strengthen tenant relationships and increase tenant loyalty."

Jack turned off the projector and faced his team, a sense of determination evident in his expression. "Managing commercial tenant relationships is not just about resolving issues—it's about fostering partnerships and ensuring tenant success. Let's approach tenant relationships with empathy, communication, and a commitment to delivering exceptional service."

The room fell silent, each team member reflecting on their role in managing commercial tenant relationships and contributing to tenant satisfaction and property success. Jack could see the determination in their eyes—a shared commitment to building strong tenant relationships and achieving excellence in commercial property management.

Maintenance and Repairs for Commercial Properties

As the team continued their journey through the intricacies of commercial property management, Jack Miller redirected their focus to the critical aspect of maintenance and repairs for commercial properties. He knew that maintaining the physical condition of commercial properties was essential for tenant satisfaction, property value, and overall operational efficiency.

"Team," Jack began, his voice filled with determination. "In our pursuit of excellence in commercial property management, maintenance and repairs play a crucial role. It's not just about fixing things—it's about preserving asset value, ensuring tenant safety, and delivering exceptional service. Let's explore the fourth subpoint: maintenance and repairs for commercial properties."

He clicked the remote, and the screen illuminated with a presentation titled "Maintenance and Repairs for Commercial Properties." "Maintaining the physical condition of commercial properties requires diligence, proactive planning, and a commitment to quality. It is the cornerstone of property performance and tenant satisfaction."

The first slide highlighted "Proactive Maintenance Planning." "1. **Proactive Maintenance Planning.** Effective maintenance and repair strategies for commercial properties begin with proactive planning. Commercial property managers must develop comprehensive maintenance plans that outline routine maintenance tasks, inspection schedules, and repair protocols for all building systems and components. This includes HVAC systems, plumbing, electrical systems, elevators, roofing, and structural elements. Proactive maintenance planning helps identify potential issues before they escalate, extends the lifespan of building systems, and minimizes disruptions to tenant operations."

Jack emphasized the importance of proactive maintenance planning in preserving property value and minimizing downtime for tenants. He recalled instances where proactive maintenance had helped prevent costly repairs and tenant dissatisfaction.

The next slide displayed "Timely Repairs and Emergency Response." "2. **Timely Repairs and Emergency Response.** In addition to routine maintenance, commercial property managers must respond promptly to repair requests and emergency situations to ensure tenant safety and satisfaction. This includes establishing clear procedures for reporting maintenance issues, prioritizing urgent repairs, and maintaining a network of qualified contractors and vendors to address maintenance needs promptly. Timely repairs and emergency response demonstrate a commitment to tenant well-being and help maintain a positive tenant experience."

Sarah, with her focus on tenant satisfaction, nodded in agreement. She understood the importance of addressing maintenance issues promptly to minimize disruptions to tenant operations and ensure tenant safety. She made a mental note to review their emergency response procedures and vendor contracts to ensure they were equipped to handle maintenance requests effectively.

The third slide depicted "Budgeting for Maintenance and Repairs." "3. **Budgeting for Maintenance and Repairs.** Commercial property managers must allocate sufficient resources for maintenance and repairs to ensure the ongoing upkeep of the property. This includes budgeting for routine maintenance expenses, planned capital improvements, and unforeseen repairs or emergencies. Commercial property managers must balance the need for cost-effective solutions with maintaining property quality and tenant satisfaction. Effective budgeting for maintenance and repairs is essential for preserving property value and maximizing long-term returns on investment."

David, always focused on maximizing returns, recognized the importance of budgeting for maintenance and repairs to ensure the ongoing upkeep of their properties. He made a mental note to review their maintenance budget and identify opportunities to optimize spending while maintaining property quality.

The next image showed "Vendor Management and Quality Control." "4. **Vendor Management and Quality Control.** Commercial property managers must carefully select and manage vendors and contractors to perform maintenance and repair work on their properties. This includes vetting vendors for qualifications, experience, and reliability, obtaining multiple bids for larger projects, and monitoring the quality of work performed. Commercial property managers must establish clear expectations, communicate effectively with vendors, and conduct regular inspections to ensure that maintenance and repair work meets quality standards and tenant expectations."

Lisa, their vendor management expert, understood the importance of selecting reliable vendors and maintaining quality control to ensure the success of maintenance and repair projects. She began reviewing their vendor selection process and establishing quality control measures to ensure consistent service delivery.

The fifth slide highlighted "Preventive Maintenance Programs." "5. **Preventive Maintenance Programs.** Implementing preventive maintenance programs is essential for minimizing the risk of unexpected breakdowns and extending the lifespan of building systems and components. This includes conducting regular inspections, lubricating moving parts, replacing worn-out components, and performing preventive maintenance tasks according to manufacturer recommendations and industry best practices. Preventive maintenance programs help identify potential issues early, reduce repair costs, and ensure the ongoing reliability and efficiency of building systems."

Jack stressed the importance of preventive maintenance programs in proactively addressing maintenance issues and preserving property value. He encouraged the team to develop tailored preventive maintenance plans for their properties to minimize downtime and tenant disruptions.

The final slide displayed "Sustainable Maintenance Practices." "6. **Sustainable Maintenance Practices.** Commercial property managers should embrace sustainable maintenance practices to reduce environmental impact, lower operating costs, and enhance property value. This includes implementing energy-efficient upgrades, water conservation measures, waste reduction initiatives, and green building certifications. Sustainable maintenance practices not only benefit the environment but also contribute to tenant satisfaction, attract environmentally conscious tenants, and differentiate the property in the market."

Jack turned off the projector and faced his team, a sense of accomplishment evident in his expression. "Maintenance and repairs are not just tasks—they're opportunities to preserve property value, ensure tenant satisfaction, and demonstrate our commitment to excellence. Let's approach maintenance with diligence, innovation, and a commitment to delivering exceptional service."

The room fell silent, each team member reflecting on their role in maintaining the physical condition of their commercial properties and contributing to tenant satisfaction and property success. Jack could see the determination in their eyes—a shared commitment to mastering maintenance and repairs and achieving excellence in commercial property management.

Financial Management of Commercial Assets

As the team delved deeper into the intricacies of commercial property management, Jack Miller redirected their focus to the critical aspect of financial management for commercial assets. He knew that effective financial management was essential for maximizing returns, minimizing risks, and ensuring the long-term success of their properties.

"Team," Jack began, his voice resonating with authority. "In our pursuit of excellence in commercial property management, financial management plays a pivotal role. It's not just about numbers—it's about strategic decision-making, risk mitigation, and maximizing asset performance. Let's explore the fifth subpoint: financial management of commercial assets."

He clicked the remote, and the screen illuminated with a presentation titled "Financial Management of Commercial Assets." "Managing the finances of commercial properties requires foresight, analysis, and a commitment to financial integrity. It is the key to unlocking the full potential of our assets and achieving long-term success."

The first slide highlighted "Budgeting and Financial Planning." "1. **Budgeting and Financial Planning.** Effective financial management begins with comprehensive budgeting and financial planning. Commercial property managers must develop annual budgets that forecast income and expenses, allocate resources for operating expenses, capital improvements, and debt service, and identify opportunities for revenue growth and cost savings. Budgeting and financial planning provide a roadmap for managing cash flow, optimizing asset performance, and achieving financial objectives."

Jack emphasized the importance of budgeting and financial planning in setting strategic priorities and aligning financial resources with property goals. He recalled instances where careful budgeting had helped them anticipate market fluctuations and allocate resources effectively.

The next slide displayed "Rent Collection Processes." "2. **Rent Collection Processes.** Timely rent collection is essential for maintaining property cash flow and meeting financial obligations. Commercial property managers must establish clear rent collection processes, communicate rent payment expectations to tenants, and implement systems for tracking rent payments and addressing delinquencies. This includes offering multiple payment options, providing incentives for on-time payments, and following up promptly on overdue accounts. Effective rent collection processes ensure consistent cash flow and minimize the risk of rent defaults."

Sarah, with her focus on financial stability, nodded in agreement. She understood the importance of establishing robust rent collection processes to maintain property cash flow and minimize revenue disruptions. She made a mental note to review their rent collection procedures and implement improvements to streamline the process.

The third slide depicted "Managing Operating Expenses." "3. **Managing Operating Expenses.** Controlling operating expenses is essential for optimizing property performance and maximizing net operating income. Commercial property managers must monitor and analyze operating expenses regularly, identify cost-saving opportunities, and implement measures to reduce unnecessary expenditures. This includes negotiating favorable contracts with vendors, implementing energy-efficient measures, and leveraging economies of scale through portfolio management. Effective management of operating expenses enhances property profitability and increases investor returns."

David, always focused on maximizing returns, recognized the importance of managing operating expenses to maintain property profitability. He made a mental note to conduct a thorough analysis of their operating expenses and identify areas for cost reduction and efficiency improvement.

The next image showed "Financial Reporting and Analysis." "4. **Financial Reporting and Analysis.** Commercial property managers must provide accurate and timely financial reporting to stakeholders, including property owners, investors, and lenders. This includes preparing monthly, quarterly, and annual financial statements, analyzing key performance indicators, and presenting financial insights and recommendations for strategic decision-making. Financial reporting and analysis enable stakeholders to assess property performance, identify trends, and make informed investment decisions."

Lisa, their financial expert, understood the importance of financial reporting and analysis in providing transparency and accountability to stakeholders. She began reviewing their financial reporting processes and identifying opportunities to enhance the quality and relevance of financial information provided to stakeholders.

The fifth slide highlighted "Handling Delinquencies and Evictions." "5. **Handling Delinquencies and Evictions.** Despite best efforts, delinquencies and evictions may occur during the lease term, impacting property cash flow and financial stability. Commercial property managers must have policies and procedures in place for handling delinquent accounts, including issuing notices, negotiating payment plans, and pursuing legal action if necessary. This includes understanding landlord-tenant laws and regulations governing evictions and ensuring compliance with due process requirements. Proactive management of delinquencies and evictions minimizes financial losses and preserves property value."

Jack stressed the importance of proactive management of delinquencies and evictions in protecting property cash flow and financial stability. He encouraged the team to develop clear policies and procedures for handling delinquent accounts and evictions to mitigate risks and protect investor interests.

The final slide displayed "Tax Considerations for Property Managers." "6. **Tax Considerations for Property Managers.** Commercial property managers must understand the tax implications of property ownership and management and develop strategies to optimize tax efficiency. This includes leveraging tax deductions and credits available for commercial real estate, such as depreciation, interest expenses, and capital improvements. Commercial property managers must work closely with tax professionals to ensure compliance with tax laws and regulations and maximize tax benefits for property owners and investors."

Jack turned off the projector and faced his team, a sense of satisfaction evident in his expression. "Financial management is not just about numbers—it's about strategic decision-making and ensuring the long-term financial health of our properties. Let's approach financial management with diligence, insight, and a commitment to maximizing returns for our stakeholders."

The room fell silent, each team member reflecting on their role in managing the finances of their commercial properties and contributing to long-term property success. Jack could see the determination in their eyes—a shared commitment to mastering financial management and achieving excellence in commercial property management.

Legal Considerations in Commercial Leasing

As the team continued their exploration of commercial property management, Jack Miller redirected their attention to the critical aspect of legal considerations in commercial leasing. He knew that navigating legal complexities was essential for mitigating risks, ensuring compliance, and protecting the interests of their properties and tenants.

"Team," Jack began, his voice filled with gravitas. "In our pursuit of excellence in commercial property management, understanding legal considerations in commercial leasing is paramount. It's not just about signing contracts—it's about safeguarding our properties, mitigating risks, and fostering positive tenant relationships. Let's explore the sixth subpoint: legal considerations in commercial leasing."

He clicked the remote, and the screen illuminated with a presentation titled "Legal Considerations in Commercial Leasing." "Navigating the legal landscape of commercial leasing demands knowledge, diligence, and a commitment to compliance. It is the foundation of responsible property management and tenant relations."

The first slide highlighted "Understanding Landlord-Tenant Laws." "1. **Understanding Landlord-Tenant Laws.**

Commercial property managers must have a thorough understanding of landlord-tenant laws and regulations governing commercial leases at the federal, state, and local levels. This includes understanding the rights and obligations of landlords and tenants, lease termination procedures, eviction laws, fair housing regulations, and other legal considerations specific to commercial leases. Knowledge of landlord-tenant laws ensures compliance, protects tenant rights, and mitigates legal risks for property owners and managers."

Jack emphasized the importance of understanding landlord-tenant laws in ensuring compliance and protecting the interests of their properties and tenants. He recalled instances where a thorough understanding of legal requirements had helped them resolve disputes and maintain positive tenant relationships.

The next slide displayed "Lease Agreements and Contracts."

"2. **Lease Agreements and Contracts.** Commercial property managers must draft clear and comprehensive lease agreements that outline the rights and responsibilities of landlords and tenants. This includes defining lease terms, rental rates, lease duration, security deposit requirements, maintenance responsibilities, and other terms and conditions of the lease. Commercial lease agreements should be reviewed by legal professionals to ensure compliance with applicable laws and regulations and protect the interests of both parties."

Sarah, with her attention to detail, nodded in agreement. She understood the importance of drafting thorough lease agreements to clarify expectations and prevent misunderstandings between landlords and tenants. She made a mental note to review their lease templates and ensure they were up-to-date and legally compliant.

The third slide depicted "Handling Evictions Legally." "3. **Handling Evictions Legally.** In the unfortunate event of lease violations or tenant non-payment, commercial property managers must follow legal procedures for evictions in accordance with landlord-tenant laws. This includes providing proper notice to tenants, filing eviction lawsuits if necessary, and adhering to due process requirements throughout the eviction process. Commercial property managers must understand the legal grounds for eviction, such as non-payment of rent, lease violations, or property damage, and ensure compliance with eviction laws to avoid legal repercussions."

David, always focused on risk mitigation, recognized the importance of handling evictions legally to protect property interests and maintain legal compliance. He made a mental note to review their eviction procedures and ensure they followed due process requirements in all eviction cases.

The next image showed "Dealing with Disputes and Litigation." "4. **Dealing with Disputes and Litigation.** Commercial property managers may encounter disputes or legal challenges with tenants, contractors, or other parties involved in property operations. In such cases, commercial property managers must take proactive steps to resolve disputes amicably through negotiation or alternative dispute resolution methods. If disputes escalate to litigation, commercial property managers should seek legal counsel and prepare a strong defense to protect property interests and minimize legal exposure."

Lisa, their legal liaison, understood the importance of

handling disputes and litigation professionally to minimize legal risks and protect property interests. She began reviewing their dispute resolution procedures and identifying opportunities to enhance their conflict resolution strategies.

The fifth slide highlighted "Ensuring Fair Housing Compliance." "5. **Ensuring Fair Housing Compliance.** Commercial property managers must adhere to fair housing laws and regulations to prevent discrimination and ensure equal housing opportunities for all tenants. This includes understanding protected classes under fair housing laws, such as race, color, national origin, religion, sex, familial status, and disability, and implementing policies and procedures to prevent discriminatory practices in tenant selection, advertising, and property management activities. Fair housing compliance is essential for maintaining legal compliance and fostering an inclusive and equitable rental environment."

Jack stressed the importance of fair housing compliance in creating an inclusive and equitable rental environment for all tenants. He encouraged the team to prioritize fair housing training and education to ensure compliance with fair housing laws and regulations.

The final slide displayed "Risk Management and Liability." "6. **Risk Management and Liability.** Commercial property managers must identify and mitigate legal risks associated with property operations to protect property owners and investors from liability. This includes implementing risk management strategies, such as maintaining adequate insurance coverage, conducting regular property inspections, addressing safety hazards, and adhering to industry standards and best practices. By proactively managing risks, commercial property managers can minimize legal exposure and safeguard property interests."

Jack turned off the projector and faced his team, a sense of resolve evident in his expression. "Legal considerations are not obstacles—they're opportunities to demonstrate our commitment to ethical and responsible property management. Let's approach legal compliance with diligence, integrity, and a commitment to protecting the interests of our properties and tenants."

The room fell silent, each team member reflecting on their role in ensuring legal compliance and mitigating risks in their commercial property operations. Jack could see the determination in their eyes—a shared commitment to mastering legal considerations and achieving excellence in commercial property management.

Chapter 12: Sustainable Property Management

Benefits of Green Buildings

As the team embarked on their exploration of sustainable property management, Jack Miller directed their attention to the first subpoint: the benefits of green buildings. He knew that understanding the advantages of environmentally friendly practices was essential for embracing sustainability and fostering positive change in their property management approach.

"Team," Jack began, his voice resonating with enthusiasm. "In our journey toward sustainable property management, understanding the benefits of green buildings is crucial. It's not just about being environmentally conscious—it's about reaping the rewards of sustainable practices for our properties, tenants, and the planet. Let's explore the first subpoint: the benefits of green buildings."

He clicked the remote, and the screen illuminated with a

presentation titled "Benefits of Green Buildings." "Embracing sustainability in property management offers a multitude of benefits that extend beyond environmental impact. It enhances property value, improves tenant satisfaction, and promotes long-term financial viability."

The first slide highlighted "Energy Efficiency and Cost Savings." "1. **Energy Efficiency and Cost Savings.** Green buildings are designed to maximize energy efficiency, reducing energy consumption and operating costs. Features such as energy-efficient lighting, HVAC systems, and insulation help minimize utility expenses, resulting in significant cost savings for property owners and tenants. By investing in energy-efficient technologies and practices, property managers can lower operating expenses, increase net operating income, and enhance property value."

Jack emphasized the importance of energy efficiency in reducing operational costs and increasing financial returns. He recalled instances where energy-saving measures had resulted in substantial cost savings and improved property performance.

The next slide displayed "Improved Indoor Air Quality and Health." "2. **Improved Indoor Air Quality and Health.** Green buildings prioritize indoor air quality by using low-emission materials, implementing effective ventilation systems, and maintaining optimal humidity levels. Improved indoor air quality enhances occupant health and well-being, reducing the risk of respiratory illnesses, allergies, and other health issues. By providing a healthier indoor environment, green buildings can improve tenant satisfaction, productivity, and retention."

Sarah, with her focus on tenant satisfaction, nodded in

agreement. She understood the importance of indoor air quality in creating a comfortable and healthy environment for tenants. She made a mental note to prioritize indoor air quality in their property management practices to enhance tenant well-being.

The third slide depicted "Enhanced Property Value and Marketability." "3. **Enhanced Property Value and Marketability.** Green buildings command higher property values and attract environmentally conscious tenants, investors, and occupants. Sustainability features such as LEED certification, energy-efficient design, and green building materials differentiate properties in the market, increasing their appeal and marketability. By investing in sustainability, property managers can enhance property value, attract premium tenants, and achieve higher rental rates and occupancy levels."

David, always focused on maximizing returns, recognized the potential for increased property value and marketability through sustainability initiatives. He made a mental note to explore opportunities for incorporating green features into their properties to capture value and attract quality tenants.

The next image showed "Reduced Environmental Impact and Carbon Footprint." "4. **Reduced Environmental Impact and Carbon Footprint.** Green buildings minimize environmental impact and contribute to sustainability goals by conserving resources, reducing greenhouse gas emissions, and promoting renewable energy use. Features such as energy-efficient appliances, water-saving fixtures, and onsite renewable energy systems help reduce carbon footprint and mitigate climate change. By prioritizing sustainability, property managers can demonstrate environmental leadership and contribute to a healthier and more sustainable future."

Lisa, their environmental advocate, understood the importance of reducing environmental impact through sustainable practices. She began researching innovative technologies and strategies for reducing carbon footprint in their properties to align with sustainability goals.

The fifth slide highlighted "Regulatory Compliance and Future-Proofing." "5. **Regulatory Compliance and Future-Proofing.** Green buildings are better positioned to comply with increasingly stringent environmental regulations and building codes. By adopting sustainable practices and green building standards, property managers can future-proof their properties against regulatory changes and market trends. Compliance with green building certifications and standards also enhances property resilience, reducing risks associated with climate change and environmental degradation."

Jack stressed the importance of regulatory compliance and future-proofing in adapting to evolving market demands and regulatory requirements. He encouraged the team to stay abreast of green building certifications and standards to ensure their properties remained competitive and resilient.

The final slide displayed "Community and Stakeholder Engagement." "6. **Community and Stakeholder Engagement.** Green buildings foster community engagement and stakeholder collaboration by promoting sustainability awareness and environmental stewardship. Property managers can engage with tenants, employees, investors, and local communities to promote sustainable practices, host educational events, and participate in green initiatives. By fostering a culture of sustainability, green buildings can strengthen community ties, enhance brand reputation, and create a positive impact on society."

Jack turned off the projector and faced his team, a sense of optimism evident in his expression. "Embracing sustainability isn't just about benefits—it's about creating a better future for our properties, tenants, and communities. Let's leverage the benefits of green buildings to drive positive change and achieve excellence in sustainable property management."

The room fell silent, each team member reflecting on the potential of green buildings to transform their approach to property management and contribute to a more sustainable future. Jack could see the determination in their eyes—a shared commitment to embracing sustainability and making a positive impact through their property management practices.

Implementing Energy Efficiency Measures

As the team delved deeper into the realm of sustainable property management, Jack Miller redirected their focus to the second subpoint: implementing energy efficiency measures. He knew that taking proactive steps to reduce energy consumption was essential for maximizing sustainability and minimizing environmental impact in their property management practices.

"Team," Jack began, his voice infused with determination. "In our quest for sustainable property management, implementing energy efficiency measures is paramount. It's not just about reducing utility bills—it's about reducing our carbon footprint and contributing to a greener future. Let's explore the second subpoint: implementing energy efficiency measures."

He clicked the remote, and the screen illuminated with a

presentation titled "Implementing Energy Efficiency Measures." "Embracing energy efficiency in property management offers a multitude of benefits, from cost savings to environmental stewardship. It's a cornerstone of sustainable property management and a catalyst for positive change."

The first slide highlighted "Energy Audit and Assessment." "1. **Energy Audit and Assessment.** Before implementing energy efficiency measures, property managers should conduct a comprehensive energy audit to identify areas of energy waste and inefficiency. This involves analyzing energy consumption patterns, assessing building systems and equipment, and identifying opportunities for improvement. An energy audit provides valuable insights into potential energy-saving measures and helps prioritize investments for maximum impact."

Jack emphasized the importance of conducting energy audits to inform strategic decision-making and identify opportunities for energy savings. He recalled instances where energy audits had revealed significant opportunities for cost savings and environmental impact reduction.

The next slide displayed "Upgrading Building Systems and Equipment." "2. **Upgrading Building Systems and Equipment.** Implementing energy-efficient building systems and equipment is key to reducing energy consumption and enhancing property performance. This includes upgrading HVAC systems, lighting fixtures, water heaters, and appliances to energy-efficient models that meet or exceed ENERGY STAR® standards. Investing in high-efficiency equipment not only reduces energy costs but also improves tenant comfort and satisfaction."

Sarah, with her focus on tenant satisfaction, nodded in

agreement. She understood the importance of upgrading building systems and equipment to create a comfortable and energy-efficient environment for tenants. She made a mental note to explore opportunities for equipment upgrades in their properties to improve energy performance.

The third slide depicted "Installing Energy-Saving Technologies." "3. **Installing Energy-Saving Technologies.** In addition to upgrading building systems, property managers can implement energy-saving technologies to further reduce energy consumption. This includes installing programmable thermostats, occupancy sensors, smart lighting controls, and building automation systems to optimize energy use and reduce waste. Energy-saving technologies enhance operational efficiency, lower utility bills, and contribute to a more sustainable built environment."

David, always focused on maximizing returns, recognized the potential for energy-saving technologies to reduce operating costs and increase property profitability. He made a mental note to explore innovative technologies for improving energy efficiency in their properties to capture cost savings and enhance asset value.

The next image showed "Promoting Energy Conservation Practices." "4. **Promoting Energy Conservation Practices.** Property managers can encourage energy conservation among tenants and building occupants through education and awareness initiatives. This includes providing energy-saving tips, conducting energy efficiency workshops, and implementing tenant engagement programs to promote sustainable behaviors. By fostering a culture of energy conservation, property managers can empower tenants to reduce their energy consumption and contribute to overall energy savings."

Lisa, their tenant engagement expert, understood the importance of promoting energy conservation practices to create a culture of sustainability within their properties. She began planning educational workshops and tenant engagement activities to raise awareness and encourage energy-saving behaviors among tenants.

The fifth slide highlighted "Monitoring and Benchmarking Energy Performance." "5. **Monitoring and Benchmarking Energy Performance.** Property managers should regularly monitor and benchmark energy performance to track progress, identify trends, and measure the impact of energy efficiency measures. This involves collecting and analyzing energy data, comparing energy usage against benchmarks and industry standards, and identifying areas for improvement. Monitoring energy performance enables property managers to identify opportunities for further energy savings and demonstrate the effectiveness of energy efficiency initiatives to stakeholders."

Jack stressed the importance of monitoring and benchmarking energy performance to evaluate the effectiveness of energy efficiency measures and identify opportunities for further improvement. He encouraged the team to establish robust energy monitoring systems and track energy usage data to inform decision-making and measure progress toward sustainability goals.

The final slide displayed "Seeking Incentives and Rebates." "6. **Seeking Incentives and Rebates.** Property managers should explore available incentives and rebates for implementing energy efficiency measures from utility companies, government agencies, and other organizations. This includes rebates for energy-efficient equipment upgrades, incentives for renewable energy installations, and financing options for energy conservation projects. Seeking incentives and rebates can help offset upfront costs and accelerate the return on investment for energy efficiency initiatives."

Jack turned off the projector and faced his team, a sense of accomplishment evident in his expression. "Implementing energy efficiency measures isn't just about reducing costs—it's about making a positive impact on the environment and enhancing property performance. Let's leverage these strategies to create a more sustainable future for our properties and communities."

The room fell silent, each team member reflecting on their role in implementing energy efficiency measures and contributing to a greener future through their property management practices. Jack could see the determination in their eyes—a shared commitment to embracing sustainability and driving positive change in their industry.

Waste Management and Recycling Programs

As the team continued their exploration of sustainable property management, Jack Miller redirected their attention to the third subpoint: waste management and recycling programs. He knew that implementing effective waste management strategies was essential for minimizing environmental impact and promoting sustainability in their property operations.

"Team," Jack began, his voice filled with conviction. "In our pursuit of sustainable property management, waste management and recycling programs play a crucial role. It's not just about disposing of waste—it's about reducing landfill waste, conserving resources, and fostering a culture of environmental responsibility. Let's explore the third subpoint: waste management and recycling programs."

He clicked the remote, and the screen illuminated with a presentation titled "Waste Management and Recycling Programs." "Embracing waste reduction and recycling initiatives in property management offers numerous benefits, from conserving resources to reducing pollution. It's a cornerstone of sustainable property management and a catalyst for positive change."

The first slide highlighted "Waste Audit and Assessment." "1. **Waste Audit and Assessment.** Before implementing waste management and recycling programs, property managers should conduct a comprehensive waste audit to assess current waste generation, disposal practices, and recycling opportunities. This involves analyzing waste streams, quantifying waste volumes, and identifying opportunities for waste reduction and recycling. A waste audit provides valuable insights into waste generation patterns and informs the development of effective waste management strategies."

Jack emphasized the importance of conducting waste audits to understand their waste generation patterns and identify opportunities for improvement. He recalled instances where waste audits had revealed significant opportunities for waste reduction and recycling.

The next slide displayed "Source Reduction and Waste Minimization." "2. **Source Reduction and Waste Minimization.** Property managers can minimize waste generation by implementing source reduction strategies and encouraging sustainable consumption practices among tenants and building occupants. This includes reducing packaging waste, implementing green purchasing policies, and promoting reusable alternatives to single-use products. By minimizing waste at the source, property managers can reduce landfill waste and conserve resources."

Sarah, with her focus on sustainability, nodded in agreement. She understood the importance of source reduction in minimizing waste generation and promoting sustainable consumption habits. She made a mental note to explore opportunities for implementing source reduction strategies in their properties to reduce waste.

The third slide depicted "Implementing Recycling Programs." "3. **Implementing Recycling Programs.** Property managers should establish comprehensive recycling programs to divert recyclable materials from landfills and promote resource recovery. This includes providing recycling bins and signage, educating tenants about recycling guidelines, and partnering with waste management companies to facilitate recycling collection and processing. Implementing recycling programs not only reduces landfill waste but also conserves natural resources and reduces greenhouse gas emissions."

David, always focused on maximizing returns, recognized the potential for implementing recycling programs to reduce waste disposal costs and promote sustainability. He made a mental note to explore opportunities for partnering with waste management companies to streamline recycling collection and processing in their properties.

The next image showed "Organic Waste Management." "4. **Organic Waste Management.** Property managers can implement organic waste management programs to divert organic waste from landfills and promote composting and organic waste recycling. This includes providing composting bins in common areas, educating tenants about composting practices, and partnering with composting facilities or community gardens to recycle organic waste. Organic waste management reduces methane emissions from landfills, conserves landfill space, and produces nutrient-rich compost for landscaping and gardening."

Lisa, their environmental advocate, understood the importance of organic waste management in reducing landfill waste and promoting sustainability. She began researching composting options and exploring partnerships with local composting facilities to implement organic waste recycling programs in their properties.

The fifth slide highlighted "Educating Tenants and Building Occupants." "5. **Educating Tenants and Building Occupants.** Property managers should educate tenants and building occupants about waste management best practices, recycling guidelines, and the importance of environmental stewardship. This includes providing educational materials, hosting workshops and events, and communicating regularly about waste reduction and recycling initiatives. By raising awareness and promoting sustainable behaviors, property managers can empower tenants to actively participate in waste reduction efforts."

Jack stressed the importance of tenant education in fostering a culture of environmental responsibility within their properties. He encouraged the team to develop educational materials and communication strategies to engage tenants and promote sustainable behaviors.

The final slide displayed "Monitoring and Evaluation." "6. **Monitoring and Evaluation.** Property managers should regularly monitor and evaluate the effectiveness of waste management and recycling programs to track progress and identify areas for improvement. This involves collecting data on waste generation, recycling rates, and program participation, and analyzing performance metrics to measure the impact of waste reduction initiatives. Monitoring and evaluation enable property managers to identify successes, address challenges, and continuously improve waste management practices."

Jack turned off the projector and faced his team, a sense of determination evident in his expression. "Implementing waste management and recycling programs isn't just about compliance—it's about making a positive impact on the environment and promoting sustainability. Let's leverage these strategies to create a greener future for our properties and communities."

The room fell silent, each team member reflecting on their role in implementing waste management and recycling programs and contributing to a more sustainable future through their property management practices. Jack could see the determination in their eyes—a shared commitment to embracing sustainability and driving positive change in their industry.

Sustainable Landscaping Practices

As the team delved deeper into sustainable property management, Jack Miller redirected their focus to the fourth subpoint: sustainable landscaping practices. He knew that implementing environmentally friendly landscaping techniques was essential for enhancing property aesthetics, conserving resources, and promoting biodiversity.

"Team," Jack began, his voice filled with enthusiasm. "In our journey toward sustainable property management, landscaping plays a vital role. It's not just about curb appeal—it's about creating vibrant outdoor spaces that support biodiversity, conserve water, and minimize environmental impact. Let's explore the fourth subpoint: sustainable landscaping practices."

He clicked the remote, and the screen illuminated with a presentation titled "Sustainable Landscaping Practices." "Embracing sustainable landscaping in property management offers numerous benefits, from reducing water consumption to enhancing property value. It's a cornerstone of sustainable property management and a catalyst for positive change."

The first slide highlighted "Water-Efficient Landscaping Design." "1. **Water-Efficient Landscaping Design.** Property managers can implement water-efficient landscaping designs that minimize water consumption and promote drought-resistant plant species. This includes selecting native or adaptive plants that require less water, incorporating water-saving irrigation systems such as drip irrigation or smart controllers, and designing landscapes to capture and retain rainwater. Water-efficient landscaping designs reduce irrigation needs, conserve water resources, and create resilient outdoor spaces."

Jack emphasized the importance of water-efficient landscaping designs in conserving water and promoting sustainability. He recalled instances where water-efficient landscaping had transformed outdoor spaces and reduced water usage significantly.

The next slide displayed "Xeriscaping and Drought-

Tolerant Plants." "2. **Xeriscaping and Drought-Tolerant Plants.** Property managers can implement xeriscaping principles and incorporate drought-tolerant plants into landscaping designs to reduce water usage and maintenance requirements. This includes selecting plants that are well-adapted to local climate conditions and soil types, mulching to retain soil moisture and suppress weed growth, and minimizing turf grass areas in favor of native ground covers and hardscapes. Xeriscaping and drought-tolerant plants reduce water consumption, minimize landscape maintenance, and enhance property resilience to drought conditions."

Sarah, with her passion for sustainability, nodded in agreement. She understood the importance of xeriscaping and drought-tolerant plants in reducing water usage and promoting environmental resilience. She made a mental note to explore opportunities for incorporating drought-tolerant landscaping into their properties to conserve water.

The third slide depicted "Integrated Pest Management (IPM) Practices." "3. **Integrated Pest Management (IPM) Practices.** Property managers can implement integrated pest management practices to minimize the use of chemical pesticides and promote natural pest control methods. This includes monitoring pest populations, identifying pest-friendly conditions, and implementing preventive measures such as proper plant selection, maintenance, and sanitation. Additionally, property managers can encourage beneficial insects and wildlife that act as natural predators to pest species. Integrated pest management reduces reliance on chemical pesticides, minimizes environmental impact, and promotes ecosystem health."

David, always focused on maximizing returns, recognized the potential for integrated pest management practices to reduce pesticide usage and minimize environmental impact. He made a mental note to explore opportunities for implementing IPM practices in their properties to promote ecosystem health and sustainability.

The next image showed "Permeable Paving and Sustainable Hardscapes." "4. **Permeable Paving and Sustainable Hardscapes.** Property managers can incorporate permeable paving materials and sustainable hardscape features into outdoor spaces to promote stormwater management and reduce runoff. This includes using permeable pavers, gravel, or porous asphalt for driveways, walkways, and patios to allow rainwater to infiltrate the ground and recharge groundwater supplies. Sustainable hardscapes reduce stormwater runoff, prevent erosion, and minimize pollution of waterways."

Lisa, their environmental advocate, understood the importance of permeable paving and sustainable hardscapes in managing stormwater and reducing runoff. She began researching permeable paving options and exploring sustainable hardscape designs to enhance stormwater management in their properties.

The fifth slide highlighted "Natural Habitat Preservation and Biodiversity." "5. **Natural Habitat Preservation and Biodiversity.** Property managers can create and preserve natural habitats within landscapes to support local wildlife and promote biodiversity. This includes preserving existing vegetation, incorporating native plants and wildlife-friendly habitats such as pollinator gardens, birdhouses, and wildlife corridors, and minimizing disturbance to natural ecosystems. Natural habitat preservation enhances biodiversity, supports ecosystem services, and creates opportunities for wildlife observation and enjoyment."

Jack stressed the importance of natural habitat preservation in promoting biodiversity and supporting local ecosystems. He encouraged the team to prioritize habitat preservation in their landscaping designs to create thriving outdoor environments for both residents and wildlife.

The final slide displayed "Educating Residents and Maintenance Staff." "6. **Educating Residents and Maintenance Staff.** Property managers should educate residents and maintenance staff about sustainable landscaping practices, water conservation techniques, and the importance of environmental stewardship. This includes providing educational materials, hosting workshops and training sessions, and communicating regularly about sustainable landscaping initiatives. By raising awareness and promoting sustainable behaviors, property managers can empower residents and staff to actively participate in sustainable landscaping efforts."

Jack turned off the projector and faced his team, a sense of optimism evident in his expression. "Implementing sustainable landscaping practices isn't just about aesthetics—it's about creating vibrant outdoor spaces that support biodiversity, conserve resources, and promote environmental stewardship. Let's leverage these strategies to enhance the beauty and sustainability of our properties."

The room fell silent, each team member reflecting on their role in implementing sustainable landscaping practices and contributing to a greener future through their property management practices. Jack could see the determination in their eyes—a shared commitment to embracing sustainability and driving positive change in their industry.

CHAPTER 12: SUSTAINABLE PROPERTY MANAGEMENT

Green Certifications and Standards

As the team continued their exploration of sustainable property management, Jack Miller redirected their attention to the fifth subpoint: green certifications and standards. He knew that obtaining green certifications and adhering to sustainable building standards was essential for demonstrating environmental leadership and enhancing property value.

"Team," Jack began, his voice resonating with determination. "In our pursuit of sustainable property management, obtaining green certifications and adhering to sustainable building standards is paramount. It's not just about compliance—it's about demonstrating our commitment to environmental stewardship and creating healthier, more sustainable buildings. Let's explore the fifth subpoint: green certifications and standards."

He clicked the remote, and the screen illuminated with a presentation titled "Green Certifications and Standards." "Embracing green certifications and standards in property management offers numerous benefits, from reducing environmental impact to enhancing marketability and tenant satisfaction. It's a cornerstone of sustainable property management and a catalyst for positive change."

The first slide highlighted "LEED Certification." "1. **LEED Certification.** Leadership in Energy and Environmental Design (LEED) certification is a globally recognized green building rating system that recognizes buildings for their sustainability performance. Property managers can pursue LEED certification for their properties by implementing energy-efficient design, water conservation measures, sustainable materials, indoor environmental quality enhancements, and innovation in design. LEED-certified buildings demonstrate environmental leadership, reduce operating costs, and attract environmentally conscious tenants and investors."

Jack emphasized the importance of LEED certification in showcasing environmental leadership and enhancing property value. He recalled instances where LEED-certified buildings had commanded premium rents and attracted high-quality tenants and investors.

The next slide displayed "Energy Star Certification." "2. **Energy Star Certification.** Energy Star certification is awarded to buildings that meet strict energy performance criteria set by the Environmental Protection Agency (EPA). Property managers can pursue Energy Star certification for their properties by implementing energy-efficient practices, using Energy Star-certified equipment and appliances, and benchmarking energy performance using the Energy Star Portfolio Manager tool. Energy Star-certified buildings are more energy-efficient, cost-effective to operate, and environmentally responsible."

Sarah, with her focus on energy efficiency, nodded in agreement. She understood the importance of Energy Star certification in recognizing energy-efficient buildings and reducing energy consumption. She made a mental note to explore opportunities for pursuing Energy Star certification in their properties to enhance energy performance.

The third slide depicted "WELL Building Standard." "3. **WELL Building Standard.** The WELL Building Standard focuses on promoting occupant health and well-being by addressing factors such as air quality, water quality, lighting, thermal comfort, and mental well-being. Property managers can pursue WELL certification for their properties by implementing features and practices that enhance occupant health and well-being, such as advanced air and water filtration systems, daylighting strategies, biophilic design elements, and wellness programs. WELL-certified buildings prioritize occupant health, productivity, and satisfaction."

David, always focused on tenant satisfaction, recognized the potential for WELL certification in promoting occupant health and well-being. He made a mental note to explore opportunities for incorporating wellness features into their properties to enhance tenant satisfaction and retention.

The next image showed "Green Globes Certification." "4. **Green Globes Certification.** Green Globes is a building certification program that assesses the environmental performance and sustainability of buildings based on criteria such as energy efficiency, water conservation, indoor environmental quality, and resource management. Property managers can pursue Green Globes certification for their properties by completing a comprehensive assessment and implementing sustainable practices that align with program requirements. Green Globes-certified buildings demonstrate commitment to sustainability, environmental responsibility, and occupant comfort."

Lisa, their environmental advocate, understood the importance of Green Globes certification in recognizing sustainable buildings and promoting environmental responsibility. She began researching Green Globes certification requirements and exploring opportunities for pursuing certification in their properties.

The fifth slide highlighted "BREEAM Certification." "5. **BREEAM Certification.** Building Research Establishment

Environmental Assessment Method (BREEAM) is a leading sustainability assessment method for master planning projects, infrastructure, and buildings. Property managers can pursue BREEAM certification for their properties by achieving high scores across various sustainability categories, including energy, water, materials, pollution, and health and well-being. BREEAM-certified buildings demonstrate superior environmental performance, resilience, and long-term sustainability."

Jack stressed the importance of BREEAM certification in assessing and recognizing sustainable buildings' environmental performance. He encouraged the team to explore opportunities for pursuing BREEAM certification in their properties to showcase their commitment to sustainability and environmental stewardship.

The final slide displayed "Compliance with Local Green Building Codes." "6. **Compliance with Local Green Building Codes.** Property managers should ensure compliance with local green building codes and regulations to meet minimum sustainability requirements and promote environmental responsibility. This includes adhering to green building ordinances, energy codes, water efficiency standards, and other sustainability mandates established by local authorities. Compliance with local green building codes demonstrates commitment to sustainability, environmental compliance, and community well-being."

Jack turned off the projector and faced his team, a sense of accomplishment evident in his expression. "Obtaining green certifications and adhering to sustainable building standards isn't just about recognition—it's about demonstrating our commitment to environmental stewardship and creating healthier, more sustainable buildings. Let's leverage these certifications and standards to enhance the sustainability and marketability of our properties."

The room fell silent, each team member reflecting on their role in pursuing green certifications and standards and contributing to a more sustainable future through their property management practices. Jack could see the determination in their eyes—a shared commitment to embracing sustainability and driving positive change in their industry.

Educating Tenants on Sustainability

As the team journeyed further into the realm of sustainable property management, Jack Miller redirected their focus to the sixth subpoint: educating tenants on sustainability. He understood that tenant education was essential for fostering a culture of environmental responsibility and promoting sustainable behaviors within their properties.

"Team," Jack began, his voice brimming with enthusiasm. "In our quest for sustainable property management, educating tenants on sustainability is crucial. It's not just about implementing green initiatives—it's about empowering our tenants to embrace sustainable practices and become active participants in our sustainability efforts. Let's explore the sixth subpoint: educating tenants on sustainability."

He clicked the remote, and the screen illuminated with a presentation titled "Educating Tenants on Sustainability." "Embracing tenant education in property management offers numerous benefits, from promoting environmental awareness to fostering a sense of community and collaboration. It's a cornerstone of sustainable property management and a catalyst for positive change."

The first slide highlighted "Creating Educational Materials."

"1. **Creating Educational Materials.** Property managers can develop educational materials such as brochures, flyers, and newsletters to communicate sustainability initiatives, tips, and resources to tenants. This includes information on energy and water conservation, waste reduction and recycling, sustainable transportation options, and green living tips. Educational materials serve as valuable resources to inform and engage tenants in sustainable practices."

Jack emphasized the importance of creating educational materials to communicate sustainability initiatives effectively. He recalled instances where informative brochures and newsletters had sparked tenant interest and participation in sustainability programs.

The next slide displayed "Hosting Workshops and Events."

"2. **Hosting Workshops and Events.** Property managers can host workshops, seminars, and events to educate tenants on sustainability topics and provide hands-on learning experiences. This includes workshops on energy-saving techniques, composting and gardening demonstrations, recycling drives, and green living expos. Hosting workshops and events creates opportunities for tenants to learn, ask questions, and engage with sustainability experts and resources."

Sarah, with her passion for community engagement, nodded in agreement. She understood the importance of hosting workshops and events to create meaningful experiences for tenants and promote sustainability awareness. She made a mental note to organize workshops and events that would resonate with their tenant community and inspire sustainable behaviors.

The third slide depicted "Implementing Green Challenges and Competitions." "3. **Implementing Green Challenges and Competitions.** Property managers can organize green challenges and competitions to motivate and incentivize tenants to adopt sustainable behaviors. This includes energy-saving challenges, recycling competitions, water conservation contests, and sustainable transportation initiatives. Implementing green challenges fosters friendly competition, encourages participation, and rewards sustainable actions."

David, always focused on tenant satisfaction, recognized the potential for green challenges and competitions to engage and motivate tenants. He made a mental note to explore opportunities for implementing green challenges and competitions that would resonate with their tenant community and drive sustainable behaviors.

The next image showed "Providing Sustainable Living Guides." "4. **Providing Sustainable Living Guides.** Property managers can provide tenants with sustainable living guides or handbooks that offer practical tips, resources, and recommendations for living a more eco-friendly lifestyle. This includes information on energy-efficient appliances, water-saving fixtures, eco-friendly cleaning products, and sustainable transportation options. Sustainable living guides empower tenants to make informed choices and adopt sustainable practices in their daily lives."

Lisa, their environmental advocate, understood the importance of providing sustainable living guides to empower tenants with practical knowledge and resources. She began compiling information and recommendations for sustainable living guides that would resonate with their tenant community and promote eco-friendly habits.

The fifth slide highlighted "Facilitating Tenant Engagement Platforms." "5. **Facilitating Tenant Engagement Platforms.** Property managers can create online platforms or community forums where tenants can share ideas, ask questions, and connect with resources related to sustainability. This includes social media groups, online forums, and community portals dedicated to sustainability topics. Facilitating tenant engagement platforms encourages collaboration, fosters a sense of community, and provides opportunities for tenants to support each other in adopting sustainable practices."

Jack stressed the importance of facilitating tenant engagement platforms to create spaces for dialogue and collaboration around sustainability. He encouraged the team to leverage technology and community-building strategies to foster meaningful connections and promote sustainable behaviors among tenants.

The final slide displayed "Engaging Tenants in Sustainable Initiatives." "6. **Engaging Tenants in Sustainable Initiatives.** Property managers should actively involve tenants in the planning, implementation, and evaluation of sustainability initiatives to foster a sense of ownership and accountability. This includes soliciting tenant feedback, forming tenant sustainability committees, and inviting tenant participation in sustainability projects and decision-making processes. Engaging tenants in sustainable initiatives promotes a sense of community ownership and empowers tenants to become champions of sustainability."

Jack turned off the projector and faced his team, a sense of determination evident in his expression. "Educating tenants on sustainability isn't just about sharing information—it's about empowering them to become active participants in our sustainability journey. Let's leverage these strategies to educate, inspire, and engage our tenants in creating a more sustainable future together."

The room fell silent, each team member reflecting on their role in educating tenants on sustainability and fostering a culture of environmental responsibility within their properties. Jack could see the determination in their eyes—a shared commitment to embracing sustainability and driving positive change in their industry.

13

Chapter 13: Handling Difficult Situations

Dealing with Problematic Tenants

As the team delved into the complexities of property management, Jack Miller redirected their attention to a critical topic: dealing with problematic tenants. He knew that effectively handling difficult situations was essential for maintaining property harmony and ensuring tenant satisfaction.

"Team," Jack began, his tone serious yet resolute. "In our line of work, dealing with problematic tenants is inevitable. It's not just about resolving conflicts—it's about maintaining a positive living environment for all residents. Let's explore the first subpoint: dealing with problematic tenants."

He clicked the remote, and the screen illuminated with a presentation titled "Dealing with Problematic Tenants." "Navigating challenging tenant situations requires empathy, communication skills, and a proactive approach. It's a crucial aspect of property management and a test of our professionalism."

The first slide highlighted "Early Intervention Strategies."

"1. **Early Intervention Strategies.** Property managers should adopt early intervention strategies to address potential issues before they escalate. This includes regular communication with tenants, addressing complaints promptly, and setting clear expectations regarding property rules and regulations. Early intervention minimizes conflicts and fosters a proactive approach to problem-solving."

Jack emphasized the importance of early intervention in preventing conflicts from escalating. He recalled instances where proactive communication had resolved potential issues before they became major concerns.

The next slide displayed "Active Listening and Empathy."

"2. **Active Listening and Empathy.** Property managers should practice active listening and empathy when dealing with problematic tenants. This involves listening attentively to tenant concerns, acknowledging their perspectives, and demonstrating understanding and compassion. Active listening and empathy build rapport, de-escalate tense situations, and facilitate constructive dialogue."

Sarah, with her strong interpersonal skills, nodded in agreement. She understood the importance of active listening and empathy in fostering positive tenant relationships. She made a mental note to approach difficult situations with patience and understanding.

The third slide depicted "Setting Boundaries and Enforcing Policies." "3. **Setting Boundaries and Enforcing Policies.** Property managers should establish clear boundaries and enforce property policies consistently. This includes communicating property rules and expectations to tenants, addressing violations promptly, and implementing consequences for repeated infractions. Setting boundaries and enforcing policies maintain order and ensure a safe and respectful living environment for all residents."

David, always focused on maintaining property standards, recognized the importance of setting boundaries and enforcing policies to uphold property integrity. He made a mental note to review property rules with tenants regularly and address any violations promptly.

The next image showed "Conflict Resolution Techniques." "4. **Conflict Resolution Techniques.** Property managers should be equipped with effective conflict resolution techniques to resolve disputes amicably. This includes identifying underlying issues, facilitating open communication between parties, and exploring mutually beneficial solutions. Conflict resolution techniques de-escalate conflicts, restore relationships, and prevent further escalation."

Lisa, their problem solver, nodded in agreement. She understood the importance of employing conflict resolution techniques to navigate challenging tenant situations. She made a mental note to approach conflicts with a solution-oriented mindset and facilitate constructive dialogue between parties.

The fifth slide highlighted "Documentation and Record-Keeping." "5. **Documentation and Record-Keeping.** Property managers should maintain thorough documentation and records of tenant communications, complaints, and resolutions. This includes documenting lease agreements, incident reports, and correspondence with tenants. Documentation provides a clear record of events, protects property interests, and serves as evidence in case of disputes or legal proceedings."

Jack stressed the importance of documentation and record-keeping in protecting property interests and mitigating risks. He encouraged the team to maintain accurate records of tenant interactions and resolutions to ensure accountability and transparency.

The final slide displayed "Seeking Legal Advice When Necessary." "6. **Seeking Legal Advice When Necessary.** Property managers should seek legal advice from qualified professionals when faced with complex or contentious tenant situations. This includes consulting with attorneys specializing in landlord-tenant law to navigate legal complexities, understand rights and responsibilities, and pursue appropriate legal remedies. Seeking legal advice ensures compliance with applicable laws and protects property interests."

Jack turned off the projector and faced his team, a sense of determination evident in his expression. "Dealing with problematic tenants requires patience, professionalism, and a proactive approach. Let's leverage these strategies to address challenges effectively and maintain a positive living environment for all residents."

The room fell silent, each team member reflecting on their role in handling difficult situations and fostering a harmonious community within their properties. Jack could see the determination in their eyes—a shared commitment to professionalism and excellence in property management.

Managing Property Crises

As the team continued their exploration of handling difficult situations in property management, Jack Miller redirected their focus to another critical aspect: managing property crises. He knew that effectively managing crises was essential for safeguarding property assets and ensuring tenant safety and satisfaction.

"Team," Jack began, his voice steady yet authoritative. "In our line of work, property crises can arise unexpectedly, posing significant challenges to our operations and reputation. It's not just about reacting—it's about implementing swift and effective crisis management strategies. Let's explore the second subpoint: managing property crises."

He clicked the remote, and the screen illuminated with a presentation titled "Managing Property Crises." "Navigating property crises requires preparation, communication, and decisive action. It's a test of our resilience and leadership in times of adversity."

The first slide highlighted "Establishing Emergency Response Protocols." "1. **Establishing Emergency Response Protocols.** Property managers should develop comprehensive emergency response protocols to address various crisis scenarios, such as natural disasters, fires, floods, and security threats. This includes establishing clear lines of communication, designating emergency contacts, and outlining procedures for evacuation, sheltering, and response coordination. Emergency response protocols ensure readiness and enable timely and effective responses to crises."

Jack emphasized the importance of establishing emergency response protocols to ensure preparedness for various crisis scenarios. He recalled instances where well-executed emergency protocols had minimized property damage and ensured tenant safety during emergencies.

The next slide displayed "Effective Communication Strategies." "2. **Effective Communication Strategies.** Property managers should implement effective communication strategies to keep tenants informed and updated during property crises. This includes establishing communication channels, such as email, phone, text messaging, and social media, for disseminating emergency alerts and instructions. Effective communication fosters trust, reduces panic, and enables coordinated responses during crises."

Sarah, with her expertise in communication, nodded in agreement. She understood the importance of clear and timely communication in mitigating panic and ensuring tenant safety during property crises. She made a mental note to review and update communication channels to enhance crisis responsiveness.

The third slide depicted "Coordinating with Emergency Services." "3. **Coordinating with Emergency Services.** Property managers should collaborate closely with emergency services, such as fire departments, police departments, and emergency medical services, during property crises. This includes establishing relationships with local emergency responders, providing them with access to property facilities and resources, and following their guidance and instructions during crisis situations. Coordinating with emergency services facilitates prompt and effective responses to emergencies."

David, always focused on property safety, recognized the importance of coordinating with emergency services to ensure swift and coordinated responses during crises. He made a mental note to establish and maintain relationships with local emergency responders and provide them with the necessary support and resources during emergencies.

The next image showed "Implementing Crisis Management Plans." "4. **Implementing Crisis Management Plans.** Property managers should develop and implement crisis management plans that outline roles, responsibilities, and procedures for responding to property crises. This includes identifying potential crisis scenarios, conducting risk assessments, and developing contingency plans and response protocols. Crisis management plans provide a structured framework for managing crises and minimizing their impact on property operations and occupants."

Lisa, their problem solver, nodded in agreement. She understood the importance of crisis management plans in providing guidance and direction during property crises. She made a mental note to review and update crisis management plans regularly to ensure relevance and effectiveness.

The fifth slide highlighted "Supporting Tenants and Staff." "5. **Supporting Tenants and Staff.** Property managers should prioritize the well-being and safety of tenants and staff during property crises. This includes providing assistance and support, such as temporary shelter, food, and medical aid, as needed. Additionally, property managers should offer psychological support and counseling services to tenants and staff affected by traumatic events. Supporting tenants and staff fosters resilience and promotes community solidarity during challenging times."

Jack stressed the importance of supporting tenants and staff during property crises to ensure their well-being and safety.

He encouraged the team to prioritize assistance and support for those affected by crises and foster a sense of community solidarity.

The final slide displayed "Conducting Post-Crisis Evaluation and Improvement." "6. **Conducting Post-Crisis Evaluation and Improvement.** Property managers should conduct post-crisis evaluations to assess the effectiveness of response efforts and identify areas for improvement. This includes analyzing response times, communication effectiveness, and resource utilization, and implementing corrective actions and enhancements to crisis management plans and protocols. Post-crisis evaluation and improvement enable continuous learning and readiness for future crises."

Jack turned off the projector and faced his team, a sense of determination evident in his expression. "Managing property crises requires preparation, coordination, and resilience. Let's leverage these strategies to navigate crises effectively and safeguard our properties and communities."

The room fell silent, each team member reflecting on their role in managing property crises and ensuring tenant safety and satisfaction. Jack could see the determination in their eyes—a shared commitment to resilience and excellence in property management.

Addressing Maintenance Emergencies

As the team delved deeper into the intricacies of property management challenges, Jack Miller redirected their focus to another critical aspect: addressing maintenance emergencies. He understood that swift and effective action was essential for minimizing damage and ensuring tenant safety and satisfaction during maintenance emergencies.

"Team," Jack began, his voice firm yet reassuring. "In our line of work, maintenance emergencies can arise unexpectedly, posing significant risks to property integrity and tenant well-being. It's not just about reacting—it's about implementing proactive measures to mitigate risks and address emergencies promptly. Let's explore the third subpoint: addressing maintenance emergencies."

He clicked the remote, and the screen illuminated with a presentation titled "Addressing Maintenance Emergencies." "Navigating maintenance emergencies requires readiness, responsiveness, and resourcefulness. It's a testament to our commitment to property safety and tenant satisfaction."

The first slide highlighted "Identifying Common Maintenance Emergencies." "1. **Identifying Common Maintenance Emergencies.** Property managers should be familiar with common maintenance emergencies that may occur in their properties, such as plumbing leaks, electrical failures, HVAC malfunctions, and structural damage. This includes conducting regular inspections and assessments to identify potential hazards and vulnerabilities. Identifying common maintenance emergencies enables proactive measures to prevent or mitigate risks."

Jack emphasized the importance of identifying common maintenance emergencies to enable proactive measures and timely responses. He recalled instances where early detection had prevented major damage and disruption to property operations.

The next slide displayed "Establishing Emergency Contacts and Procedures." "2. **Establishing Emergency Contacts and Procedures.** Property managers should establish emergency contacts and procedures for addressing maintenance emergencies. This includes maintaining a list of reliable contractors, vendors, and service providers who can respond to emergencies promptly. Additionally, property managers should outline procedures for notifying tenants, coordinating repairs, and documenting incidents. Establishing emergency contacts and procedures ensures readiness and enables swift responses to maintenance emergencies."

Sarah, with her attention to detail, nodded in agreement. She understood the importance of establishing emergency contacts and procedures to facilitate swift responses to maintenance emergencies. She made a mental note to review and update emergency contact lists regularly to ensure reliability and responsiveness.

The third slide depicted "Prioritizing Safety and Tenant Well-being." "3. **Prioritizing Safety and Tenant Well-being.** Property managers should prioritize safety and tenant well-being during maintenance emergencies. This includes promptly addressing hazards and risks, such as water leaks, electrical issues, and structural damage, to ensure tenant safety and prevent further damage. Additionally, property managers should provide clear instructions and guidance to tenants on safety procedures and evacuation protocols. Prioritizing safety and tenant well-being minimizes risks and fosters trust and confidence among tenants."

David, always focused on property safety, recognized the importance of prioritizing safety and tenant well-being during maintenance emergencies. He made a mental note to conduct regular safety inspections and provide tenants with clear instructions on emergency procedures.

The next image showed "Coordinating Repairs and Restoration." "4. **Coordinating Repairs and Restoration.** Property managers should coordinate repairs and restoration efforts promptly to address maintenance emergencies effectively. This includes contacting reliable contractors and service providers to assess and address the issue promptly. Additionally, property managers should oversee repair and restoration efforts to ensure quality and timeliness. Coordinating repairs and restoration minimizes downtime and disruption to property operations and tenant activities."

Lisa, their problem solver, nodded in agreement. She understood the importance of coordinating repairs and restoration efforts to minimize downtime and disruption during maintenance emergencies. She made a mental note to maintain open communication with contractors and oversee repair activities closely.

The fifth slide highlighted "Communicating with Tenants." "5. **Communicating with Tenants.** Property managers should communicate with tenants promptly and transparently during maintenance emergencies. This includes notifying tenants of the emergency, providing updates on repair progress, and offering guidance on safety precautions and alternative arrangements, such as temporary accommodations. Additionally, property managers should be available to address tenant concerns and questions promptly. Communicating with tenants fosters trust, reduces anxiety, and promotes cooperation during emergencies."

Jack stressed the importance of communicating with tenants promptly and transparently during maintenance emergencies to ensure their well-being and cooperation. He encouraged the team to provide regular updates and guidance to tenants to alleviate concerns and foster trust.

The final slide displayed "Conducting Post-Emergency Evaluation and Improvement." "6. **Conducting Post-Emergency Evaluation and Improvement.** Property managers should conduct post-emergency evaluations to assess the effectiveness of response efforts and identify areas for improvement. This includes analyzing response times, communication effectiveness, and repair outcomes, and implementing corrective actions and enhancements to emergency procedures and protocols. Post-emergency evaluation and improvement enable continuous learning and readiness for future emergencies."

Jack turned off the projector and faced his team, a sense of determination evident in his expression. "Addressing maintenance emergencies requires readiness, responsiveness, and resourcefulness. Let's leverage these strategies to navigate emergencies effectively and ensure property safety and tenant satisfaction."

The room fell silent, each team member reflecting on their role in addressing maintenance emergencies and safeguarding property integrity and tenant well-being. Jack could see the determination in their eyes—a shared commitment to excellence in property management.

Financial Troubleshooting

As the team delved further into the complexities of property management challenges, Jack Miller redirected their focus to another critical aspect: financial troubleshooting. He understood that navigating financial difficulties was essential for maintaining property stability and ensuring long-term success.

"Team," Jack began, his voice composed yet resolute. "In our line of work, financial troubles can arise unexpectedly, posing significant risks to property operations and profitability. It's not just about reacting—it's about implementing proactive measures to address financial challenges and ensure financial stability. Let's explore the fourth subpoint: financial troubleshooting."

He clicked the remote, and the screen illuminated with a presentation titled "Financial Troubleshooting." "Navigating financial troubles requires diligence, creativity, and strategic thinking. It's a test of our financial acumen and resilience in times of uncertainty."

The first slide highlighted "Identifying Financial Warning Signs." "1. **Identifying Financial Warning Signs.** Property managers should be vigilant in identifying financial warning signs that may indicate underlying issues, such as declining revenue, increasing expenses, or cash flow disruptions. This includes conducting regular financial reviews and analyses to assess property performance and identify areas for improvement. Identifying financial warning signs enables proactive measures to address potential financial challenges before they escalate."

Jack emphasized the importance of identifying financial warning signs to enable proactive measures and timely interventions. He recalled instances where early detection had prevented major financial setbacks and ensured property stability.

The next slide displayed "Implementing Cost-Saving Measures." "2. **Implementing Cost-Saving Measures.** Property managers should implement cost-saving measures to reduce expenses and improve property profitability. This includes renegotiating vendor contracts, optimizing utility usage, and implementing energy-saving initiatives. Additionally, property managers can explore creative solutions, such as shared services or outsourcing non-essential functions, to reduce overhead costs. Implementing cost-saving measures preserves financial resources and enhances property profitability."

Sarah, with her knack for efficiency, nodded in agreement. She understood the importance of implementing cost-saving measures to optimize property finances and improve profitability. She made a mental note to explore opportunities for renegotiating contracts and implementing energy-saving initiatives.

The third slide depicted "Maximizing Revenue Generation." "3. **Maximizing Revenue Generation.** Property managers should explore opportunities to maximize revenue generation and enhance property income streams. This includes optimizing rental rates, leasing vacant units promptly, and implementing value-added services or amenities to attract tenants and increase rental income. Additionally, property managers can explore alternative revenue streams, such as advertising or partnership opportunities, to diversify income sources. Maximizing revenue generation boosts property profitability and financial resilience."

David, always focused on property performance, recognized the importance of maximizing revenue generation to enhance property income streams. He made a mental note to review rental rates and explore opportunities for leasing vacant units promptly.

The next image showed "Negotiating with Lenders and Stakeholders." "4. **Negotiating with Lenders and Stake-**

holders. Property managers should proactively engage with lenders, investors, and stakeholders to address financial challenges and explore restructuring or refinancing options. This includes communicating openly about financial difficulties, presenting recovery plans or mitigation strategies, and negotiating favorable terms or extensions to loan agreements. Negotiating with lenders and stakeholders preserves property interests and facilitates financial recovery."

Lisa, their problem solver, nodded in agreement. She understood the importance of negotiating with lenders and stakeholders to address financial challenges and preserve property interests. She made a mental note to review loan agreements and engage with lenders proactively.

The fifth slide highlighted "Exploring Financial Assistance Programs." "5. **Exploring Financial Assistance Programs.** Property managers should explore financial assistance programs or resources offered by government agencies or industry organizations to support property operations during financial difficulties. This includes researching grants, loans, or subsidies available for property rehabilitation, energy efficiency upgrades, or rental assistance programs. Additionally, property managers can collaborate with community organizations or nonprofit agencies to access additional financial resources or support services. Exploring financial assistance programs provides additional support and resources to navigate financial challenges effectively."

Jack stressed the importance of exploring financial assistance programs to access additional support and resources during financial difficulties. He encouraged the team to research available programs and collaborate with relevant organizations to access assistance.

The final slide displayed "Conducting Financial Performance Reviews." "6. **Conducting Financial Performance Reviews.** Property managers should conduct regular financial performance reviews to monitor property financial health and evaluate the effectiveness of financial strategies and interventions. This includes analyzing key performance indicators, such as occupancy rates, revenue growth, and expense ratios, to assess property performance and identify areas for improvement. Conducting financial performance reviews enables informed decision-making and proactive adjustments to financial strategies."

Jack turned off the projector and faced his team, a sense of determination evident in his expression. "Addressing financial troubles requires diligence, creativity, and strategic thinking. Let's leverage these strategies to navigate financial challenges effectively and ensure property stability and success."

The room fell silent, each team member reflecting on their role in addressing financial challenges and safeguarding property stability. Jack could see the determination in their eyes—a shared commitment to financial resilience and excellence in property management.

Conflict Mediation and Resolution

As the team progressed through their exploration of property management challenges, Jack Miller redirected their attention to another crucial aspect: conflict mediation and resolution. He understood that effectively managing conflicts was essential for maintaining tenant satisfaction and fostering a positive living environment.

"Team," Jack began, his tone measured yet firm. "In our line of work, conflicts among tenants or between tenants and management can arise, impacting property harmony and tenant satisfaction. It's not just about addressing conflicts—it's about facilitating constructive dialogue and finding mutually acceptable solutions. Let's explore the fifth subpoint: conflict mediation and resolution."

He clicked the remote, and the screen illuminated with a presentation titled "Conflict Mediation and Resolution." "Navigating conflicts requires empathy, communication skills, and a commitment to fairness. It's a test of our ability to foster understanding and cooperation among stakeholders."

The first slide highlighted "Understanding Conflict Dynamics." "1. **Understanding Conflict Dynamics.** Property managers should understand the underlying dynamics of conflicts, including their causes, triggers, and escalation factors. This includes recognizing common sources of conflict, such as communication breakdowns, competing interests, or perceived injustices. Understanding conflict dynamics enables property managers to address conflicts effectively and prevent their escalation."

Jack emphasized the importance of understanding conflict dynamics to facilitate effective conflict resolution. He recalled instances where insight into conflict triggers had enabled swift resolution and prevented further escalation.

The next slide displayed "Facilitating Constructive Dialogue." "2. **Facilitating Constructive Dialogue.** Property managers should facilitate constructive dialogue among conflicting parties to explore underlying issues, perspectives, and interests. This includes creating a safe and neutral space for dialogue, actively listening to each party's concerns, and reframing conflicts as opportunities for mutual understanding and collaboration. Facilitating constructive dialogue fosters empathy, builds trust, and promotes cooperative problem-solving."

Sarah, with her expertise in communication, nodded in agreement. She understood the importance of facilitating constructive dialogue to foster understanding and cooperation among conflicting parties. She made a mental note to create opportunities for dialogue and mediation when conflicts arose.

The third slide depicted "Identifying Common Conflict Resolution Techniques." "3. **Identifying Common Conflict Resolution Techniques.** Property managers should be familiar with common conflict resolution techniques to address conflicts effectively. This includes techniques such as negotiation, mediation, arbitration, and consensus-building. Each technique offers different approaches to resolving conflicts, depending on the nature and complexity of the issues involved. Identifying common conflict resolution techniques enables property managers to choose the most appropriate approach for each conflict situation."

David, always focused on finding practical solutions, recognized the importance of employing various conflict resolution techniques to address conflicts effectively. He made a mental note to adapt his approach based on the specific circumstances of each conflict.

The next image showed "Seeking Win-Win Solutions." "4. **Seeking Win-Win Solutions.** Property managers should strive to seek win-win solutions that address the interests and concerns of all conflicting parties. This involves exploring creative options and compromises that meet the underlying needs and objectives of each party while preserving property interests and community harmony. Seeking win-win solutions fosters cooperation, builds relationships, and promotes long-term peace and stability."

Lisa, their problem solver, nodded in agreement. She understood the importance of seeking win-win solutions to promote cooperation and harmony among conflicting parties. She made a mental note to explore creative options and compromises to resolve conflicts effectively.

The fifth slide highlighted "Implementing Conflict Resolution Protocols." "5. **Implementing Conflict Resolution Protocols.** Property managers should establish clear protocols and procedures for addressing conflicts among tenants or between tenants and management. This includes outlining steps for conflict resolution, identifying responsible parties or mediators, and establishing timelines for resolution. Implementing conflict resolution protocols ensures consistency, fairness, and transparency in resolving conflicts."

Jack stressed the importance of implementing conflict resolution protocols to ensure fair and transparent resolution processes. He encouraged the team to review and update conflict resolution protocols regularly to adapt to evolving needs and challenges.

The final slide displayed "Promoting Conflict Prevention Strategies." "6. **Promoting Conflict Prevention Strategies.** Property managers should promote conflict prevention strategies to mitigate the risk of conflicts arising in the first place. This includes fostering open communication channels, setting clear expectations and boundaries, and addressing potential sources of conflict proactively. Additionally, property managers can provide conflict resolution training or resources to tenants to enhance conflict management skills and promote a culture of cooperation and respect."

Jack turned off the projector and faced his team, a sense of determination evident in his expression. "Managing conflicts requires empathy, communication skills, and a commitment to fairness. Let's leverage these strategies to navigate conflicts effectively and foster a positive living environment for our tenants."

The room fell silent, each team member reflecting on their role in facilitating conflict resolution and promoting community harmony. Jack could see the determination in their eyes—a shared commitment to excellence in property management.

Learning from Past Mistakes

As the team delved deeper into their discussion on property management challenges, Jack Miller redirected their attention to the importance of learning from past mistakes. He understood that reflecting on past experiences was essential for growth and improvement in property management practices.

"Team," Jack began, his tone reflective yet determined. "In our line of work, mistakes are inevitable, but what truly matters is how we learn from them and use them to become better property managers. It's not just about avoiding mistakes—it's about embracing them as opportunities for growth and improvement. Let's explore the sixth subpoint: learning from past mistakes."

He clicked the remote, and the screen illuminated with

a presentation titled "Learning from Past Mistakes." "Navigating challenges requires humility, self-reflection, and a commitment to continuous improvement. It's a testament to our resilience and dedication to excellence."

The first slide highlighted "Conducting Post-Mortem Analyses." "1. **Conducting Post-Mortem Analyses.** Property managers should conduct post-mortem analyses following major incidents, mistakes, or failures to identify root causes, contributing factors, and lessons learned. This includes analyzing what went wrong, why it happened, and what could have been done differently to prevent or mitigate the issue. Conducting post-mortem analyses enables property managers to extract valuable insights and identify opportunities for improvement."

Jack emphasized the importance of conducting post-mortem analyses to extract valuable insights from past mistakes. He recalled instances where post-mortem analyses had led to significant process improvements and prevented similar mistakes from occurring in the future.

The next slide displayed "Implementing Corrective Actions." "2. **Implementing Corrective Actions.** Property managers should implement corrective actions and preventive measures based on the findings of post-mortem analyses to address root causes and mitigate recurrence of past mistakes. This includes developing action plans, assigning responsibilities, and establishing timelines for implementing corrective actions. Implementing corrective actions demonstrates a commitment to learning and continuous improvement."

Sarah, with her eye for detail, nodded in agreement. She understood the importance of implementing corrective actions to address root causes and prevent recurrence of past mistakes. She made a mental note to develop action plans based on the team's post-mortem analyses.

The third slide depicted "Promoting a Culture of Accountability." "3. **Promoting a Culture of Accountability.** Property managers should promote a culture of accountability where team members take ownership of their actions and decisions. This includes fostering open communication, encouraging feedback and transparency, and holding individuals accountable for their performance and conduct. Promoting a culture of accountability creates a supportive environment where mistakes are viewed as learning opportunities rather than failures."

David, always focused on teamwork, recognized the importance of promoting a culture of accountability to foster a supportive environment. He made a mental note to encourage open communication and feedback among team members.

The next image showed "Providing Ongoing Training and Development." "4. **Providing Ongoing Training and Development.** Property managers should provide ongoing training and development opportunities to equip team members with the knowledge, skills, and tools needed to succeed. This includes offering training programs, workshops, and seminars on relevant topics, such as conflict resolution, customer service, and risk management. Providing ongoing training and development enhances team competency and resilience in handling challenges."

Lisa, their problem solver, nodded in agreement. She understood the importance of providing ongoing training and development to enhance team competency and resilience.

She made a mental note to explore training opportunities on conflict resolution and risk management for the team.

The fifth slide highlighted "Encouraging Innovation and Creativity." "5. **Encouraging Innovation and Creativity.** Property managers should encourage innovation and creativity in problem-solving and decision-making processes. This includes empowering team members to propose new ideas, experiment with different approaches, and challenge existing norms and practices. Encouraging innovation and creativity fosters a culture of continuous improvement and adaptation to changing circumstances."

Jack stressed the importance of encouraging innovation and creativity to foster a culture of continuous improvement. He encouraged the team to embrace new ideas and approaches to problem-solving.

The final slide displayed "Celebrating Successes and Progress." "6. **Celebrating Successes and Progress.** Property managers should celebrate successes and progress made in learning from past mistakes and implementing improvements. This includes recognizing and rewarding individuals or teams for their contributions to problem-solving and innovation. Celebrating successes and progress reinforces a culture of learning and achievement."

Jack turned off the projector and faced his team, a sense of determination evident in his expression. "Learning from past mistakes requires humility, self-reflection, and a commitment to continuous improvement. Let's leverage these strategies to become better property managers and achieve excellence in our work."

The room fell silent, each team member reflecting on their role in learning from past mistakes and driving continuous improvement. Jack could see the determination in their eyes—a shared commitment to growth and excellence in property management.

Chapter 14: Scaling Your Property Management Business

Identifying Growth Opportunities

As the team gathered to explore the nuances of scaling a property management business, Jack Miller set the stage for an insightful discussion on identifying growth opportunities. He understood that strategic growth was essential for expanding business operations and maximizing profitability.

"Team," Jack began, his voice resonating with anticipation. "In our journey to scale our property management business, it's imperative to identify and capitalize on growth opportunities that align with our vision and objectives. Let's embark on a journey to explore the first subpoint: identifying growth opportunities."

He clicked the remote, and the screen illuminated with a presentation titled "Identifying Growth Opportunities." "Scaling our business requires vision, foresight, and a keen understanding of market dynamics. It's about recognizing potential avenues for expansion and seizing them with confidence."

The first slide highlighted "Market Analysis and Research."

"1. **Market Analysis and Research.** Property managers should conduct comprehensive market analysis and research to identify growth opportunities within their target markets. This includes analyzing market trends, demand-supply dynamics, and competitive landscape to pinpoint areas of unmet demand or underserved niches. Market analysis and research provide valuable insights for strategic decision-making and expansion planning."

Jack emphasized the importance of market analysis and research in identifying growth opportunities. He recalled instances where thorough market analysis had led to the discovery of untapped market segments and lucrative business prospects.

The next slide displayed "Portfolio Diversification Strategies." "2. **Portfolio Diversification Strategies.** Property managers should explore portfolio diversification strategies to expand their service offerings and reach new customer segments. This includes diversifying into different property types, such as residential, commercial, or vacation rentals, or offering specialized services, such as property maintenance, asset management, or real estate investment consulting. Portfolio diversification strategies enhance business resilience and create opportunities for revenue growth."

Sarah, with her strategic mindset, nodded in agreement. She understood the importance of portfolio diversification in expanding service offerings and reaching new customer segments. She made a mental note to explore opportunities for diversification in their business strategy.

The third slide depicted "Strategic Partnerships and Alliances." "3. **Strategic Partnerships and Alliances.** Property managers should establish strategic partnerships and alliances with complementary businesses or industry stakeholders to leverage synergies and unlock growth opportunities. This includes collaborating with real estate agents, contractors, or technology providers to enhance service capabilities or access new markets. Strategic partnerships and alliances facilitate business expansion and market penetration."

David, always focused on collaboration, recognized the importance of strategic partnerships in unlocking growth opportunities. He made a mental note to explore potential partnerships with industry stakeholders to expand their business reach.

The next image showed "Geographical Expansion Plans." "4. **Geographical Expansion Plans.** Property managers should consider geographical expansion as a strategic growth opportunity to enter new markets or expand their presence in existing ones. This includes conducting market assessments, regulatory analysis, and feasibility studies to evaluate the potential for expansion into new regions or territories. Geographical expansion plans enable property managers to diversify their revenue streams and mitigate market risks."

Lisa, their problem solver, nodded in agreement. She understood the potential benefits of geographical expansion in diversifying revenue streams and mitigating market risks. She made a mental note to explore opportunities for expansion into new regions.

The fifth slide highlighted "Technology Integration Initiatives." "5. **Technology Integration Initiatives.** Property managers should embrace technology integration initiatives to streamline operations, enhance service delivery, and drive business growth. This includes adopting property management software, implementing smart home technologies, or leveraging data analytics for informed decision-making. Technology integration initiatives improve operational efficiency and scalability, enabling property managers to manage larger portfolios effectively."

Jack stressed the importance of technology integration initiatives in driving business growth and scalability. He encouraged the team to embrace technology solutions that aligned with their business objectives and customer needs.

The final slide displayed "Customer Feedback and Innovation." "6. **Customer Feedback and Innovation.** Property managers should actively seek customer feedback and foster a culture of innovation to identify new service opportunities and improve customer satisfaction. This includes soliciting feedback through surveys, focus groups, or social media channels, and leveraging customer insights to innovate service offerings or business processes. Customer feedback and innovation drive continuous improvement and competitive differentiation."

Jack turned off the projector and faced his team, a sense of determination evident in his expression. "Identifying growth opportunities requires vision, innovation, and a willingness to adapt to changing market dynamics. Let's leverage these strategies to scale our property management business and achieve sustainable growth."

The room fell silent, each team member reflecting on their role in identifying and seizing growth opportunities. Jack could see the determination in their eyes—a shared commitment to excellence and expansion in property management.

Expanding Your Property Portfolio

As the team delved deeper into their exploration of scaling strategies, Jack Miller shifted their focus to the second subpoint: expanding the property portfolio. He understood that diversifying and growing the portfolio was essential for increasing revenue streams and market presence.

"Team," Jack began, his voice resonating with enthusiasm. "Expanding our property portfolio is key to our growth strategy. It's about identifying opportunities to acquire new properties and diversify our holdings to maximize returns. Let's explore how we can expand our property portfolio effectively."

He clicked the remote, and the screen illuminated with a presentation titled "Expanding Your Property Portfolio." "Expanding our portfolio requires strategic vision, financial acumen, and a thorough understanding of market dynamics. It's about seizing opportunities and building a diverse portfolio that generates sustainable returns."

The first slide highlighted "Market Research and Opportunity Analysis." "1. **Market Research and Opportunity Analysis.** Property managers should conduct comprehensive market research and opportunity analysis to identify potential properties for acquisition. This includes analyzing market trends, property prices, rental demand, and investment potential in target locations. Market research and opportunity analysis provide valuable insights for identifying lucrative investment opportunities and mitigating risks."

Jack emphasized the importance of market research and

opportunity analysis in identifying properties with strong investment potential. He recalled instances where thorough research had led to successful property acquisitions and lucrative investment returns.

The next slide displayed "Financial Planning and Budgeting." "2. **Financial Planning and Budgeting.** Property managers should develop detailed financial plans and budgets to assess their capacity for property acquisition and expansion. This includes evaluating financing options, projecting cash flows, and setting investment criteria and benchmarks. Financial planning and budgeting ensure that property acquisitions are aligned with business objectives and financial goals."

Sarah, with her expertise in financial analysis, nodded in agreement. She understood the importance of financial planning and budgeting in assessing investment opportunities and ensuring financial feasibility. She made a mental note to refine their financial models for property acquisitions.

The third slide depicted "Acquisition Strategies and Criteria." "3. **Acquisition Strategies and Criteria.** Property managers should establish clear acquisition strategies and criteria to guide their property selection process. This includes defining target property types, locations, size, condition, and investment returns. Acquisition strategies and criteria enable property managers to focus their efforts on properties that align with their investment objectives and portfolio diversification goals."

David, always focused on strategy, recognized the importance of establishing clear acquisition criteria to guide their property selection process. He made a mental note to refine their acquisition strategies based on market trends and investment opportunities.

The next image showed "Negotiation and Due Diligence Processes." "4. **Negotiation and Due Diligence Processes.** Property managers should conduct thorough due diligence and negotiation processes before finalizing property acquisitions. This includes assessing property condition, conducting property inspections, reviewing financial documents, and negotiating purchase terms and agreements. Negotiation and due diligence processes ensure that property acquisitions are conducted efficiently and mitigate potential risks."

Lisa, their problem solver, nodded in agreement. She understood the importance of thorough due diligence and negotiation processes in mitigating risks associated with property acquisitions. She made a mental note to streamline their due diligence workflows for efficiency.

The fifth slide highlighted "Asset Management and Optimization Strategies." "5. **Asset Management and Optimization Strategies.** Property managers should implement effective asset management and optimization strategies to maximize the value and performance of acquired properties. This includes implementing property improvements, optimizing rental rates, minimizing vacancies, and enhancing tenant satisfaction. Asset management and optimization strategies ensure that acquired properties generate sustainable returns and contribute to portfolio growth."

Jack stressed the importance of asset management and optimization strategies in maximizing the value and performance of acquired properties. He encouraged the team to focus on continuous improvement and innovation in their asset management practices.

The final slide displayed "Risk Management and Contingency Planning." "6. **Risk Management and Contingency Planning.** Property managers should develop robust risk management and contingency plans to address potential risks associated with property acquisitions. This includes identifying risks, implementing risk mitigation measures, and developing contingency plans to address unforeseen challenges. Risk management and contingency planning safeguard property investments and ensure business continuity."

Jack turned off the projector and faced his team, a sense of determination evident in his expression. "Expanding our property portfolio requires diligence, foresight, and a commitment to excellence. Let's leverage these strategies to grow our portfolio strategically and achieve long-term success."

The room fell silent, each team member reflecting on their role in expanding the property portfolio. Jack could see the determination in their eyes—a shared commitment to growth and excellence in property management.

Hiring and Training Staff

As the team delved deeper into their exploration of scaling strategies, Jack Miller shifted their focus to the critical aspect of hiring and training staff. He understood that building a competent and motivated team was essential for managing a growing property portfolio effectively.

"Team," Jack began, his voice filled with conviction. "Our success in scaling our property management business hinges on the strength of our team. It's imperative that we focus on hiring the right talent and providing them with the necessary training to excel in their roles. Let's delve into how we can effectively hire and train staff to support our growth."

He clicked the remote, and the screen illuminated with a presentation titled "Hiring and Training Staff." "Building a high-performing team requires strategic recruitment, comprehensive training, and ongoing development. It's about investing in our people and empowering them to contribute to our collective success."

The first slide highlighted "Strategic Recruitment Practices." "1. **Strategic Recruitment Practices.** Property managers should adopt strategic recruitment practices to attract top talent that aligns with the company culture and values. This includes defining job roles and responsibilities, crafting compelling job descriptions, and leveraging multiple recruitment channels to reach a diverse pool of candidates. Strategic recruitment practices ensure that the right candidates are selected for key positions within the organization."

Jack emphasized the importance of strategic recruitment in identifying candidates who not only possess the necessary skills but also align with the company culture and values. He recalled instances where strategic recruitment had led to the hiring of exceptional team members who contributed significantly to the company's success.

The next slide displayed "Comprehensive Onboarding Processes." "2. **Comprehensive Onboarding Processes.** Property managers should implement comprehensive onboarding processes to integrate new hires seamlessly into the organization and set them up for success. This includes providing orientation sessions, introducing them to company policies and procedures, and assigning mentors or buddies to support their transition. Comprehensive onboarding processes ensure that new hires feel welcomed and equipped to perform their roles effectively from day one."

Sarah, with her focus on organizational development, nodded in agreement. She understood the importance of comprehensive onboarding processes in ensuring that new hires acclimate quickly and become productive members of the team. She made a mental note to enhance their onboarding program to provide a more seamless experience for new hires.

The third slide depicted "Continuous Training and Development Initiatives." "3. **Continuous Training and Development Initiatives.** Property managers should prioritize continuous training and development initiatives to enhance the skills and capabilities of their team members. This includes offering regular training sessions, workshops, and professional development opportunities to keep employees updated on industry trends and best practices. Continuous training and development initiatives foster a culture of learning and growth within the organization."

David, always focused on skill-building, recognized the importance of continuous training and development in keeping team members engaged and motivated. He made a mental note to explore additional training opportunities to further develop the team's skills and capabilities.

The next image showed "Performance Management and Feedback Systems." "4. **Performance Management and Feedback Systems.** Property managers should implement robust performance management and feedback systems to provide regular performance evaluations and constructive feedback to their team members. This includes setting clear performance expectations, conducting regular performance reviews, and providing coaching and support for improvement. Performance management and feedback systems enable property managers to identify strengths and areas for development and support career growth."

Lisa, their problem solver, nodded in agreement. She understood the importance of performance management and feedback systems in helping team members reach their full potential. She made a mental note to enhance their performance evaluation process to provide more actionable feedback to employees.

The fifth slide highlighted "Employee Recognition and Rewards Programs." "5. **Employee Recognition and Rewards Programs.** Property managers should implement employee recognition and rewards programs to acknowledge and celebrate the contributions of their team members. This includes recognizing achievements, milestones, and exceptional performance through awards, bonuses, or public acknowledgment. Employee recognition and rewards programs boost morale, motivation, and job satisfaction within the organization."

Jack stressed the importance of employee recognition and rewards programs in fostering a positive work environment and retaining top talent. He encouraged the team to regularly recognize and appreciate the efforts of their colleagues.

The final slide displayed "Succession Planning and Career Development." "6. **Succession Planning and Career Development.** Property managers should develop succession plans and career development pathways to groom future leaders and retain top talent within the organization. This includes identifying high-potential employees, providing them with opportunities for growth and advancement, and creating clear career paths and development plans. Succession planning and career development initiatives ensure continuity and stability within the organization."

Jack turned off the projector and faced his team, a sense of determination evident in his expression. "Hiring and training staff is a cornerstone of our growth strategy. Let's invest in our people and empower them to succeed. Together, we'll build a team that drives our business forward and achieves our goals."

The room fell silent, each team member reflecting on their role in hiring and training staff to support the company's growth. Jack could see the determination in their eyes—a shared commitment to building a strong and capable team.

Outsourcing vs. In-House Services

As the team continued their exploration of scaling strategies, Jack Miller redirected their focus to the critical decision between outsourcing and in-house services. He understood that choosing the right approach could significantly impact the efficiency and effectiveness of their operations.

"Team," Jack began, his voice filled with contemplation. "One of the key decisions we need to make as we scale our property management business is whether to outsource certain services or keep them in-house. It's a decision that requires careful consideration of various factors. Let's delve into the nuances of outsourcing versus in-house services."

He clicked the remote, and the screen illuminated with a presentation titled "Outsourcing vs. In-House Services." "Determining the optimal mix of outsourcing and in-house services is crucial for optimizing resource allocation and achieving operational excellence. It's about finding the right balance that aligns with our business objectives and supports our growth trajectory."

The first slide highlighted "Cost Analysis and Efficiency." "1. **Cost Analysis and Efficiency.** Property managers should conduct a comprehensive cost analysis to compare the financial implications of outsourcing versus keeping services in-house. This includes evaluating direct costs, such as labor, equipment, and overhead, as well as indirect costs, such as training, supervision, and quality control. Cost analysis helps property managers identify cost-saving opportunities and optimize resource allocation for maximum efficiency."

Jack emphasized the importance of cost analysis in making informed decisions about outsourcing versus in-house services. He recalled instances where cost-saving opportunities had been identified through thorough analysis, leading to more efficient operations.

The next slide displayed "Core Competencies and Specialization." "2. **Core Competencies and Specialization.** Property managers should assess their core competencies and areas of specialization to determine which services are best kept in-house and which can be outsourced to specialized vendors or contractors. This includes evaluating the complexity and criticality of services, as well as the availability of external expertise and resources. Focusing on core competencies enables property managers to leverage their strengths and deliver superior value to clients."

Sarah, with her focus on strategic planning, nodded in agreement. She understood the importance of focusing on core competencies to maintain a competitive edge in the market. She made a mental note to assess their areas of specialization and explore outsourcing opportunities for non-core services.

The third slide depicted "Scalability and Flexibility." "3. **Scalability and Flexibility.** Property managers should consider the scalability and flexibility of outsourcing versus in-house services in relation to their growth objectives and market dynamics. This includes assessing the ability to scale services up or down based on fluctuating demand, as well as the flexibility to adapt to changing business requirements. Scalability and flexibility ensure that property managers can effectively respond to market opportunities and challenges."

David, always focused on adaptability, recognized the importance of scalability and flexibility in ensuring operational agility. He made a mental note to evaluate the scalability of their current service model and explore outsourcing options that offered greater flexibility.

The next image showed "Quality Control and Service Standards." "4. **Quality Control and Service Standards.** Property managers should establish robust quality control mechanisms and service standards to maintain consistency and accountability in service delivery, whether services are outsourced or kept in-house. This includes defining performance metrics, conducting regular audits, and implementing feedback mechanisms to monitor service quality and customer satisfaction. Quality control and service standards ensure that service providers meet or exceed expectations and uphold the brand reputation."

Lisa, their problem solver, nodded in agreement. She understood the importance of quality control and service standards in ensuring consistent service delivery and customer satisfaction. She made a mental note to review their quality control processes and explore outsourcing options that aligned with their service standards.

The fifth slide highlighted "Risk Management and Compliance." "5. **Risk Management and Compliance.** Property managers should assess the risk management and compliance implications of outsourcing versus in-house services to mitigate potential risks and liabilities. This includes evaluating the reliability and reputation of service providers, as well as their adherence to industry regulations and standards. Risk management and compliance measures safeguard property managers against legal and reputational risks associated with service delivery."

Jack stressed the importance of risk management and compliance in selecting service providers, whether outsourced or in-house. He encouraged the team to prioritize reliability and adherence to regulations when evaluating outsourcing options.

The final slide displayed "Customer Experience and Satisfaction." "6. **Customer Experience and Satisfaction.** Property managers should prioritize customer experience and satisfaction in their decision-making process, whether outsourcing or keeping services in-house. This includes considering the impact of service delivery models on the overall customer experience, as well as the ability to meet customer expectations and preferences. Prioritizing customer experience ensures that property managers maintain high levels of customer satisfaction and loyalty."

Jack turned off the projector and faced his team, a sense of contemplation evident in his expression. "Choosing between outsourcing and in-house services requires careful consideration of various factors, including cost, efficiency, scalability, and customer experience. Let's assess our options thoughtfully and make decisions that support our long-term growth and success."

The room fell silent, each team member reflecting on the complexities of the outsourcing versus in-house services decision. Jack could see the wheels turning in their minds—a shared commitment to making the best choices for the company's future.

Building a Strong Brand

As the team continued their journey through the intricacies of scaling strategies, Jack Miller redirected their focus to the crucial aspect of building a strong brand. He understood that a powerful brand could differentiate their business in a competitive market and attract both clients and top talent.

"Team," Jack began, his voice resonating with determination. "In our quest to scale our property management business, one of our most valuable assets will be our brand. It's the essence of who we are, what we stand for, and the promise we make to our clients and stakeholders. Let's explore how we can build a strong brand that sets us apart and drives our success."

He clicked the remote, and the screen illuminated with a presentation titled "Building a Strong Brand." "Building a strong brand is about crafting a compelling identity, fostering trust and credibility, and delivering exceptional experiences that resonate with our target audience. It's about creating a lasting impression that inspires loyalty and advocacy."

The first slide highlighted "Brand Identity and Values." "1. **Brand Identity and Values.** Property managers should define their brand identity and core values to establish a strong foundation for their brand. This includes articulating their mission, vision, and unique selling propositions, as well as identifying key brand attributes and personality traits. Brand identity and values provide a framework for consistent messaging and communication that resonates with their target audience."

Jack emphasized the importance of defining their brand identity and values as the cornerstone of their branding efforts. He recalled instances where a clear brand identity had helped businesses stand out in crowded markets and forge strong connections with their audience.

The next slide displayed "Brand Messaging and Communication." "2. **Brand Messaging and Communication.** Property managers should develop compelling brand messaging and communication strategies to effectively convey their value proposition and engage with their audience. This includes crafting clear and concise messaging that communicates their brand story, benefits, and differentiation, as well as selecting appropriate communication channels to reach their target audience. Brand messaging and communication build awareness, credibility, and trust in the marketplace."

Sarah, with her expertise in communication, nodded in agreement. She understood the importance of crafting compelling brand messaging that resonated with their audience and differentiated their business from competitors. She made a mental note to refine their brand messaging to better communicate their value proposition.

The third slide depicted "Brand Experience and Customer Service." "3. **Brand Experience and Customer Service.** Property managers should prioritize delivering exceptional brand experiences and customer service that exceed customer expectations and foster loyalty. This includes providing personalized and attentive service, resolving issues promptly and effectively, and going above and beyond to delight customers at every touchpoint. Brand experience and customer service build trust, loyalty, and advocacy among customers."

David, always focused on customer satisfaction, recognized the importance of delivering exceptional brand experiences and customer service. He made a mental note to empower their team to prioritize customer satisfaction and exceed expectations at every opportunity.

The next image showed "Brand Consistency and Cohesion."
"4. **Brand Consistency and Cohesion.** Property managers should maintain consistency and cohesion across all brand touchpoints and channels to reinforce their brand identity and messaging. This includes ensuring consistency in visual elements, such as logo, colors, and typography, as well as tone of voice, messaging, and customer interactions. Brand consistency and cohesion enhance brand recognition, credibility, and memorability."

Lisa, their problem solver, nodded in agreement. She understood the importance of brand consistency in building trust and credibility with their audience. She made a mental note to review their brand guidelines and ensure consistency across all communication channels.

The fifth slide highlighted "Brand Reputation and Trust."
"5. **Brand Reputation and Trust.** Property managers should prioritize building a positive brand reputation and earning the trust of their audience through transparency, integrity, and reliability. This includes delivering on promises, addressing concerns and feedback openly and honestly, and actively engaging with their community and stakeholders. Brand

reputation and trust are invaluable assets that drive customer loyalty and business growth."

Jack stressed the importance of building a positive brand reputation and earning the trust of their audience. He encouraged the team to prioritize integrity and reliability in all their interactions, both internally and externally.

The final slide displayed "Brand Differentiation and Innovation." "6. **Brand Differentiation and Innovation.** Property managers should focus on brand differentiation and innovation to stand out in a crowded market and drive continuous improvement. This includes identifying unique selling propositions, exploring new service offerings or business models, and staying ahead of industry trends and customer preferences. Brand differentiation and innovation foster a culture of creativity and excellence that propels the brand forward."

Jack turned off the projector and faced his team, a sense of determination evident in his expression. "Building a strong brand is a journey that requires dedication, creativity, and a relentless focus on delivering value to our customers. Let's leverage these strategies to build a brand that resonates with our audience and drives our success."

The room fell silent, each team member reflecting on their role in building a strong brand for the company. Jack could see the determination in their eyes—a shared commitment to creating a brand that would leave a lasting impression on their audience and propel the company forward.

Strategic Planning for the Future

As the team delved deeper into their exploration of scaling strategies, Jack Miller redirected their focus to the critical aspect of strategic planning for the future. He understood that successful scaling required a clear vision and strategic roadmap to guide their actions and decisions.

"Team," Jack began, his voice filled with anticipation. "As we chart our course for growth and expansion, strategic planning will be paramount. It's about setting a clear direction, identifying opportunities, and aligning our resources and efforts to achieve our long-term objectives. Let's explore how we can develop a strategic plan that propels us toward our vision for the future."

He clicked the remote, and the screen illuminated with a presentation titled "Strategic Planning for the Future." "Strategic planning is a dynamic process that involves assessing the current state of the business, defining future goals and objectives, and developing actionable strategies to achieve them. It's about anticipating challenges, seizing opportunities, and staying agile in a rapidly evolving landscape."

The first slide highlighted "Vision and Mission." "1. **Vision and Mission.** Property managers should articulate a compelling vision and mission that define the purpose and direction of the organization. This includes envisioning where the company wants to be in the future and articulating its core values and guiding principles. A clear vision and mission provide a roadmap for decision-making and aligning the efforts of the team towards common goals."

Jack emphasized the importance of a compelling vision and mission in guiding their strategic planning efforts. He recalled instances where a strong vision had inspired teams to overcome challenges and achieve ambitious goals.

The next slide displayed "SWOT Analysis." "2. **SWOT Analysis.** Property managers should conduct a comprehensive SWOT analysis to assess the strengths, weaknesses, opportunities, and threats facing the business. This includes identifying internal strengths and weaknesses, such as market position, resources, and capabilities, as well as external opportunities and threats, such as market trends, competition, and regulatory changes. A SWOT analysis provides valuable insights for developing strategies that leverage strengths, mitigate weaknesses, capitalize on opportunities, and address threats."

Sarah, with her focus on strategic analysis, nodded in agreement. She understood the importance of a SWOT analysis in identifying strategic priorities and crafting actionable strategies. She made a mental note to lead their team through a thorough SWOT analysis to inform their strategic planning process.

The third slide depicted "Goal Setting and Objective Alignment." "3. **Goal Setting and Objective Alignment.** Property managers should establish clear and measurable goals and objectives that support the organization's vision and mission. This includes defining specific, achievable, relevant, and time-bound goals that align with the company's strategic priorities. Goal setting and objective alignment provide a roadmap for tracking progress and evaluating success."

David, always focused on goal achievement, recognized the importance of setting clear objectives to guide their actions and measure their progress. He made a mental note to collaborate with the team to establish ambitious yet

CHAPTER 14: SCALING YOUR PROPERTY MANAGEMENT BUSINESS

achievable goals for the future.

The next image showed "Resource Allocation and Budgeting." "4. **Resource Allocation and Budgeting.** Property managers should allocate resources strategically and develop budgets that support the implementation of their strategic plan. This includes aligning financial resources, human capital, and other assets with strategic priorities and investing in initiatives that drive growth and innovation. Resource allocation and budgeting ensure that the organization's priorities are supported by adequate resources and funding."

Lisa, their problem solver, nodded in agreement. She understood the importance of resource allocation in executing their strategic plan effectively. She made a mental note to optimize their budgeting process to ensure that resources were allocated to initiatives with the highest strategic impact.

The fifth slide highlighted "Risk Management and Contingency Planning." "5. **Risk Management and Contingency Planning.** Property managers should identify potential risks and develop contingency plans to mitigate their impact on strategic objectives. This includes assessing the likelihood and impact of various risks, such as market volatility, regulatory changes, and operational disruptions, and developing proactive measures to manage and mitigate them. Risk management and contingency planning safeguard the organization against unforeseen challenges and disruptions."

Jack stressed the importance of risk management and contingency planning in ensuring the resilience of their strategic plan. He encouraged the team to anticipate potential risks and develop proactive measures to mitigate their impact.

The final slide displayed "Monitoring and Evaluation." "6. **Monitoring and Evaluation.** Property managers should establish mechanisms for monitoring progress and evaluating the effectiveness of their strategic plan. This includes defining key performance indicators (KPIs) and benchmarks for tracking progress, conducting regular performance reviews, and making adjustments as needed to stay on course. Monitoring and evaluation ensure that the organization remains agile and responsive to changing market dynamics and strategic priorities."

Jack turned off the projector and faced his team, a sense of determination evident in his expression. "Strategic planning is a continuous process that requires ongoing assessment, adaptation, and alignment with our vision for the future. Let's leverage these strategies to develop a roadmap that guides us toward our goals and propels us to new heights of success."

The room fell silent, each team member reflecting on their role in shaping the future of the company through strategic planning. Jack could see the determination in their eyes—a shared commitment to realizing their vision and achieving their objectives.

15

Chapter 15: Achieving Excellence in Property Management

Setting and Achieving High Standards

As the team embarked on the final chapter of their journey towards excellence in property management, Jack Miller redirected their focus to the crucial aspect of setting and achieving high standards. He understood that excellence was not a destination but a continuous pursuit fueled by a commitment to excellence in every aspect of their operations.

"Team," Jack began, his voice resonating with determination. "As we strive for excellence in property management, setting and achieving high standards will be paramount. It's about raising the bar for ourselves and exceeding the expectations of our clients, tenants, and stakeholders. Let's explore how we can set and achieve high standards that define our commitment to excellence."

He clicked the remote, and the screen illuminated with a

presentation titled "Setting and Achieving High Standards." "Achieving excellence in property management requires a relentless focus on quality, professionalism, and continuous improvement. It's about setting ambitious goals, holding ourselves accountable, and relentlessly pursuing excellence in everything we do."

The first slide highlighted "Defining High Standards." "1. **Defining High Standards.** Property managers should establish clear and measurable standards of excellence that reflect the highest industry benchmarks and exceed the expectations of their stakeholders. This includes defining quality benchmarks for service delivery, operational efficiency, customer satisfaction, and regulatory compliance. Defining high standards sets the foundation for excellence and provides a benchmark for performance."

Jack emphasized the importance of defining high standards as the cornerstone of their pursuit of excellence. He recalled instances where adherence to high standards had differentiated businesses and earned them a reputation for excellence in the industry.

The next slide displayed "Commitment to Continuous Improvement." "2. **Commitment to Continuous Improvement.** Property managers should foster a culture of continuous improvement that encourages innovation, learning, and adaptation. This includes soliciting feedback from clients, tenants, and stakeholders, analyzing performance metrics, and identifying opportunities for optimization and innovation. Commitment to continuous improvement ensures that property managers stay ahead of the curve and continually raise the bar for excellence."

Sarah, with her focus on innovation, nodded in agreement.

She understood the importance of fostering a culture of continuous improvement in driving innovation and staying competitive in the market. She made a mental note to encourage their team to embrace change and seek out opportunities for improvement.

The third slide depicted "Training and Development Initiatives." "3. **Training and Development Initiatives.** Property managers should invest in training and development initiatives that empower their team members with the skills and knowledge needed to deliver exceptional service and achieve high standards. This includes providing regular training sessions, workshops, and certifications, as well as fostering a culture of learning and growth within the organization. Training and development initiatives equip property managers with the tools they need to excel in their roles and exceed expectations."

David, always focused on skill-building, recognized the importance of investing in training and development initiatives to empower their team members. He made a mental note to prioritize training opportunities that aligned with their strategic objectives and helped their team members reach their full potential.

The next image showed "Quality Assurance and Performance Monitoring." "4. **Quality Assurance and Performance Monitoring.** Property managers should implement robust quality assurance mechanisms and performance monitoring systems to ensure adherence to high standards and identify areas for improvement. This includes conducting regular audits, inspections, and performance reviews, as well as analyzing performance metrics and benchmarking against industry standards. Quality assurance and performance monitoring enable property managers to maintain consistency, identify trends, and drive continuous improvement."

Lisa, their problem solver, nodded in agreement. She understood the importance of quality assurance and performance monitoring in maintaining high standards of service delivery. She made a mental note to enhance their quality assurance processes to ensure that they were meeting and exceeding expectations.

The fifth slide highlighted "Client and Tenant Satisfaction." "5. **Client and Tenant Satisfaction.** Property managers should prioritize client and tenant satisfaction as the ultimate measure of their success and adherence to high standards. This includes soliciting feedback from clients and tenants, addressing concerns and issues promptly and effectively, and proactively seeking out opportunities to enhance the customer experience. Client and tenant satisfaction are key indicators of the effectiveness of property managers' efforts to achieve excellence."

Jack stressed the importance of prioritizing client and tenant satisfaction in their pursuit of excellence. He encouraged the team to go above and beyond to delight their clients and tenants and exceed their expectations at every opportunity.

The final slide displayed "Recognition and Rewards for Excellence." "6. **Recognition and Rewards for Excellence.** Property managers should recognize and reward individuals and teams that demonstrate a commitment to excellence and consistently exceed high standards. This includes celebrating achievements, acknowledging exceptional performance, and providing incentives and rewards for outstanding contributions. Recognition and rewards motivate and inspire team members to strive for excellence and uphold high standards."

CHAPTER 15: ACHIEVING EXCELLENCE IN PROPERTY MANAGEMENT

Jack turned off the projector and faced his team, a sense of determination evident in his expression. "Achieving excellence in property management is not just about meeting expectations—it's about exceeding them. Let's commit ourselves to setting and achieving high standards that define our commitment to excellence and drive our success."

Continuous Learning and Professional Development

As the team delved deeper into their pursuit of excellence, Jack Miller redirected their focus to the crucial aspect of continuous learning and professional development. He understood that in an ever-evolving industry, staying ahead meant constantly updating their skills and knowledge.

"Team," Jack began, his voice infused with enthusiasm. "In our journey towards excellence, one of our most valuable assets will be continuous learning and professional development. It's about embracing a mindset of growth and seizing every opportunity to expand our skills and knowledge. Let's explore how we can cultivate a culture of continuous learning that propels us towards excellence."

He clicked the remote, and the screen illuminated with a presentation titled "Continuous Learning and Professional Development." "Continuous learning and professional development are essential for staying relevant, adapting to change, and driving innovation in property management. It's about investing in ourselves and empowering our team members to reach their full potential."

The first slide highlighted "Embracing a Growth Mindset." "1. **Embracing a Growth Mindset.** Property managers should foster a culture of continuous learning by embracing a growth mindset that values curiosity, resilience, and adaptability. This includes encouraging team members to seek out new challenges, learn from failures, and embrace feedback as opportunities for growth. Embracing a growth mindset empowers property managers to adapt to change, overcome obstacles, and achieve their full potential."

Jack emphasized the importance of cultivating a growth mindset as the foundation for continuous learning and professional development. He recalled instances where a growth mindset had fueled innovation and resilience in the face of adversity.

The next slide displayed "Investing in Training and Development." "2. **Investing in Training and Development.** Property managers should invest in training and development initiatives that equip their team members with the skills and knowledge needed to excel in their roles and adapt to changing industry trends. This includes providing access to workshops, courses, certifications, and conferences, as well as creating opportunities for mentorship and coaching. Investing in training and development ensures that property managers stay ahead of the curve and deliver exceptional value to their clients and tenants."

Sarah, with her focus on innovation, nodded in agreement. She understood the importance of investing in training and development initiatives to foster a culture of continuous learning and drive innovation. She made a mental note to explore opportunities for professional development that aligned with their strategic objectives.

The third slide depicted "Encouraging Lifelong Learning." "3. **Encouraging Lifelong Learning.** Property managers should encourage team members to pursue lifelong learning opportunities that align with their interests, goals, and aspirations. This includes providing access to resources and tools for self-directed learning, such as online courses, industry publications, and professional networks, as well as creating a supportive environment that values and rewards continuous learning. Encouraging lifelong learning empowers property managers to stay curious, informed, and adaptable in a rapidly changing industry."

David, always eager to learn, recognized the importance of encouraging lifelong learning among their team members. He made a mental note to create opportunities for sharing knowledge and best practices within the team and fostering a culture of continuous learning.

The next image showed "Staying Current with Industry Trends." "4. **Staying Current with Industry Trends.** Property managers should stay abreast of emerging industry trends, best practices, and technological innovations that impact the field of property management. This includes attending industry conferences and events, participating in professional associations and networks, and subscribing to industry publications and newsletters. Staying current with industry trends enables property managers to anticipate change, identify opportunities, and proactively adapt their strategies and practices."

Lisa, their problem solver, nodded in agreement. She understood the importance of staying current with industry trends to remain competitive and innovative in the market. She made a mental note to allocate time for staying informed about emerging trends and best practices.

The fifth slide highlighted "Seeking Feedback and Mentoring." "5. **Seeking Feedback and Mentoring.** Property managers should actively seek feedback from mentors, peers, clients, and tenants to identify areas for improvement and opportunities for growth. This includes soliciting feedback on performance, seeking mentorship from experienced professionals, and participating in peer learning groups and networks. Seeking feedback and mentoring provides valuable insights, guidance, and support for continuous learning and professional development."

Jack stressed the importance of seeking feedback and mentoring as valuable opportunities for growth and development. He encouraged the team to be proactive in seeking out mentors and leveraging feedback to enhance their skills and knowledge.

The final slide displayed "Celebrating Learning Milestones."

"6. **Celebrating Learning Milestones.** Property managers should celebrate learning milestones and achievements as a way to recognize and reinforce the value of continuous learning and professional development. This includes acknowledging certifications, skills development, and knowledge acquisition through internal recognition programs, team celebrations, and rewards. Celebrating learning milestones fosters a culture of appreciation and motivates team members to continue investing in their growth and development."

Jack turned off the projector and faced his team, a sense of determination evident in his expression. "Continuous learning and professional development are not just individual pursuits—they're integral to our collective success as a team. Let's commit ourselves to embracing a growth mindset, investing in our development, and supporting each other on our journey towards excellence."

The room fell silent, each team member reflecting on

their commitment to continuous learning and professional development. Jack could see the determination in their eyes—a shared commitment to embracing growth, seizing opportunities, and achieving excellence in property management.

Adopting Best Practices

As the team ventured further into their quest for excellence, Jack Miller redirected their focus to the pivotal aspect of adopting best practices. He understood that excellence wasn't just about individual efforts but also about leveraging proven methods and strategies.

"Team," Jack began, his voice resonating with conviction. "In our journey towards excellence, adopting best practices will be instrumental. It's about learning from the successes and failures of others, embracing tried-and-tested methods, and continuously refining our approach to deliver exceptional results. Let's explore how we can adopt best practices that elevate our performance and set us apart in the industry."

He clicked the remote, illuminating the screen with a presentation titled "Adopting Best Practices." "Adopting best practices is essential for optimizing efficiency, minimizing risks, and maximizing value in property management. It's about learning from industry leaders, benchmarking against top performers, and implementing strategies that drive success."

The first slide highlighted "Learning from Industry Leaders." "1. **Learning from Industry Leaders.** Property managers should study the practices of industry leaders and top performers to glean insights into what sets them apart. This includes analyzing case studies, attending industry conferences, and seeking out opportunities to learn from experienced professionals. By learning from industry leaders, property managers can identify best practices and innovative strategies that can be applied to their own operations."

Jack emphasized the importance of studying the practices of industry leaders as a source of inspiration and learning. He recalled instances where insights from industry leaders had inspired breakthroughs and driven success in their own operations.

The next slide displayed "Benchmarking Against Top Performers." "2. **Benchmarking Against Top Performers.** Property managers should benchmark their performance against top performers in the industry to identify areas for improvement and opportunities for growth. This includes analyzing key performance indicators (KPIs), such as occupancy rates, rental yields, and tenant satisfaction scores, and comparing them to industry benchmarks and peer group averages. Benchmarking against top performers enables property managers to set ambitious goals, track progress, and drive continuous improvement."

Sarah, with her focus on innovation, nodded in agreement. She understood the importance of benchmarking against top performers to identify opportunities for improvement and set ambitious goals. She made a mental note to conduct a thorough analysis of their performance metrics and benchmark them against industry standards.

The third slide depicted "Implementing Standard Operating Procedures (SOPs)." "3. **Implementing Standard Operating Procedures (SOPs).** Property managers should develop and implement standardized processes and procedures for key aspects of their operations to ensure consistency, efficiency, and compliance. This includes documenting workflows, creating checklists, and establishing protocols for routine tasks, such as leasing, maintenance, and tenant relations. Implementing SOPs streamlines operations, reduces errors, and enhances overall performance."

David, always focused on efficiency, recognized the importance of implementing SOPs to standardize their operations. He made a mental note to collaborate with the team to document their workflows and create standardized procedures for key tasks.

The next image showed "Staying Abreast of Regulatory Changes." "4. **Staying Abreast of Regulatory Changes.** Property managers should stay informed about changes to laws, regulations, and industry standards that impact the field of property management. This includes monitoring updates from regulatory authorities, attending training sessions on compliance requirements, and consulting with legal experts as needed. Staying abreast of regulatory changes ensures that property managers remain compliant and mitigate legal risks in their operations."

Lisa, their problem solver, nodded in agreement. She understood the importance of staying abreast of regulatory changes to ensure compliance and mitigate legal risks. She made a mental note to establish protocols for monitoring regulatory updates and disseminating relevant information to the team.

The fifth slide highlighted "Embracing Technology Solutions." "5. **Embracing Technology Solutions.** Property managers should leverage technology solutions to streamline operations, enhance efficiency, and improve service delivery. This includes implementing property management software, mobile apps, and digital communication platforms to automate routine tasks, streamline communication, and provide tenants with self-service options. Embracing technology solutions empowers property managers to stay competitive, deliver value-added services, and enhance the tenant experience."

Jack stressed the importance of embracing technology solutions as a means of driving efficiency and innovation in property management. He encouraged the team to explore technology solutions that aligned with their strategic objectives and enhanced their operations.

The final slide displayed "Continuous Improvement Through Feedback." "6. **Continuous Improvement Through Feedback.** Property managers should solicit feedback from clients, tenants, and stakeholders to identify areas for improvement and opportunities for innovation. This includes conducting satisfaction surveys, holding focus groups, and encouraging open communication channels for feedback and suggestions. Continuous improvement through feedback enables property managers to adapt to changing needs and preferences and deliver exceptional value to their clients and tenants."

Jack turned off the projector and faced his team, a sense of determination evident in his expression. "Adopting best practices is not just about following the crowd—it's about leveraging proven methods and strategies to drive success in our operations. Let's commit ourselves to learning from industry leaders, benchmarking against top performers, and continuously refining our approach to deliver exceptional results."

The room fell silent, each team member reflecting on

their commitment to adopting best practices and driving excellence in property management. Jack could see the determination in their eyes—a shared commitment to continuous improvement and delivering exceptional value to their clients and tenants.

Building a Reputation for Excellence

As the team delved deeper into their pursuit of excellence, Jack Miller redirected their focus to the pivotal aspect of building a reputation for excellence. He understood that in a competitive market, reputation was paramount in attracting clients and tenants.

"Team," Jack began, his voice infused with determination. "In our journey towards excellence, building a reputation for excellence will be key. It's about consistently delivering exceptional service, exceeding expectations, and earning the trust and respect of our clients and tenants. Let's explore how we can build a reputation for excellence that sets us apart in the industry."

He clicked the remote, illuminating the screen with a presentation titled "Building a Reputation for Excellence." "Building a reputation for excellence is essential for establishing credibility, attracting clients, and fostering loyalty in property management. It's about delivering on our promises, cultivating positive relationships, and going above and beyond to exceed expectations."

The first slide highlighted "Delivering Consistent Quality Service." "1. **Delivering Consistent Quality Service.** Property managers should prioritize delivering consistent, high-quality service to every client and tenant. This includes setting clear expectations, providing timely and responsive communication, and proactively addressing concerns and issues. By consistently delivering quality service, property managers can build trust and confidence in their abilities and establish a reputation for excellence."

Jack emphasized the importance of delivering consistent quality service as the foundation of their reputation for excellence. He recalled instances where their commitment to quality had earned them repeat business and glowing testimonials from satisfied clients.

The next slide displayed "Exceeding Expectations at Every Opportunity." "2. **Exceeding Expectations at Every Opportunity.** Property managers should strive to exceed expectations at every opportunity by going above and beyond to deliver value-added services and personalized experiences. This includes anticipating needs, anticipating needs, and preferences, and proactively offering solutions and enhancements. By consistently exceeding expectations, property managers can differentiate themselves from competitors and solidify their reputation for excellence."

Sarah, with her focus on innovation, nodded in agreement. She understood the importance of exceeding expectations to delight their clients and tenants and differentiate themselves in the market. She made a mental note to brainstorm ideas for value-added services that would elevate their service delivery.

The third slide depicted "Cultivating Positive Relationships." "3. **Cultivating Positive Relationships.** Property managers should prioritize building and nurturing positive relationships with clients, tenants, and stakeholders based on trust, integrity, and transparency. This includes actively listening to their needs and concerns, being responsive and accessible, and treating them with respect and professionalism. Cultivating positive relationships fosters loyalty and advocacy, resulting in a strong reputation for excellence."

David, always focused on relationships, recognized the importance of cultivating positive relationships in building their reputation for excellence. He made a mental note to prioritize building rapport and trust with their clients and tenants through open communication and attentive service.

The next image showed "Seeking Feedback and Continuous Improvement." "4. **Seeking Feedback and Continuous Improvement.** Property managers should actively seek feedback from clients, tenants, and stakeholders to identify areas for improvement and opportunities for innovation. This includes conducting satisfaction surveys, holding regular meetings, and implementing feedback mechanisms to gather input and suggestions. By soliciting feedback and embracing continuous improvement, property managers can demonstrate their commitment to excellence and responsiveness to evolving needs."

Lisa, their problem solver, nodded in agreement. She understood the importance of seeking feedback to drive continuous improvement and enhance their service delivery. She made a mental note to implement feedback mechanisms to gather input from clients and tenants regularly.

The fifth slide highlighted "Showcasing Success Stories and Testimonials." "5. **Showcasing Success Stories and Testimonials.** Property managers should showcase success stories and testimonials from satisfied clients and tenants to build credibility and trust in their services. This includes creating case studies, testimonials, and reviews that highlight their achievements, client satisfaction, and positive experiences. Showcasing success stories and testimonials reinforces their reputation for excellence and attracts new clients and tenants."

Jack stressed the importance of showcasing success stories and testimonials as powerful endorsements of their reputation for excellence. He encouraged the team to collect and share stories of their successful collaborations and satisfied clients to build credibility and trust.

The final slide displayed "Consistent Branding and Messaging." "6. **Consistent Branding and Messaging.** Property managers should maintain consistent branding and messaging across all channels to reinforce their reputation for excellence and professionalism. This includes aligning their brand identity, values, and messaging with their commitment to delivering exceptional service and exceeding expectations. Consistent branding and messaging create a strong, cohesive brand image that resonates with clients, tenants, and stakeholders."

Jack turned off the projector and faced his team, a sense of determination evident in his expression. "Building a reputation for excellence is not just about what we do—it's about how we do it. Let's commit ourselves to delivering consistent quality service, exceeding expectations, and cultivating positive relationships that set us apart as leaders in the industry."

The room fell silent, each team member reflecting on their role in building a reputation for excellence. Jack could see the determination in their eyes—a shared commitment to delivering exceptional service, exceeding expectations, and earning the trust and respect of their clients and tenants.

Case Studies of Successful Managers

As the team progressed further into their pursuit of excellence, Jack Miller redirected their focus to the enlightening aspect of studying case studies of successful managers. He understood the power of learning from real-world examples and drawing inspiration from those who had achieved remarkable success in the field.

"Team," Jack began, his voice resonating with enthusiasm. "In our journey towards excellence, studying case studies of successful managers can provide invaluable insights and inspiration. It's about learning from their experiences, strategies, and challenges, and applying those lessons to our own endeavors. Let's explore how we can glean wisdom from the journeys of successful managers and leverage it to elevate our own performance."

He clicked the remote, illuminating the screen with a presentation titled "Case Studies of Successful Managers." "Studying case studies of successful managers allows us to gain a deeper understanding of the strategies and practices that have propelled them to success. It's about drawing inspiration from their achievements and applying those lessons to our own operations."

The first slide highlighted "The Journey of James Reynolds: Innovating Through Technology." "1. **The Journey of James Reynolds: Innovating Through Technology.** James Reynolds, a successful property manager, revolutionized his operations by embracing technology solutions. He implemented property management software to streamline processes, improve communication, and enhance tenant experiences. By leveraging technology, James was able to increase efficiency, reduce costs, and deliver exceptional service to his clients and tenants."

Jack emphasized the importance of innovation through technology as demonstrated by James Reynolds. He encouraged the team to explore how they could leverage technology solutions to optimize their operations and enhance their service delivery.

The next slide displayed "The Success Story of Emily Carter: Building Strong Relationships." "2. **The Success Story of Emily Carter: Building Strong Relationships.** Emily Carter, a renowned property manager, attributes her success to her ability to build and nurture positive relationships. She prioritizes open communication, transparency, and integrity in her interactions with clients, tenants, and stakeholders. By cultivating strong relationships based on trust and respect, Emily has earned the loyalty and advocacy of her clients and tenants."

Sarah, with her focus on relationships, nodded in agreement. She understood the importance of building strong relationships as demonstrated by Emily Carter. She made a mental note to prioritize fostering positive relationships with their clients, tenants, and stakeholders.

The third slide depicted "The Leadership of Michael Johnson: Empowering His Team." "3. **The Leadership of Michael Johnson: Empowering His Team.** Michael Johnson, a visionary property manager, credits his success to his leadership style focused on empowering his team. He fosters a culture of trust, collaboration, and innovation, where team members are encouraged to take ownership, share ideas, and contribute to the success of the organization. By empowering his team, Michael has built a high-performing, motivated workforce that drives excellence in property management."

David, always focused on leadership, recognized the importance of empowering the team as demonstrated by Michael Johnson. He made a mental note to cultivate a culture of trust and empowerment within their own team.

The next image showed "The Strategic Approach of Sarah Adams: Setting Ambitious Goals." "4. **The Strategic Approach of Sarah Adams: Setting Ambitious Goals.** Sarah Adams, a strategic property manager, achieves success by setting ambitious goals and executing strategic plans to achieve them. She conducts thorough market research, identifies growth opportunities, and develops action plans to capitalize on them. By setting ambitious goals and maintaining a strategic focus, Sarah has achieved remarkable growth and success in property management."

Lisa, their problem solver, nodded in agreement. She understood the importance of setting ambitious goals and maintaining a strategic focus as demonstrated by Sarah Adams. She made a mental note to collaborate with the team to set clear goals and develop strategic plans for achieving them.

The fifth slide highlighted "The Customer-Centric Approach of David Martinez: Prioritizing Tenant Satisfaction." "5. **The Customer-Centric Approach of David Martinez: Prioritizing Tenant Satisfaction.** David Martinez, a customer-centric property manager, places a strong emphasis on tenant satisfaction in his operations. He actively listens to tenant feedback, responds promptly to their needs and concerns, and continuously seeks ways to enhance their experience. By prioritizing tenant satisfaction, David has cultivated a loyal tenant base and earned a reputation for excellence in property management."

Jack stressed the importance of prioritizing tenant satisfaction as demonstrated by David Martinez. He encouraged the team to adopt a customer-centric approach and prioritize the needs and concerns of their tenants.

The final slide displayed "Drawing Inspiration from Success." "6. **Drawing Inspiration from Success.** Studying case studies of successful managers allows us to draw inspiration from their journeys, strategies, and achievements. It's about learning from their successes and challenges, and applying those lessons to our own endeavors. By drawing inspiration from success, we can elevate our performance, drive innovation, and achieve excellence in property management."

Jack turned off the projector and faced his team, a sense of determination evident in his expression. "Studying case studies of successful managers is not just about admiring their achievements—it's about learning from their experiences and applying those lessons to our own journey towards excellence. Let's commit ourselves to drawing inspiration from success and leveraging it to elevate our performance in property management."

The room fell silent, each team member reflecting on the insights gleaned from the case studies of successful managers. Jack could see the determination in their eyes—a shared commitment to learning, growing, and achieving excellence in property management.

Future Trends and Innovations in Property Management

As the team ventured deeper into their pursuit of excellence, Jack Miller redirected their focus to the forward-thinking aspect of exploring future trends and innovations in property management. He understood the importance of staying ahead of the curve and embracing emerging technologies and strategies to maintain a competitive edge in the industry.

"Team," Jack began, his voice brimming with anticipation. "In our journey towards excellence, it's crucial to keep our eyes on the horizon and anticipate future trends and innovations in property management. It's about embracing change, leveraging technology, and adopting new strategies to stay ahead of the curve. Let's explore how we can position ourselves as leaders in the industry by embracing future trends and innovations."

He clicked the remote, illuminating the screen with a presentation titled "Future Trends and Innovations in Property Management." "Exploring future trends and innovations allows us to anticipate changes in the industry, adapt to evolving needs, and capitalize on emerging opportunities. It's about embracing innovation and staying at the forefront of the property management landscape."

The first slide highlighted "The Rise of Proptech: Embracing Technology Solutions." "1. **The Rise of Proptech: Embracing Technology Solutions.** The property management industry is undergoing a digital transformation with the rise of Proptech—technology solutions designed specifically for real estate professionals. From property management software to smart home technologies, Proptech offers innovative tools to streamline operations, enhance tenant experiences, and optimize asset performance. By embracing Proptech, property managers can increase efficiency, reduce costs, and deliver value-added services to their clients and tenants."

Jack emphasized the importance of embracing Proptech as a means of driving efficiency and innovation in property management. He encouraged the team to explore emerging Proptech solutions and identify opportunities to integrate them into their operations.

The next slide displayed "The Shift Towards Sustainable Practices: Implementing Green Initiatives." "2. **The Shift Towards Sustainable Practices: Implementing Green Initiatives.** With growing concerns about environmental sustainability, property managers are increasingly adopting green initiatives to reduce energy consumption, minimize waste, and promote eco-friendly practices. From energy-efficient appliances to sustainable landscaping, green initiatives not only reduce operating costs but also attract environmentally-conscious tenants and enhance property value. By implementing green initiatives, property managers can demonstrate their commitment to sustainability and differentiate their properties in the market."

Sarah, with her focus on innovation, nodded in agreement. She understood the importance of implementing green initiatives to align with evolving environmental trends and attract eco-conscious tenants. She made a mental note to explore opportunities for integrating sustainable practices into their properties.

The third slide depicted "The Evolution of Tenant Experience: Enhancing Digital Engagement." "3. **The Evolution of Tenant Experience: Enhancing Digital Engagement.**

As tenant expectations continue to evolve, property managers are leveraging digital technologies to enhance tenant experiences and engagement. From online portals for rent payments to virtual property tours, digital engagement tools provide convenience, accessibility, and transparency for tenants. By embracing digital engagement, property managers can improve tenant satisfaction, retention, and loyalty, ultimately driving long-term success."

David, always focused on relationships, recognized the importance of enhancing digital engagement to meet the evolving needs of tenants. He made a mental note to explore digital engagement tools that would enhance their tenants' experiences and streamline communication.

The next image showed "The Emergence of Data Analytics: Leveraging Insights for Decision-Making." "4. **The Emergence of Data Analytics: Leveraging Insights for Decision-Making.** With the proliferation of data in the digital age, property managers are increasingly leveraging data analytics to gain valuable insights into property performance, market trends, and tenant preferences. By analyzing data on occupancy rates, rental yields, and tenant satisfaction scores, property managers can make informed decisions, identify opportunities for optimization, and drive operational efficiency. By embracing data analytics, property managers can gain a competitive edge and achieve superior outcomes."

Lisa, their problem solver, nodded in agreement. She understood the importance of leveraging data analytics to inform decision-making and drive operational efficiency. She made a mental note to explore data analytics tools that would provide valuable insights into their property performance and market trends.

The fifth slide highlighted "The Integration of Artificial Intelligence: Automating Routine Tasks." "5. **The Integration of Artificial Intelligence: Automating Routine Tasks.** Artificial intelligence (AI) is revolutionizing property management by automating routine tasks, such as maintenance scheduling, rent collection, and tenant inquiries. AI-powered chatbots and virtual assistants provide instant support and personalized interactions for tenants, while predictive analytics algorithms optimize maintenance schedules and resource allocation. By integrating AI, property managers can streamline operations, improve efficiency, and enhance the tenant experience."

Jack stressed the importance of integrating artificial intelligence as a means of automating routine tasks and enhancing operational efficiency. He encouraged the team to explore AI-powered solutions that would optimize their operations and improve the tenant experience.

The final slide displayed "Anticipating Future Trends: Staying Ahead of the Curve." "6. **Anticipating Future Trends: Staying Ahead of the Curve.** Exploring future trends and innovations allows property managers to anticipate changes in the industry, adapt to evolving needs, and capitalize on emerging opportunities. By embracing innovation and staying at the forefront of the property management landscape, property managers can position themselves as leaders in the industry and drive long-term success."

Jack turned off the projector and faced his team, a sense of anticipation evident in his expression. "Exploring future trends and innovations is not just about staying current—it's about staying ahead of the curve. Let's commit ourselves to embracing change, leveraging technology, and adopting new strategies that will position us as leaders in the industry."

The room fell silent, each team member reflecting on the exciting possibilities presented by future trends and innovations in property management. Jack could see the enthusiasm in their eyes—a shared commitment to embracing innovation and driving excellence in property management.

About the Author

Goodson Mumba is a multifaceted individual known for his diverse expertise and prolific contributions across various fields. As an infopreneur, thought leader, and spiritual leader, he has inspired countless individuals through his insightful teachings and impactful writings. Mumba is also an accomplished author, with several notable works to his name, including "Understanding Corporate Worship," "The Years I Spent in a Week," "Management By Harmony," "The CEO's Diary," "Change to Change" and "Creative Thinking for results" His literary works span topics ranging from business management to personal development and spirituality, reflecting his broad range of interests and insights.

With a Master of Business Leadership (MBL) and a Bachelor of Arts in Theology (BTh), Mumba brings a unique blend of business acumen and spiritual wisdom to his work. His educational background is further enriched by a Group Diploma in Management Studies, providing him with a solid foundation in organizational dynamics and leadership principles. Additionally, Mumba holds diplomas in Education

Psychology, Leadership and Management Styles, Organizational Behaviour, Financial Accounting, Economic Growth and Development, and Project Management, showcasing his commitment to continuous learning and professional development.

Mumba's expertise extends beyond traditional academic disciplines, encompassing areas such as Neuro-Linguistic Programming (NLP) and Positive Psychology. His diverse skill set is complemented by a range of certifications, including Creative Problem Solving and Decision Making, Life Coaching Fundamentals and Techniques, Professional Life Coaching, and Performance Management System Design. These certifications reflect Mumba's dedication to equipping himself with the tools and knowledge necessary to empower others and drive positive change.

As an author, Mumba's writings reflect his deep understanding of human nature, organizational dynamics, and spiritual principles. His works offer practical insights, actionable strategies, and inspirational guidance for individuals seeking personal growth, professional success, and spiritual fulfillment. Mumba's holistic approach to life and leadership resonates with readers worldwide, making him a respected figure in both the business and spiritual communities.

Overall, Goodson Mumba's diverse background, extensive knowledge, and profound insights make him a sought-after speaker, mentor, and author. His commitment to excellence, lifelong learning, and service to others continues to inspire individuals to unlock their full potential and lead lives of purpose and significance.

Goodson Mumba is renowned for initiating the concept of Management by Harmony, revolutionizing traditional management practices with a focus on balanced and holistic approaches. He has authored two influential books on this subject: "Introduction to Management by Harmony" and its sequel, "Management by Harmony."

Mumba's work has significantly impacted the field, offering innovative strategies for fostering organizational harmony and efficiency. His contributions continue to shape contemporary management theories and practices.

www.ingramcontent.com/pod-product-compliance
Lightning Source LLC
Chambersburg PA
CBHW071825210526
45479CB00001B/1